# Robin Hood

J. C. Holt

# Robin Hood

*Revised and enlarged edition*

*with 52 illustrations
and 4 maps*

*Thames and Hudson*

# Contents

# Preface to Second Edition

This new edition embodies some important changes. In the first edition of 1982 I advanced a number of arguments to suggest that the Robin Hood legend originated in the thirteenth century – well before the time of the most frequently advocated 'original' who lived in Wakefield in the first decades of the fourteenth century. The case really rested on the appearance of Robinhood surnames as early as 1296. It is now quite certain that this was so. More such names have been found. They not only carry the legend back to 1261–2, but also show how it intermingled with the activities of real criminals and thereby provide a clue to the manner in which fact and legend were mixed in the mature tales of Robin Hood of the fifteenth century. At the same time this newly secured chronology allows more to be said about the medieval historian's knowledge of Robin, about the relation of the tales to other literature and about the sources of the legend.

In addition, further consideration of Robin's role in the May Games or Spring Festival, especially as revealed in a number of church wardens' accounts, has suggested an origin of the notion that he robbed the rich and gave to the poor. For it is plain that by the beginning of the sixteenth century he had become the leading figure in what the British call a Flag Day.

These matters are discussed in the Postscript. Minor changes have also been embodied in the earlier chapters, and the Notes and Sources and further reading have been brought up to date. The other additions of any length are at page 13 and at pages 157–8 where I introduce a passage from the Anonimalle Chronicle which so far has escaped the attention of scholars interested in Robin Hood. I am grateful to Professor Takeshi Kido of the University of Tokyo who brought it to my notice.

In addition I have been helped in a number of ways in the preparation of this new edition. Professor Derek Brewer kindly revised all the translations. Dr Rivkah Zim brought to my attention all the problems surrounding the authorship of the Letter of Robert Langham. Dr Henry Summerson generously provided me with Robinhood surnames from his collection of criminal nicknames. Dr David Crook sent me further information concerning Roger Godberd and other matters; I have also benefited from reading some of his own work on Robin Hood prior to publication. Reviewers of the first edition made corrections; friends made suggestions. To all these I am grateful. It need scarcely be said that such errors as remain are my own. It should certainly be added that the changes in this new edition do not undermine the arguments of the original book: indeed they reinforce them.

J. C. HOLT
*August 1988*                                         *Fitzwilliam College, Cambridge*

# I
# Prologue

This book is about a legend rather than a man. The legend began more than seven hundred years ago. The man, if he existed at all, lived even earlier. He has survived as a hero in ballad, book, poem and play ever since.

He cannot be identified. There is a quiverful of possible Robin Hoods. Even the likeliest is little better than a shot in the gloaming. To substantiate an identity, the earliest tales of Robin's doings have to be matched with information from other sources. This is scanty. Moreover, even in the earliest stories there is no sure way of sifting fact from fiction. Hence who he might have been is inseparable from what he was thought to have been: any search for a man involves an analysis of the legend.

The identity of the man matters less than the persistence of the legend. That is the most remarkable thing about him. And the perpetuation of the legend involves others: those who told the stories and those who listened to them. But while the legend survived, the performers and the audience changed from one generation to the next. So also did the circumstances in which they came together. What began as an oral tradition ended as a television script.

The legend endured through adaptation. In each generation it acquired new twists from shifts in the composition, outlook and interests of the audience, or changes in the level of literacy, or developments in the means of communication. New tales were added to the story. New characters were introduced to the plot. Fresh historical contexts were invented. Minor features of the older tales were expanded into major themes; important elements in the earlier tales were later jettisoned. The legend snowballed, collecting fragments of other stories as it rolled along. The central character was repeatedly remodelled. At his first appearance Robin was a yeoman. He was then turned into a nobleman unjustly deprived of his inheritance, later into an Englishman protecting his native countrymen from the domination

7

of the Normans, and finally into a social rebel who, in the peasant's struggle against the grasping landlord, retaliates against the person and property of the oppressor. He is usually heroic, sometimes romantic, occasionally, as a participant in rustic buffoonery, merely ridiculous, or even just a thief.

The legend is now very different from what it was originally. Both in popular imagination and sociological jargon Robin has come to provide a stereotype for robbing the rich and giving to the poor. Nothing has taken firmer hold in his modern reputation than this unlikely activity. Yet there is very little warrant for it in the earliest stories. In one of them Robin lends money to a knight and recovers it by robbing an abbot, but that is only one tale among many. The rest are simple adventure stories, tales of combat, contest, disguise and stratagem. They have nothing to do with robbing the rich and giving to the poor. They are not specifically concerned with class grievances, with needy knights or grasping abbots, still less with discontented, overburdened peasants.

To say this is not to deprive the legend in its origin of all social content. Its heroes are outlaws. They are placed in the world of the hardened criminal who roamed the countryside, of the defeated rebel, peasant, knight or noble, who took to the woods rather than submit, of the felon in the strict legal sense who incurred outlawry, rightly or wrongly, in the course of legal process through his failure to appear before the courts or his unwillingess or inability to find the money for paying bribes or pecuniary penalties. The outlaws are engaged in a running battle with the sheriff and his men who are the real villains of the tale. The woods where they live and roam were, both in legend and real life, the haunt of criminal and guerrilla alike. They live off the king's deer which were the object of widespread poaching. Their story evokes a multiplicity of local scenes: the archery of the municipal butts, the fencing demonstrations of the banquet hall and market-place, the halls, the kitchens and the prison cells of castles. It relies in realistic fashion on familiar activities: not ploughing or reaping, but feasting, fighting, buying and selling, hunting, worshipping. In short it would strike many chords in the audience's sensibilities.

Yet it does so with a light touch. It is useful to compare it as an outlaw tale with another *Outlaw's Song* written in Anglo-Norman shortly after 1305, when the legend of Robin had already begun to take shape. The two have common features: they both praise the delights of the greenwood; and the author of *The Outlaw's Song* knows that the forest is the haunt of companies of archers which he may be driven to join. But by the side of Robin's legend his plaint is quite precise. He names the justices responsible for his outlawry; he specifically condemns the royal ordinance which gave them their commission; he makes it perfectly

The medieval outlaw in sixteenth-century dress after an
engraving by Thomas Bewick, *c*.1795, from Ritson's
*Robin Hood*.

clear that he has been 'indicted out of malice' by a body of false jurors.
The piece is specific to a particular time and context. It was not isolated;
there are other fragments similar in tone; none of them initiated or
contributed to a legend. Robin's tale, by contrast, is imprecise. He is an
outlaw, but no one explains why. He is in conflict with the sheriff but
no reason is ever given; it is simply that the sheriff represents the law
and Robin stands outside it. His story is less committed to immediate
circumstances. This is one reason why it proved so durable.

The legend was varied and adaptable. These qualities went together.
It would arouse diverse responses in the audience. It could also invade
and absorb other entertainments. At a very early date, certainly by the
middle of the fifteenth century, the tales or gests were turned into plays;
some have argued that the plays came first. At the same time, Robin
was adopted into the May Games, from which his legend in its turn
gained fresh characters. In its greenwood theme it mingled in one
direction with Teutonic myth and a world of woodland sprites, whilst
in another it contributed to the conventional setting which Shakespeare
used in *As You Like It*.

This helps to explain the tale's potential. To explain why the
potential was realized, to understand why stories which seem on the
face of it so artless and shallow, should have proved so compelling to
generation after generation, it is necessary to turn from the social issues
which went into their making to the general terms in which those issues
were expressed. They may lack depth, but again and again they play on

9

sensitivities and arouse responses which transcend era, age and social background.

At first sight the legend is about justice. Robin is at once an embodiment of honour and an agent of retribution. He corrects the evil which flows from the greed of rich clerics and the corruption of royal officials. But he does not seek to overturn social conventions. On the contrary, he sustains those conventions against the machinations of the wicked and the powerful who exploit, flout and undermine them. He keeps his word, unlike the treacherous sheriff. He is devout, unlike the worldly clerics. He is generous, unlike the avaricious abbot. He is courteous, unlike the churlish monks whom he entertains to dinner. He makes his world conform to the principles which are supposed to underlie it. Inevitably he wins. Honourable men triumph. Villains get tit for tat. Some are compelled to honour the code by which they have failed to live. Others receive their just deserts from a well-directed arrow. It is all very satisfying.

Robin also foreshadows the world of superman and the comic strip. He has no practical scheme for improving the human condition. There is no sense at any stage of the legend's history that man's lot might be improved by the sweat of his brow. Robin simply intervenes. He succeeds because he is a superlative archer, a consummate swordsman and a master of disguise and stratagem. Only the king and, in some traditions, the rustics, beggars or tradesmen whom he attacks and often persuades to join his band, are his equals. He is invulnerable except to treachery. Robin belongs to that world of heroes and villains in which the heroes are so supreme, so magical in their mastery that they will always win. Many of the stories, far from embodying social protest, turn on this and nothing else. The sheriff hunts the outlaws; Robin turns the tables; the outlaws win. In such simple adventures lies the legend's continuing juvenile appeal.

Originally, however, the tale had another meaning. What is now pure adventure to the young or laudable social protest to the radical was at first a glorification of violence to young and old alike. Robin, whether real or legendary, was a product of a society where the threshold which separated lawful behaviour from self-help by force of arms was indistinct and easily crossed. It was a society where the exercise of local office and the enforcement of the law were often an instrument of political faction, a society where the defeated party might easily pay the penalty with their heads, a society in which men took to robbery and pillage under the pressure of famine and other adverse circumstances, a society in which crime was tolerated, in which local juries protected the criminals and in which gangs of knightly bandits might gain royal pardon for extortion, kidnapping and murder. Now

Robin and his gang vindicate such activity by presenting it as honourable and meritorious. They confound it with other behaviour likely to inspire sympathy; there would be few who would not approve of their poaching of the king's deer. They deck it out with the conventions of the day: chivalry towards women, devotion to the Virgin, generosity, courtesy, loyalty, obedience, in all matters except his deer, to the king. But it cannot be camouflaged totally. Robin kills bloodily and with zest. He not only shoots the sheriff but beheads him for his treachery. He not only slays Guy of Gisborne with the sword but carries his defaced head on his bow's end, pretending that it is his own. Violent death is accepted with almost casual brutality. Much the Miller's son beheads the monk's little page simply to silence him. No one sheds a tear for him. The knight is in debt because his son, fond of jousting, had the misfortune to slay a knight and a squire. No one mourns for them.

This violence takes two directions. One is towards rebellion: not rebellion against authority, for the outlaws are at one in their veneration of the king, but against the local exercise of that authority by the sheriff. All will be well for them if they can gain access to the king and obtain his pardon. He will appreciate their real value and understand, not so much the justice of their cause, for they have none, but the injustice of their exclusion from his peace and favour which the sheriff and his men deny to them.

The other route is criminal. The most realistic early tradition of Robin is that he extorted money from travellers whom he waylaid on the Great North Road. They are forced to disgorge under duress. True, those who truthfully admit what they are carrying are allowed to retain it; it is only those who deny their wealth who are forced to hand it over. But it just so happens that the poor and impoverished tell the truth while the wealthy always lie. By such ingenious but transparent logic the victim's untruth is used to give moral justification to his captor's crime of highway robbery.

In Robin Hood the criminal is made heroic. This, too, helped to prolong the life of the legend, for the myth of Robin contributed to those concocted around the names of Jesse James and Billy the Kid. They also were supposed to kill chivalrously and in self-defence. For them too it was claimed that they robbed the rich and gave to the poor. 'Billy the Kid was good to Mexicans. He was like Robin Hood; he'd steal from the white people and give it to the Mexicans. So they thought he was all right.'[1] And

> *Jesse was a man, a friend of the poor,*
> *He would never see a man suffer pain;*
> *And with his brother Frank he robbed the Chicago bank,*
> *And stopped the Glendale train.*[2]

From such a smoke-screen no one benefits more than the criminals themselves. After all, what looks like robbing the rich in order to give to the poor may in reality amount to giving to the poor in order to facilitate robbing the rich. It does not matter that neither the James gang nor Billy the Kid lived up to their legend. What matters is that in Missouri and New Mexico in the nineteenth century, as in England in the fifteenth century, men were ready to argue, perhaps even to believe, that criminals behaved with such becoming charity. If the love of justice and adventure contributes to the survival of such tales, so also do human failings: gullibility and self-deception.

*The Outlaw's Song* is a realistic statement of the outlaw's plight and plaint. The tale of Robin Hood, by contrast, injects make-believe into an everyday environment. It makes violence natural. It presents it as unusually successful, for the outlaws' arrows rarely miss. It makes crime honourable, for the outlaws' victims always deserve what they get. It has Robin stand for justice against the corruption and venality of the sheriff; he forces the real world to conform to the ideal. It even transforms the real discomfort suffered by those who took to the woods into the idyllic life of the greenwood in which it never rains and where, with the king's deer to hand, every meal is a feast. And this tale took root in communities which submitted petition after petition to the king in parliament deploring the 'lack of governance' from which the realm of England suffered. Men voiced their longing for a more orderly life free from 'injustice' in practical fashion, if often to little effect, through the usual channels of government. They also took flight in their imagination with an outlawed hero who, at one and the same time, symbolized disorder and set it all to rights. The first person known to have asserted that Robin was 'a good man' was a sheriff's clerk writing a parliamentary return in 1432.[3]

Who then first relished this rough and ready, but unreal world of Robin Hood? Criminals, outlaws and rowdies, certainly, for some of them masqueraded under the name of Robin Hood. But the audience was larger than that, wide though the criminal fraternity extended in the Middle Ages. The legend is about yeomen and, as I shall show, not the yeoman freeholder, but the yeoman servant of the feudal household. In its formation and dissemination the structure of the great feudal estates played a part, especially one such estate, the combined honours of Lancaster and Lacy assembled by Thomas earl of Lancaster, in the reign of Edward I.[4] It was spread by minstrels who were themselves employed in the households of the aristocracy. Through them it was broadcast from the hall to the market-place, the tavern and the inn, wherever a worthwhile audience might collect. In this fashion it traversed class boundaries. It was played before knights and was sung by peasants. To men who could cock a snook at the sheriff as the enforcer of the law and the agent of the crown, to men who lived in or on the fringe of murderous political conflict, to men ever ready to transgress the line between violent politics and violent crime, to men who partook in the almost national pastime of poaching deer, to all those who shared the widespread aversion to usury, it provided a brittle moral fibre. In time it became a harmless tale fit for children. In its origin it served a bloodier purpose.

Myth and legend are matters for the anthropologist. This book is concerned merely with one such story. Yet one social phenomenon is worth noting at this stage. Ask any audience attending a lecture on Robin Hood the following questions: to each there will be an entirely predictable answer. Who present has never read a tale of Robin Hood or listened to one being read, or seen a film or television programme featuring his adventures? Answer: no-one. Who has read the stories as an adult other than to children? Answer: no-one. Who has ever read the stories in the original versions? Answer: no-one. In one form or another the tales have been told to children by adults who themselves learned them as children. That holds good for the last two hundred years, probably for much longer. It is thus that the legend has been transmitted and transmuted; and has endured.

An old story-teller and a young listener after an engraving by
Thomas Bewick, *c.*1795, from Ritson's *Robin Hood*.

# ¶Here begynneth a lytell geste of Ro= byn hode

Frontispiece to Wynkyn de Worde's edition of the *Gest*, 1492–1534.

# II
# The Legend

Practically all that is known of the medieval legend of Robin Hood is derived from five surviving poems or ballads and a fragment of a play. The earliest of these, which describes itself as the 'talkyng of the munke and Robyn Hode', and is conventionally known as *Robin Hood and the Monk*, is found in a manuscript collection written about 1450, in which the piece is included with a prayer against thieves and robbers and a treatise on the seven deadly sins, in a very mixed bag of poetic and moralistic material. Another tale, entitled *Robin Hood and the Potter*, forms part of a manuscript collection of romances and moralistic pieces probably written shortly after 1503. These two stories are chance survivals.

By this time, however, the legend was well enough known to attract the attention of the early printers. Between the last years of the fifteenth and the middle of the sixteenth century there appeared no less than five editions of a lengthy poem describing the deeds of Robin Hood. Of these, one, which supplies only half the text, was possibly derived from an Antwerp press between 1510 and 1515; another, which is complete, comes from the press of the famous English printer, Wynken de Worde, who worked between 1492 and 1534. Between them these two provide a text which the one describes as *A Gest of Robyn Hode* and the other as *A Lyttell Geste of Robyn Hode*; the remaining three versions, all later, supply corrections or minor additions. These five printed versions were all derived, directly or indirectly, from a single written source.[1] What it was is uncertain. Who wrote it is unknown. However, the balance of probability is that the *Gest* was first composed, in something very close to its present form, in the fifteenth century, perhaps even as early as 1400.[2]

Two other early tales were found in a manuscript which Thomas Percy, bishop of Dromore, Ireland (1782–1811), rescued from destruction in a Shropshire house and used for his *Reliques of Ancient English Poetry*, published in 1765. The manuscript, which has become famous as the Percy Folio, was written in the middle of the seventeenth century, but it contains two stories which are certainly very much earlier. One, *Robin Hoode his Death*, is closely related to the closing verses of the *Gest*. The other, *Robin Hood and Guy of Gisborne*, is archaic in form and language, and shares some of its subject-matter with a play about Robin Hood, a fragment of which survives in a manuscript of *c*.1475, which possibly belonged to the Paston family. The Percy Folio also contains a ballad called *Robin Hood and the Curtal Friar*.[3] This is less archaic in style than *Guy of Gisborne* and, as it stands, can scarcely be counted with the other early tales. However, the dramatic fragment of *c*.1475 mentions Friar Tuck as a member of Robin's company, so some story of Robin and a Friar was in circulation in the fifteenth century; its origin, as will be shown later, can be dated to *c*.1417.[4]

Stories of Robin were current long before these surviving pieces were composed. In a text of William Langland's *Piers Plowman*, written in or about 1377, one of the characters, Sloth, is made to say:

> *I kan noght parfitly my Paternoster as the preest it syngeth,*
> *But I kan rymes of Robyn hood and Randolf Erl of Chestre.*[5]

I do not know my paternoster perfectly as the priest sings it.
But I know rhymes of Robin Hood and Randolph, earl of Chester.

This is the earliest literary reference to Robin.[6] It implies that 'rhymes' of Robin Hood were already widely disseminated in the last quarter of the fourteenth century. Other evidence, which I shall discuss in the Postscript, indicates that the legend was known over a century earlier, in 1261–2. Hence between the origin of the legend and the first surviving versions of *c*. 1450 there was an interval of over two hundred years.

The surviving stories can only be properly understood with this interval in mind. They spring, not from the point of origin of the legend, but from different stages in its growth. They emphasize different aspects of Robin's activities. They introduce different characters. They reflect different geographic backgrounds. They may have been directed to different audiences. Diversification came easily. In every generation performers and authors assessed their audience afresh and combined their own inventiveness and powers of expression with what came down to them as a literary tradition or by word of mouth. Composition and repetition were intermingled. Each tale contains both old and new components, old social assumptions and conventions which descended with the poetic material to mix with those of the author's own day. Hence these robust simple stories constitute singularly delicate and complex evidence: about Robin, what he was thought to have been, and about the social context in which the telling of his deeds was born and nurtured.

## A Gest of Robyn Hode

The *Gest* is a long poem of 456 four-line stanzas, divided into eight cantos or 'fyttes'. Some of these form chapters of a continuously developing story; in others new themes and scenes are introduced. The author attempted to bring them together by means of retrospective allusions and the inclusion of short linking passages at the beginning and end of some of the fyttes. But the poem is episodic in structure and the links between the episodes are sometimes very artificial. The author also composed an introduction and a single concluding stanza to round off the whole work; these come closer to defining Robin's social 'objectives' than any other sections of the early tales.[7]

The first two and fourth fyttes are the most coherent sections of the poem. In fytte one the scene is set in the outlaws' camps in Barnsdale and the story opens abruptly: Robin will not dine until he has welcomed an unexpected guest to the feast. Little John, Much the Miller's son and Will Scarlok are sent out to bring in a guest and they soon encounter a knight who (23):

| | |
|---|---|
| *– rode in symple aray;* | – rode in simple array; |
| *A soriar man than he was one* | There never was a worse dressed man |
| *Rode never in somer day.* | To ride on a summer's day. |

The knight accepts the invitation to dinner which is lavish and which he much enjoys. At the end of the meal Robin suggests that he should pay for it and the sad condition of the knight is then made plain (38):

| | |
|---|---|
| *'I have nought in my coffers', saide* | 'I have nothing in my coffers', said |
| *the knyght,* | the knight, |
| *'That I may profer for shame.'* | 'Which I would shame not to offer.' |

His immediate resources, indeed, amount to a mere ten shillings. On Little John verifying this, Robin seeks an explanation of his guest's anomalous poverty, and this opens up the main plot of these three fyttes: in order to go bail for his son, who has committed a homicide, the knight has had to sell his goods and mortgage his estates for £400 to the abbot of St Mary's, York. Robin decides to lend him the money, the repayment pledged on the name of the Virgin Mother, and with this advance and the provision of a suitable horse and raiment, the knight is sent on his way, accompanied by Little John as his servant.

In the second fytte the scene shifts to York where the abbot of St Mary's and his crony, the 'high justice' of England, await the coming of the knight or rather sit relishing the final day for the payment of the debt after which the knight's land will be forfeit; only the prior has any pang of conscience. At length the knight appears, poorly dressed by deliberate intent. There is much play on the abbot's lack of charity: he will not grant delay or accept the knight's service in return for the land; he even keeps the knight kneeling throughout the interchange. At length the knight casts dissemblance aside (120–1):

| | |
|---|---|
| *He stert hym to a borde anone,* | He went over to a table then, |
| *Tyll a table rounde,* | To a table round, |
| *And there he shoke oute of a bagge* | And there shook out of a bag |
| *Even four hundred pound.* | As much as four hundred pound. |
| *'Have here thi golde, sir abbot', saide the knight,* | 'Take here your gold, Sir abbot', said the knight, |
| *'Which that thou lentest me;* | 'Which you lent to me; |
| *Had thou ben curtes at my comynge,* | If you had been courteous on my arrival, |
| *Rewarded shuldest thou have be.'* | Rewarded you would have been.' |

That spoils the abbot's day (122):

| | |
|---|---|
| *The abbot sat styll, and ete no more,* | The abbot sat still, and ate no more, |
| *For all his ryall fare;* | For all his royal fare; |
| *He cast his hede on his shulder,* | He leaned his head on his shoulder, |
| *And fast began to stare.* | And soon began to stare. |

His discomfiture is complete. The justice will not even return the fee he received to take the abbot's side. The knight returns home in triumph. There he accumulates £400 and the fytte closes with his setting forth to Barnsdale to repay the debt to Robin.

The fourth fytte at first duplicates the first. Once more Little John, Much and Will are sent out by Robin to find a guest for dinner. This time their guest is less willing; he is a monk who is only persuaded to come by force after his escort has been put to flight. At dinner he is revealed as the high cellarer of St Mary's, and Robin and his men at once agree that, as a monk of St Mary, he has been sent to repay the debt pledged in her name (241–2):

| | |
|---|---|
| *'Thou toldest with thyn owne tonge* | 'You told with your own tongue, |
| *Thou may not say nay,* | And you may not deny, |
| *How thou arte her servaunt,* | How you are her servant, |
| *And servest her every day.* | And serve her every day. |
| *'And thou art made her messengere,* | 'And you are made her messenger, |
| *My money for to pay;* | My money to repay; |
| *Therfore I cun the more thanke* | Therefore I thank you all the more |
| *Thou arte come at thy day.'* | That you have come on your appointed day.' |

However, the cellarer who earlier at York had revelled in the knight's impending default, now denies all knowledge of the debt and, when questioned about his coffers, only admits to carrying a mere 20 marks. As with the knight, Robin asks Little John to open his baggage and this time the result is different: the monk is carrying £800; the outlaws rejoice; the Virgin Mother has repaid the loan twofold (249–50):

| | |
|---|---|
| *'I make myn avowe to God', sayd*<br>   *Robyn –*<br>*'Monke, what tolde I the? –*<br>*Our Lady is the trewest woman*<br>*That euer yet founde I me.* | 'I make my vow to God', said<br>   Robin,<br>'Monk, what did I tell you?<br>Our Lady is the truest woman<br>That I have ever found. |
| *'By dere worthy God', sayd Robyn,*<br>*'To seche all England*<br>   *thorowe,*<br>*Yet founde I neuer to my pay*<br>*A much better borowe.'* | 'By dear worthy God', said Robin,<br>'I might search throughout all<br>   England,<br>And never find to my pleasure<br>A better security.' |

The rueful monk is sent on his way to London without his £800 and, to conclude the fytte, the knight returns to repay Robin's loan. Instead, Robin gives him the extra £400 acquired over and above the initial advance and so all ends happily (280):

| | |
|---|---|
| *Thus than holpe hym good Robyn,*<br>*The knyght all of his care:*<br>*God that syt in heuen hye,*<br>*Graunte us well to fare!* | Robin thus relieved<br>The knight of all his care:<br>God who sits in Heaven high,<br>Grant us well to fare! |

It will be noticed that, in all this, Little John moves about in mercurial fashion. He is with the knight at York in fytte two and once more with Robin in Barnsdale in fytte four. This is partly because a very different element is introduced into the poem in fytte three. Here Little John takes part in an archery contest observed by the sheriff of Nottingham. His archery is masterly (146–7):

| | |
|---|---|
| *Thre tymes Litell Johnn shet aboute,*<br>*And alwey he slet the wande;*<br>*The proude sherif of Notingham*<br>*By the markes can stande.* | Three times Little John shot about,<br>And always he slit the wand;<br>The proud sheriff of Nottingham<br>By the marks did stand. |
| *The sherif swore a full greate othe:*<br>*'By hym that dyede on a tre,*<br>*This man is the best arschere*<br>*That ever yet saw we.'* | The sheriff swore an enormous oath;<br>'By him that died on the cross,<br>This man is the best archer<br>That we have ever seen.' |

The sheriff thereupon invites John into his service. Little John, under the alias of Reynold Greenlefe, accepts. He is determined to pay the sheriff out, although it is not clear for what; at this stage the outlaws' inveterate hostility to the sheriff is taken for granted. In his new role Little John soon quarrels with the cook while the sheriff is away hunting. They fight and the cook proves so doughty an adversary that John asks him to join Robin's band. This he agrees to do and, after helping themselves to the sheriff's valuables, the two of them join

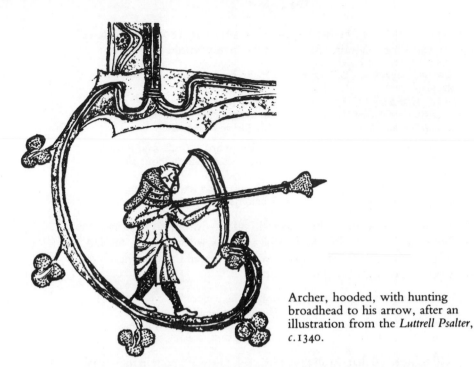

Archer, hooded, with hunting broadhead to his arrow, after an illustration from the *Luttrell Psalter*, *c.*1340.

Robin in the forest. There Little John 'hym bethought on a shrewd wyle' and goes off in search of the sheriff. By the promise of good hunting he lures him into the arms of Robin. The sheriff is compelled to sup from his own looted plate and to spend the night sleeping in outlaw fashion in a green cloak 'under the grene-woode tree'. One night is enough for him (200–1):

| | |
|---|---|
| 'Or I be here another nyght', sayde the sherif, | 'Before I stay here another night', said the sheriff, |
| 'Robyn, nowe pray I the, | 'Robin, I now pray thee, |
| Smyte of mijn hede rather to-morowe, | I would rather you strike off my head this morning, |
| And I forgyve it the. | And I will forgive it to thee. |
| | |
| 'Lat me go', than sayde the sherif, | 'Let me go', then said the sheriff, |
| 'For saynte charite, | 'For holy charity, |
| And I wol be the best frende | And I will be the best friend |
| That ever yet had ye.' | That you have ever had.' |

So in the morning he is released after swearing on Robin's sword never to harm Robin or do other than aid his men.

Fytte four then completes the tale of the endebted knight and the monks of St Mary's. Fytte five opens with yet another archery contest, arranged this time by the sheriff of Nottingham who promises a gold and silver arrow for the victor. Robin and his men take part and inevitably Robin wins. The hue and cry is then raised against them; they have been betrayed by the sheriff and, although they are able to hold off his posse, Little John is wounded in the knee and the outlaws have to take refuge in the castle of Sir Richard at the Lee, who is identified with the knight of fyttes one, two and four. The knight welcomes them, the castle gates are shut, and they feast in safety.

The sixth fytte opens with the castle under siege by the sheriff, but this is soon brought to an end. After an altercation with the knight, the sheriff goes off to London to appeal to the king. Robin and Little John, now recovered from his wound, return to the forest. The sheriff reappears only to find that they have eluded him and he promptly takes revenge by waylaying and capturing the knight whilst he is out hawking. The knight's wife tells Robin, who musters his men, pursues the sheriff to Nottingham and kills him (347–8):

| | |
|---|---|
| *Robyn bent a full goode bowe,* | Robin bent a very good bow, |
| *An arrowe he drowe at wyll;* | An arrow he drew at will; |
| *He hit so the proude sherife* | He so hit the proud sheriff |
| *Upon the grounde he lay full still.* | That upon the ground he lay quite still. |
| | |
| *And or he myght up aryse,* | And before he could rise, |
| *On his fete to stonde,* | On his feet to stand, |
| *He smote of the sherifs hede* | He struck off the sheriff's head |
| *With his brighte bronde* | With his bright blade. |

The outlaws drive off the sheriff's men and release the knight who returns to the greenwood with them until Robin can obtain pardon for them from the king.

In the seventh fytte the king resolves the fate of the outlaws and their knightly ally. He comes to Nottingham (354):

| | |
|---|---|
| *With knyghtes in grete araye,* | With knights in great array, |
| *For to take that gentyll knyght* | In order to take that gentle knight |
| *And Robyn Hode, and yf he may.* | And Robin Hood, if he could. |

But he finds that he cannot deal with the knight by depriving him of his lands, for no one will accept a gift which might prove fatal with Robin Hood still at large. His temper is not softened by the state of his forests, which Robin has depleted of deer (366):

| | |
|---|---|
| *But alway went good Robyn* | And always went good Robin |
| *By halke and eke by hyll,* | Both by hideout and by hill |
| *And alway slewe the kynges dere* | And always slew the king's deer |
| *And welt them at his wyll.* | And dealt with them at his will. |

At length the king is persuaded to use guile. He enters the forest with a small company all disguised as monks. The familiar scenes are then repeated: Robin waylays him and entertains him, believing him to be an abbot sent by the king to invite the outlaws to Nottingham. After the usual feast, the outlaws hold an archery contest with a clout on the head as a penalty for those who miss the target. Robin buffets his men with gusto only to have to submit in the end to the abbot's chastisement as his own shooting falters. The abbot's blow is wondrous lusty and he stands revealed as the king. The outlaws immediately submit. They are pardoned and enter the royal service.

The eighth fytte opens with the king and the outlaws returning to Nottingham all dressed in Lincoln green. The knight is restored to his land, but Robin, after a year or more in the king's service, begins to find life stale. All his men have left him except Little John and Scathelocke, and he has exhausted his wealth in the rich world of the court. Above all he laments (437–8):

| | |
|---|---|
| *'Somtyme I was an archere good,* | 'Once I was an archer good, |
| *A styffe and eke a stronge;* | Stout and also strong; |
| *I was compted the best archere* | I was counted the best archer |
| *That was in mery Englonde.* | That there was in merry England. |
| | |
| *'Alas!' then sayd good Robyn,* | 'Alas!' then said good Robin, |
| *'Alas and well a woo!* | 'Alas and well a'woe, |
| *Yf I dwele lenger with the kynge,* | If I dwell longer with the king, |
| *Sorowe wyll me sloo.'* | Sorrow will be the death of me.' |

He obtains permission to visit a chapel which he founded in Barnsdale. Once there the scene is too tempting (447):

| | |
|---|---|
| *Robyn slewe a full grete harte;* | Robin slew a very great hart; |
| *His horne than gan he blow,* | Then his horn he did blow, |
| *That all the outlawes of that forest* | That all the outlaws of that forest |
| *That horne coud they knowe.* | That horn might recognize. |

He is reunited with his band and lives in the greenwood for twenty-two years. In the end he is slain by treachery. He visits his relative, the **prioress of Kirklees, for medical treatment.** She has a secret lover, Sir Roger of Doncaster, and the two of them plot the outlaw's death. The *Gest* ends briefly in pathos and with a pious prayer for Robin's soul.[8]

The *Gest* is a long, rambling narrative. One critic has commented enthusiastically on 'the poem's remarkable unity and above all its narrative symmetry' and concludes that it 'is the work of a skilled artist'.[9] but this is only really applicable to the tale of Robin and the indebted knight in the first, second and fourth fyttes. This certainly is a well-integrated, nicely balanced piece. It is held together stylistically by the use of recurrent scenes: Robin's refusal to dine without guests, the dispatch of his men in search of them, the ritual of the dinner, the request for payment, the opening of the guest's money-bags and so on.

This is emphasized by verbal repetition. Compare, for example, the discovery of the knight's resources with that of the monk's in fyttes one and four. First the knight's (42–3):

| | |
|---|---|
| *Lytell John sprede downe hys mantell* | Little John spread his mantle down |
| *Full fayre upon the grounde,* | Very fair upon the ground |
| *And there he fonde in the knyghtes cofer* | And there he found in the knight's coffer |
| *But even halfe a pounde.* | No more than half a pound. |
| | |
| *Littell Johnn let it lye full styll,* | Little John let it lie quite still, |
| *And went to hys maysteer full lowe;* | And humbly sought his master; |
| *'What tydinges, Johnn?' sayde Robyn;* | 'What tidings, John?' said Robin; |
| *'Sir, the knyght is true inowe.'* | 'Sir, the knight is true enough.' |

Then the monk's (247–8):

| | |
|---|---|
| *Lytell Johnn spred his mantell downe,* | Little John spread his mantle down, |
| *As he had done before,* | As he had done before, |
| *And he tolde out of the monkes male* | And counted out of the monk's bag |
| *Eyght hondred pounde and more.* | Eight hundred pounds and more. |
| | |
| *Lytell John let it lye full styll,* | Little John let it lie quite still, |
| *And went to his mayster in hast;* | And went to his master in haste; |
| *'Syr,' he sayd, 'the monke is trewe ynowe,* | 'Sir,' said he, 'the monk is true enough, |
| *Our Lady hath doubled your cast.'* | Our Lady has doubled your throw.' |

Such repetition reinforces the moral lesson of the story. The knight tells the truth and Robin helps him; the monk lies (for it is only in repaying a debt pledged on the Virgin that the monk is 'trewe') and Robin robs him. The contrast lies not simply in truthfulness but in the courtesy of Robin and the knight on the one hand and the discourtesy and churlishness of the abbot and the monks on the other. It is underlain by a unifying religious theme. Robin is devoted to the Virgin Mother, and it is in her name that his loan to the knight is pledged. The knight's debt is to the abbot of St Mary's, and it is through a monk of her abbey that St Mary returns Robin's loan with interest.

New material was intruded into this tale in at least two stages. The second fytte ends with the knight riding out to repay Robin, his company well decked, bearing gifts of bows and arrows for the outlaws. He then tarries at a wrestling match where he rescues the victor who is a stranger yeoman in danger from the home crowd. This is used as a device to delay his return to Robin, but it is not essential to the main plot since he has already 'dwelled fayre at home' before setting out; that it was an integral part of the original story is unlikely.

Much more obviously intrusive is the tale of Little John in the third fytte. Here the plot is wrenched into an entirely new context in the first three stanzas (144–5):

| | |
|---|---|
| *Lyth and lystyn, gentilmen,* | Give ear and listen, gentlemen, |
| *All that nowe be here;* | All who now are here; |
| *Of Lytell Johnn, that was the knightes man,* | Of Little John, that was the knight's man, |
| *Goode myrth ye shall here.* | Good mirth you shall hear. |
| *It was upon a mery day* | It was upon a merry day |
| *That yonge men wolde go shete;* | When young men would go to shoot; |
| *Lytell John fet his bowe anone,* | Little John forthwith fetched his bow, |
| *And sayde he wolde them mete.* | And said he would with them meet. |

The return to the theme of the knight and his debt is achieved almost equally artificially at the beginning of fytte four (205–6):

| | |
|---|---|
| *The sherif dwelled in Notingham;* | The sheriff stayed in Nottingham; |
| *He was fayne he was agone;* | He was glad he had escaped; |
| *And Robyn and his mery men* | And Robin and his merry men |
| *Went to wode anone.* | Went to the wood forthwith. |
| *'Go we to dyner', sayde Littell Johnn;* | 'Let's go to dinner', said Little John; |
| *Robyn Hode sayde, 'Naye,* | Robin Hood said, 'Nay, |
| *For I drede Our Lady be wroth with me,* | For I fear Our Lady is angry with me, |
| *For she sent me nat my pay'.* | For she has not sent me my pay'. |

That tale is nicely rounded off and yet another abrupt shift is made to revert to the sheriff in fytte five (281–3):

| | |
|---|---|
| *Now hath the knyght his leve i-take,* | Now the knight has taken his leave, |
| *And wente hym on his way;* | And departed on his way; |
| *Robyn Hode and his mery men* | Robin Hood and his merry men |
| *Dwelled styll full many a day.* | Stayed quiet for many a day. |
| *Lyth and lysten, gentil men,* | Give ear and listen gentlemen, |
| *And herken what I shall say.* | And hark to what I shall say. |
| *How the proude sheryfe of Notyngham* | How the proud sheriff of Nottingham |
| *Dyde crye a full fayre play;* | Proclaimed a splendid game; |
| *That all the best archers of the north* | That all the best archers of the north |
| *Sholde come upon a day,* | Should come on a certain day, |
| *And he that shoteth allther best* | And he who would shoot the best of all |
| *The game shall bere a way.* | Would bear the prize away. |

Thereafter the narrative moves more easily through the quarrel with the sheriff to the arrival of the king and the subsequent dénouement.

These contrived linking passages suggest very strongly that the *Gest* contains not one, but at least two stories, or groups of stories: first, the tale of the knight, the outlaws and the monks of St Mary's; and second, the more miscellaneous material about the sheriff and the king. They differ not only in subject-matter, but also in geographic setting, for the first is based in Barnsdale and the second in Sherwood and Nottingham.[10]

Some attempt was made to give the whole work unity. The tale of Little John and the sheriff is inserted into the middle of the story of the indebted knight rather than crudely tacked on the end. Sir Richard at the Lee of fytte five is carefully, if somewhat unconvincingly, identified with the indebted knight of fyttes one, two and four. The author brought sufficient sophistication to his task for it to be difficult to distinguish between those unifying elements which he himself contributed and those derived from the similarities of situation, theme and versification already present in the material he used. Yet he was still unable to produce a work in which the component elements were fully amalgamated. The second story of the outlaws and the sheriff is plainly less well constructed than the first concerning the knight and his debt. The tale of Little John in fytte three duplicates, in less precise fashion, the sheriff's archery contest in fytte five; fytte three adds little to the whole plot except to place the sheriff under an oath of friendship which he treacherously breaks in fytte five. The continuity here is merely formal. The sheriff of fytte five is menacing and villainous. The sheriff of fytte three is a laughing stock.

In much of this, critics have differed, and will continue to differ, about the extent of the unifying contribution of the author of the *Gest* or about the number of distinct component elements which went into its making.[11] There is room for argument, if only because none of the components survive other than in the *Gest*. Of all the early tales only one, *Robin Hoode his Death*, comes close enough to the *Gest* to suggest direct interdependence. Each of the others embodies a distinct and independent tradition of its own.

## Robin Hoode his Death

Derived from a damaged section of the Percy Folio, this is a fragment of twenty-seven verses. It lacks half a page after verse 8 and again after verse 18, so the tale is fragmentary and in its present form amounts to perhaps half the original. It opens brusquely with Robin declaring that he will visit Kirklees ('Church Lees') to have his blood let. He is warned by Will Scarlett, but insists on going without a bodyguard other than Little John. They set out (7–8):

| | |
|---|---|
| *Untill they came to blacke water,* | Until they came to dark water, |
| *And over it laid a planke.* | Over which was laid a plank. |
| | |
| *Upon it there kneeled an old woman,* | Upon it there kneeled an old woman, |
| *Was banning Robin Hoode;* | Who was cursing Robin Hood; |
| *'Why dost thou bann Robin Hoode?'* | 'Why do you curse Robin Hood?' |
| *said Robin . . .* | said Robin . . . |

Kirklees gatehouse in the nineteenth century after an etching
from Ritson's *Robin Hood*.

What precisely the 'ban' was is a mystery, for at this point the page is damaged. When the tale takes up Robin is arguing that he need fear no harm from the prioress since she is his cousin. They arrive at Kirklees, the bleeding begins and Robin soon realizes his cousin's treachery (16–17):

| | |
|---|---|
| *Shee laid the blood-irons to Robin Hoods vaine,* | She laid the blood-irons to Robin Hood's vein, |
| *Alack, the more pitye!* | Alack, the more the pity! |
| *And pearct the vaine, and let out the bloode,* | And pierced the vein, and let out the blood, |
| *That full red was to see.* | That was very red to see. |
| | |
| *And first it bled, the thicke, thicke bloode,* | And first it bled, the thick, thick blood, |
| *And afterwards the thinne,* | And afterwards the thin, |
| *And well then wist good Robin Hoode* | And well then knew good Robin Hood, |
| *Treason there was within.* | That there was treason within. |

Once again the fragment breaks off with Robin informing Little John of what has happened. In the last and final section Robin fights and slays Red Roger. He then makes his peace with God, refuses to avenge himself on the prioress and commands Little John to bear him to his grave (27):

| | |
|---|---|
| *And sett my bright sword at my head,* | And set my bright sword at my head, |
| *Mine arrowes at my feete.* | My arrows at my feet. |
| *And lay my yew bow by my side,* | And lay my yew-bow by my side, |
| *My met-yard wi . . .* | My measuring-rod wi . . . |

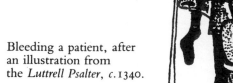

Bleeding a patient, after
an illustration from
the *Luttrell Psalter, c.*1340.

There the fragment breaks off yet again and for the last time.

There is no real doubt that this tale stems from the same source as the concluding stanzas of the *Gest*.[12] They both relate the visit to Kirklees, the blood-letting, the relationship of the treacherous prioress to Robin and the intrusion of a man called Roger, Red Roger in the one, Roger of Donkesley or Doncaster in the other. What that source was, how far the author of the *Gest* refashioned it, how much was altered as it passed down to the form revealed in the Percy Folio, all that is guesswork. Yet the close proximity of the two, the one a fragment and the other a much condensed summary, is a remarkable testimony to the durability of the legend of Robin's death.

## Robin Hood and the Monk

*Robin Hoode his Death* is grim, full of foreboding. *Robin Hood and the Monk* is by contrast a blood-and-thunder adventure in which the real hero is Little John. It is of common stock, with some sections of the *Gest*, and also overlaps the *Death*, but the connections with both are distant and limited: in its essentials *Robin Hood and the Monk* is an independent story. It is lengthy, extending to ninety stanzas with at least one considerable omission, and it is an intricate yarn fit to stand comparison with the main sections of the *Gest*.

The poem opens with a conventional introduction in praise of the greenwood and the splendour of a May morning. Little John's enjoyment of the day is not shared by Robin Hood who has not been to church for a fortnight and hence decides to go to Nottingham. Much advises him to take twenty of his yeomen, but Robin will have none of it. As in *Robin Hoode his Death*, he insists on going with Little John as his sole companion. On their journey they wager their skill in archery. Little John claims to have won five shillings which Robin refuses to pay. They quarrel, Robin strikes him and they part, Robin to Nottingham, John to Sherwood. On entering St Mary's church, Robin is spotted by a 'gret-heded monke' who raises the alarm, bars the town gates and alerts the sheriff. The sheriff's men break into the church and a fight ensues. Robin kills twelve of them but disaster follows (28–9):

| | |
|---|---|
| *His sworde upon the schireff hed* | His sword upon the sheriff's head |
| *Sertanly he brake in too;* | For sure he broke in two: |
| *'The smyth that the made', seid Robyn,* | 'The smith who made thee', said Robin |
| *'I pray to God wyrke hym woo!* | 'I pray God to bring him woe! |

| | |
|---|---|
| *'Ffor now am i weppynlesse', seid Robyn,* | 'For now I am weaponless', said Robin, |
| *'Alasse! agayn my wylle;* | 'Alas! against my will; |
| *But if I may fle these traytors fro,* | Unless I from these traitors flee, |
| *I wot thei wil me kyll.'* | I know they will me kill.' |

At this point there is a considerable omission in the surviving version of the poem, for without explanation the scene shifts to the outlaws who are aghast at the news of Robin's capture. Little John, stout-hearted in his trust that Our Lady will protect Robin, proposes action. He and Much set out to find the monk who they know has been sent to report Robin's capture to the king. They meet him, beguile him and then slay both him and his page (50–2):

| | |
|---|---|
| *Litull John was sore agrevyd,* | Little John was very aggrieved, |
| *And drew owt his swerde in hye;* | And drew out his sword in haste; |
| *This munke saw he shulde be ded,* | This monk saw he would be dead, |
| *Lowd mercy can he crye.* | And 'mercy' loud he cried. |
| | |
| *'He was my maister', seid Litull John,* | 'He was my master', said Little John, |
| *'That thou hase browght in bale;* | 'To whom you have brought such harm; |
| *Shalle thou never cum at our kyng,* | You shall never get to our king, |
| *Ffor to telle hym tale.'* | To tell him the tale.' |
| | |
| *John smote of the munkis hed,* | John struck off the monk's head, |
| *No longer wolde he dwell;* | No longer would he wait; |
| *So did Moch the litull page,* | Much did the same to the little page, |
| *Ffor ferd lest he wolde tell.* | For fear that he might tell. |

Little John and Much then carry the monk's letter to the king, who makes them yeomen of the crown and sends them back to Nottingham with the royal seal as authority that they are to bring Robin to him. The sheriff receives them well and, after dinner, with the sheriff in a drunken sleep, they visit the gaol. There they rouse the gaoler with the cry that Robin has escaped. He takes the bait and lets them in. Little John kills him, finds Robin and releases him; they leap the castle walls and return to Sherwood.

The remainder of the tale is crude moral comment. Little John has repaid a bad turn with a good. He now intends to leave, but Robin will not have it so and offers him command of the outlaw band. John refuses the offer but decides to stay. The sheriff fears that he will be hanged for his dereliction, but the king appreciates that they have both been beguiled. The last word lies with him (87–9):

| | |
|---|---|
| *'I gaf theym grith', then seid oure kyng;* | 'I pardoned them', then said our king; |
| *'I say, so mot I the,* | I say, so may I thrive, |
| *Ffor sothe soch a yeman as he is on* | For sooth, such a yeomen as he is one |
| *In all Ingolnd are not thre.* | In the whole of England there are not three.' |

29

| | |
|---|---|
| *'He is trew to his maister', seid our kyng;*<br>*'I sey, be swete Seynt John,*<br>*He lovys better Robyn Hode*<br>*Then he dose us ychon.* | 'He is true to his master', said our king;<br>'I say, by sweet Saint John,<br>He loves Robin Hood better<br>Than he does any one of us. |
| *'Robyn Hode is ever bond to hym,*<br>*Bothe in strete and stalle;*<br>*Speke no more of this mater', seid oure kyng,*<br>*'But John has begyled us alle.'* | 'Robin Hood is ever bound to him,<br>Wherever he roams or stays;<br>Speak no more this matter', said our king,<br>'But John has beguiled us all'. |

*Robin Hood and the Monk* ends thus, with a paean for loyal service. It is a shallow tale, but one well and crisply told.

## Robin Hood and Guy of Gisborne

This is a much deeper and more mysterious story. It is a lengthy narrative of fifty-eight stanzas which survives only in the Percy Folio in a corrupt text marred by omissions and inconsequential intrusions. Like *The Monk* it opens with verses in praise of the greenwood. These break off and the story takes up with Robin recounting a dream in which he was captured and disarmed by two yeomen. He vows vengeance and, accompanied by Little John, sets off in search of them. Presently they espy a stranger (6–7):

| | |
|---|---|
| *There were the ware of a wight yeoman,*<br>*His body leaned to a tree.*<br>*A sword and a dagger he wore by his side,*<br>*Had beene many a mans bane,*<br>*And he was cladd in his capull-hyde,*<br>*Topp, and tayle, and mayne.* | There was the gear of a lusty yeoman,<br>Who was leaning against a tree.<br>A sword and a dagger he wore by his side,<br>Which had been the bane of many a man,<br>And he was clad in horse-hide,<br>Top, tail and main. |

Little John offers to investigate the stranger, but Robin turns down this suggestion in an overbearing manner. They quarrel and John returns to Barnsdale only to find himself in the midst of catastrophe. Two of the band have been slain and Will Scarlett is in flight from the sheriff's men. John takes his bow, aims a shaft which kills one of the sheriff's men, William a' Trent, but then the bow breaks and he is taken. The sheriff has him bound to a tree to await summary execution (20):

| | |
|---|---|
| *'Thou shalt be drawen by dale and downe,*<br>*And hanged hye on a hill:'*<br>*'But thou may ffayle', quoth Little Iohn*<br>*'If itt be Christ's owne will.'* | 'You shall be drawn by dale and down,<br>And hanged high on a hill:'<br>'But you may fail', said Little John,<br>'If it be Christ's own will.' |

Robin Hood and Guy of Gisborne, after an engraving by Thomas Bewick, *c.*1795, from Ritson's *Robin Hood*.

The story then reverts to Robin Hood and the mysterious yeoman, now identified as Guy of Gisborne. The encounter begins with polite exchanges: Robin offers to act as Guy's guide, and Guy informs him that he is hunting an outlaw – 'men call him Robin Hood'. They compete in friendly fashion at archery and Robin proves the better. Thereupon Guy seeks to know more about his companion (32–5):

'God's blessing on thy heart!' sayes Guye,
'Goode ffellow, thy shooting is goode;
For an thy hart be as good as thy hands,
Thou were better then Robin Hood.

'Tell me thy name, good ffellow', quoth Guy,
'Under the leaves of lyne:'
'Nay, by my faith', quoth good Robin,
'Till thou have told me thine.'

'I dwell by dale and downe', quoth Guye,
'And I have done many a curst turne;
And he that calles me by my right name
Calles me Guye of good Gysborne.'

'God's blessing on your heart', said Guy,
'Good fellow, your shooting is good;
If your heart were as good as your hands,
You would be better than Robin Hood.

'Tell me your name, good fellow', said Guy,
'Under the leaves of this tree.'
'No, by my faith', said good Robin,
'Till you have told me yours.'

'I dwell by dale and down', said Guy,
'And I have done many a cursed turn;
And he who calls me by my right name
Calls me Guy of good Gisborne.'

| | |
|---|---|
| 'My dwelling is in the wood', sayes<br>  Robin;<br>'By thee I set right nought;<br>My name is Robin Hood of<br>  Barnesdale,<br>A ffellow thou hast long sought.' | 'My dwelling is in the wood', says<br>  Robin;<br>'Of you I reckon nothing;<br>My name is Robin Hood of<br>  Barnsdale,<br>A fellow you have long sought.' |

They set to immediately (37):

| | |
|---|---|
| To have seene how these yeomen<br>  together fought,<br>Two howers of a summers day;<br>Itt was neither Guy nor Robin Hood<br>That ffettled them to flye away. | To have seen how these yeomen<br>  fought,<br>Two hours of a summer's day;<br>And neither Guy nor Robin Hood<br>Was ready to flee away. |

Robin stumbles and is wounded but he calls on Our Lady and wondrously invigorated by her support, he renews the attack and slays Guy. He then maltreats the corpse (41–2):

| | |
|---|---|
| He tooke Sir Guys head by the hayre,<br>And sticked itt on his bowes end:<br>'Thou has beene traytor all thy liffe,<br>Which thing must have an ende.'<br><br>Robin pulled forth an Irish kniffe,<br>And nicked Sir Guy in the fface,<br>That he was never on a woman borne<br>Cold tell who Sir Guye was. | He took Sir Guy's head by the hair,<br>And stuck it on the end of his bow:<br>'You have been a traitor all your life,<br>To which there must come an end.'<br><br>Robin pulled out an Irish knife,<br>And slashed Sir Guy in the face,<br>So that no one of a woman born<br>Could tell who Sir Guy was. |

With this gruesome trophy Robin returns to Barnsdale disguised in Guy's cloak of hide. A blast on Guy's horn announces his coming to the sheriff who takes it to mean that Robin has been slain. The disguised Robin will only take one reward (50):

| | |
|---|---|
| 'I'le none of thy gold', sayes Robin<br>  Hood,<br>'Nor I'le none of it have.<br><br>'But now I have slaine the master', he<br>  sayd,<br>'Let me goe strike the knave;<br>This is all the reward I aske,<br>Nor no other will I have.' | 'I'll none of your gold', says Robin<br>  Hood,<br>'No, I'll have none of it.<br><br>'But now I have slain the master', he<br>  said,<br>Let me go strike the knave;<br>This is all the reward I ask,<br>And no other will I have.' |

The astonished sheriff grants the request. Robin then cuts Little John loose, gives him Guy's bow which he is still carrying and together the two put the sheriff and his men to flight. The sheriff is not quick enough (58):

| | |
|---|---|
| *But he cold neither soe fast goe,* | But he could neither walk so fast, |
| *Nor away soe fast runn,* | Nor run away so swiftly, |
| *But Little Iohn, with an arrow broade,* | And Little John, with an arrow broad, |
| *Did cleave his heart in twinn.* | Did cleave his heart in twain. |

With that the poem ends abruptly.

## The dramatic fragment of c.1475

The verse-play of Robin Hood is a mere fragment of twenty-one lines written on the back of a half sheet of paper recording financial receipts for the year 1475–6.[13] It does no more than overlap part of the story told in *Guy of Gisborne*. It opens abruptly with an arrangement between the sheriff and a knight who promises to capture Robin Hood in return for 'gold and fee'. The knight meets Robin. They compete at archery, casting a stone and wrestling. Robin wins. The knight then identifies Robin, they fight and Robin slays and beheads him. He then disguises himself:

| | |
|---|---|
| *This knyghtys clothis wolle i were* | This knight's clothes will I wear |
| *And in my hode his hede woll bere.* | And in my hood his head will bear. |

The scene then shifts to a more confused picture in which Little John, Will Scarlett and Friar Tuck fight with the sheriff's men. They are captured. Robin does not reappear, but it is rumoured that he too has been taken. With that the fragment ends.

## Robin Hood and the Potter

This is a poem in a much lighter vein. The plot opens with an encounter with a 'proud potter'. Little John warns Robin that the potter is a tough customer whom he has already encountered to his cost, and they wager on Robin's ability to make him pay a levy for passing through Barnsdale. Robin waylays the potter, demands a charge and they fight. Robin is armed with a sword and buckler against the potter's staff, but he is soon defeated, and the potter reads him a lesson in good manners with which Robin ruefully agrees.

The tale then takes a new twist. Impressed by the potter's prowess, Robin befriends him and suggests that they exchange clothing. The potter agrees and in the potter's dress Robin journeys to Nottingham where he makes a splash by selling his wares at cut prices. There is a dramatic run on his pots until he has only five left which he presents as a gift to the sheriff's wife. The gift leads, somewhat improbably, to an invitation to dine with the sheriff. At dinner there is talk of an archery contest. The pseudo-potter expresses interest and they adjourn to the butts where, after the rest have shot, he is provided with a bow. He shoots with splendid accuracy and inquiry reveals that he knows Robin Hood; indeed he has a bow of Robin's in his cart and has shot with him a hundred times under his 'trysting tree'. He promises to take the sheriff there on the morrow.

In the morning the company sets out in style, the pseudo-potter presenting the sheriff's wife with a gold ring. They reach the forest, the pseudo-potter sounds his horn and the outlaws appear. The sheriff now regrets his wish to encounter Robin (69–70):

| | |
|---|---|
| *The screffe had lever nar a hundred ponde* | The sheriff would rather have given a hundred pounds |
| *He had never sene Roben Hode.* | Than have ever seen Robin Hood. |
| *'Had I west that befforen,* | 'Had I known this before, |
| *At Notynggam when we were,* | When we were at Nottingham, |
| *Thow scholde not com yn ffeyre fforest* | You would not have returned to the fair forest |
| *Of all thes thowsande eyre'* | In a thousand years.' |

He is deprived of his horse and would have suffered worse but for his wife's kind hospitality to Robin (73, 75):

| | |
|---|---|
| *'Hether ye cam on hors ffoll hey,* | 'Hither you came high on a horse, |
| *And hom schall ye go on ffote;* | And home you shall go on foot; |
| *And grete well they weyffe at home,* | And greet well your wife at home, |
| *The woman ys ffoll godde.* | For the woman is very good. |
| *Y schall her sende a wheyt palffrey,* | I shall send her a white palfrey, |
| *Het hambellet as the weynde;* | That gallops as the wind; |
| *Nere ffor the loffe of yowre weyffe,* | But for the love of your wife, |
| *Off more sorow scholde yow seyng.'* | Of more sorrow would you sing.' |

The sheriff returns disconsolate, much to his wife's amusement, and the poem ends with Robin paying the potter for his wares.

It is a trite tale very dependent on comic situations: Robin's sale of the pots, his entertainment by the sheriff and the preparation for the archery contest in which Robin finds that the bow provided for him is 'ryght weke gere'. However, it contains one important novel feature: in the fight with the potter Robin is defeated. That set the pattern for many later tales in which Robin challenged a poor traveller, tradesman or rustic.

These early stories share many features. Introductory verses in praise of the greenwood occur in *The Monk, Guy of Gisborne* and *The Potter*; they are conventional, appearing in a variety of pastoral verse. Dramatic artifice requires that Robin should set forth in the sole company of Little John; he rejects equally the bodyguard proposed by Much the Miller's son in *The Monk* and by Will Scarlett in *Robin Hoode his Death*. Robin and Little John quarrel, albeit on different grounds, in both *The Monk* and *Guy of Gisborne*. Robin Hood is bested by the potter in *The Potter*; Little John is matched by the cook in the *Gest*. Robin and his men enter the king's service in the *Gest*; Little John and Much are made yeomen of the crown in *The Monk*. Robin's devotion to the Virgin Mother recurs in the *Gest*, *The Monk* and *Guy of Gisborne*. Throughout, disguise is an important dramatic device: the king figures as an abbot, Little John as Reynold Greenleaf and Robin, variously, as Guy of Gisborne and the potter. The character incognito is an even hardier subterfuge: in the *Gest* both Robin and Little John, not to mention the other outlaws, compete in archery contests at Nottingham with their real identity necessarily, but implausibly, hidden; in *The Monk* Little John beguiles monk, king and sheriff without revealing his true identity and loyalties; Robin himself plays a similar role in *The Potter*, whilst in *Guy of Gisborne* Guy and Robin meet, talk and shoot in competition before Robin reveals his true identity. Throughout, much of the excitement and humour depends on the listener knowing the identity and purpose of the heroes while the villains remain in impotent and rueful ignorance. Robin as the potter deludes the sheriff thus (55–8):

| | |
|---|---|
| 'Yn mey cart y haffe a bowe, | 'In my cart I have a bow, |
| Ffor soyt,' he seyde, 'and that a godde; | Forsooth,' he said, 'and that a good one; |
| Yn mey cart ys the bow | In my cart there is the bow |
| That gaffe me Robyn Hode.' | That Robin Hood gave me.' |
| | |
| 'Knowest thou Robyn Hode,' seyde the screffe, | 'Do you know Robin Hood,' said the sheriff, |
| 'Potter, y prey the tell thow me;' | 'Potter, I pray you tell me;' |
| 'A hundred torne y haffe schot with hem, | 'A hundred bouts I have shot with him, |
| Under hes tortyll-tre.' | Under his trysting-tree.' |
| | |
| 'Y had lever nar a hundred ponde,' seyde the screffe, | 'I had rather than a hundred pounds,' said the sheriff, |
| 'And sware be the Trenite, | 'And I swear by the Trinity, |
| . . . . . . . . . . . | . . . . . . . . . . . |
| That the ffals owtelawe stod be me.' | That the false outlaw stood next to me.' |

The listeners can anticipate the outcome. They enjoy a joke hidden from and at the expense of the villain. It was on such simple stratagems that the tales depended.

Yet the stories are not entirely of common stock. They vary widely in atmosphere. The tale of Robin, the knight and the abbot of St Mary's is a moralistic romance. *Guy of Gisborne* is a grim yarn of the bloody end of a medieval bounty-hunter. *The Monk* tells of brutal retribution for monkish treachery. By the side of these *The Potter* is a burlesque. It is difficult to believe that these tales all stemmed from a single origin, whether in literary fiction or in the adventures of a particular person. Moreover, there is no obvious or easy method of determining which of them embodies the earliest or the most authentic account of Robin's activities. The legend is not like a settled archaeological site where the earlier deposits lie underneath the later. It is like a hoard amassed from different sources, probably at different times, perhaps for different purposes. There is no way of knowing for sure how much of the hoard remains or how haphazard that residue is.

How much of the medieval legend has come down to modern times? The survival of medieval literature was often hazardous. In the case of Robin Hood, simple survival was complicated by word-of-mouth transmission and even more by the living quality of the stories, which meant that as they descended from generation to generation old tales were revised and new tales invented. Early and late versions which illustrate this process survive for *Robin Hoode his Death*, *Robin Hood and the Potter* (the second version of which is in dramatic form), *Robin Hood and the Curtal Friar*, and many of the later tales.[14] It is possible that some late tales overlie and completely obscure earlier versions. It is certain that some stories have simply been lost. It is usually assumed, not unreasonably, that the early stories which remain are a typical and perhaps considerable part of the whole legend. The main ground for thinking this lies in the *Gest*, for it is nothing less than a deliberate attempt to collect the tales into a single poem of epic length. Yet the author either did not know or chose to ignore *Guy of Gisborne*, *The Monk* and *The Potter*. He could just as easily have passed by other stories which have not survived.

Yet this is no licence for guesswork. Nothing has confused the story of Robin so much as the imposition of modern anachronism on the medieval legend. It is well to summarize what the medieval stories do *not* contain. First, but least important, they lack a number of striking incidents which have accrued subsequently. For example, in the earliest version of *Robin Hoode his Death* Robin does not summon Little John by three blasts of his horn, nor does he shoot a final arrow to mark the site of his grave; that comes into the story in the eighteenth century.

Secondly, Robin and his men, their bows apart, fight with the sword. It is only in *The Potter* that combat with the staff appears and there it is the potter alone who uses it. Robin himself does not stoop to this weapon until in *Robin Hood and Little John*, a tale derived from an eighteenth-century garland, both he and Little John set to work on each other with staffs (16):

As if they had been threshing of corn.

Thirdly, there is no Maid Marian. Marian only made her way into the legend via the May Games and that not certainly until the sixteenth century. It was not simply that Robin's devotion to the Virgin Mother left no room for other women. It was rather that there was no place for them in the context of the tales. Only the sheriff's wife in *The Potter* cuts any kind of figure. Her hospitality to Robin and his respect for her may carry a distant echo of courtly love. That apart, there is no sex and no family.

Fourthly, the only king mentioned is 'Edward our comely king'. There is nothing at all in the early stories to associate Robin with Richard I (the Lionheart) or with his brother and successor of evil repute, John count of Mortain.

Fifthly, the only tax mentioned anywhere in the early stories is the 'pavage' or toll which Robin attempts to levy on the potter. The only example of financial oppression is by the abbot of St Mary's on the knight. The early stories are simply not concerned with the burdens of medieval government, central or local, royal, baronial or ecclesiastical.

Sixthly, there is not the slightest indication that Robin played any part in English resistance to the Norman conquerors who settled in England after 1066. Of all the fictions about Robin this is the most fictitious.

Seventhly, there is no doubt about Robin's status. He is a yeoman, not a peasant, nor a knight, still less a dispossessed nobleman.

Eighthly, there is nothing in these early tales to support those social historians who have claimed Robin as 'the archetype of the social rebel . . . essentially a peasant rebelling against landlords, usurers, and other representatives of what Thomas More called "the conspiracy of the rich"',[15] whose 'most endearing activities to his public were the robbery and killing of landowners, in particular church landowners'. Equally, there is nothing to suggest that the legend was a by-product of the agrarian struggle over rents, manorial services and social status which culminated in the Peasants' Revolt of 1381.[16] To be sure, there is nothing to exclude social historians from contributing to the legend. Indeed, these views of Robin have spilled over into the latest dramatic and artistic representations of the outlaw. But they simply do not fit the original. Robin is not a peasant. He does not kill landowners or advocate such action. Nowhere does he mention any conspiracy by the rich. There is nothing in the ballads of the great economic and social issues which led to the peasants' rising of 1381; nothing of manorial lordship, nothing of villeinage, nothing of rent or labour-services. The rising was centred on Kent and East Anglia; Robin is based on South

Yorkshire and Nottinghamshire, and the ballad genre as a whole belongs essentially to northern England and Scotland. Songs bemoaning the peasants' lot survive. They complain of misfortunes both natural and man-made: bad harvests, the demands of bailiffs and beadles, and the burden of royal taxes:

| | |
|---|---|
| *To seche selver to the kyng y mi seed solde* | To find money for the king I sold my seed, |
| *Forthi my lond leye lith ant leorneth to slepe.* | Wherefore my land lies fallow and learns to sleep. |

Thus the *Husbandman's Song* of *c.*1317.[17] No such plaint ever appears in the tales of Robin Hood. On the contrary, the king is 'our comely king' with whom Robin makes his peace.

Finally, there is very little about robbing the rich and giving to the poor. There is some hint of it in the opening and concluding stanzas of the *Gest*, which are additions made by the compiler, not integral parts of the component stories. The ending is short, its message simple (456):

| | |
|---|---|
| *Cryst have mercy on his soule,* | Christ have mercy on his soul, |
| *That dyed on the rode.* | That died on the rood. |
| *For he was a good outlawe,* | For he was a good outlaw, |
| *And dyde pore men moch god.* | And did poor men much good. |

The introduction, however, is lengthy, and in it the poet has Little John ask Robin who is to be robbed and who is to be left in peace. Robin's answer is explicit (13–15):

| | |
|---|---|
| *'But loke ye do no husbonde harme,* | 'But make sure you do no husbandman harm |
| *That tilleth with his ploughe.* | Who tilleth with his plough. |
| *'No more ye shall no gode yeman* | Nor shall you harm any good yeoman |
| *That walketh by grene-wode shawe:* | Who walks by greenwood grove: |
| *Ne no knyght ne no squyer* | Nor any knight nor any squire |
| *That wol be a gode felawe.* | Who will be a good fellow. |
| *'These bisshoppes and these archebishoppes,* | These bishops and these archbishops, |
| *Ye shall them bete and bynde;* | You shall them beat and bind; |
| *The hye sherif of Notyingham* | The high sheriff of Nottingham |
| *Hym holde ye in your mynde.'* | You keep him in your mind.' |

Now this is different from the modern stereotype, in that there is no positive intention to help the poor. Moreover, the line drawn is not between rich and poor. Robin distinguishes bishops, archbishops and the sheriff of Nottingham as his enemies and potential victims, and associates knights and squires, 'that wol be a gode felawe', with yeomen and husbandmen, as his friends. This is not mere rhetoric, detached from the content of the tale. The *Gest* is a story of Robin's befriending of a knight who was a 'good fellow', of the redemption of the knight's lands from the hands of the abbot of St Mary's, of their joint battle against the sheriff of Nottingham, and of their final reconciliation with the king. The abbot may have been rich, but not all the rich were abbots. Though the knight enters the tale impoverished, his knighthood was scarcely a symbol of poverty. In time the abbot came to stand for the one, and the knight, less convincingly, for the other.

That is the nearest approach in the original legend to the later conceit that Robin robbed the rich to give to the poor. The tale is only part of the *Gest* and the *Gest* is only one of the earliest surviving stories. But none of the extant ballads, early or late, presents the outlaws robbing a secular landlord; and none is concerned with robbing the rich, whether clerk or lay, *in order to* give to the poor. Such an objective was not part of Robin's original make-up. It is a posthumous cosmetic. More will be said of this in the Postscript.

# III
# *Who was Robin Hood?*

Robin Hood enjoys a unique distinction. He was accorded in the *Dictionary of National Biography* an article devoted entirely to arguing that he never existed. The author, Sidney Lee, who was also the editor of the dictionary, believed that Robin was purely mythical and tried to write him out of history. Yet obstinately he remains within it. From the first he was believed to be a real historical person.

Belief is one thing; certain knowledge quite another. Robin's activities were not recorded by any contemporary chronicler. No one says that he knew him or had seen him. No one could point to authentic records of his activities. Hence the earliest attempts to identify him had mixed results. Andrew de Wyntoun who, by 1420, had completed a rhyming chronicle of Scotland up to 1408, referred to Robin and Little John under the years 1283–5:

| | |
|---|---|
| *Than litill Iohne and Robyne Hude* | Then Little John and Robin Hood |
| *Waichmen were commendit* | As forest outlaws were well |
| *gud,* | renowned, |
| *In Yngilwode and Bernysdale* | In Inglewood and Barnsdale |
| *And usit this tyme thar travale.*[1] | All this time they plied their trade. |

Some twenty years later, in the 1440s, another Scotsman, Walter Bower, engaged on a continuation of John Fordun's fourteenth-century *Scotichronicon*, inserted under the year 1266:

Then arose the famous murderer, Robert Hood, as well as Little John, together with their accomplices from among the dispossessed, whom the foolish populace are so inordinately fond of celebrating both in tragedy and comedy.[2]

That was not far from Wyntoun's dating, and it placed Robin in a possible historical context among the disinherited supporters of Simon de Montfort, earl of Leicester, who continued in rebellion after his defeat and death at the battle of Evesham in 1265. A third Scotsman, John Major, who published a *History of Greater Britain* in 1521, chose yet another date, assigning Robin and Little John to 1193–4 when Richard I, following his crusade, was in captivity in Germany.[3]

On the face of it there is nothing to choose between these dates. However, in time it was Major's date of 1193–4 that gained general acceptance. It was not reinforced by argument, evidence or proof. It was simply recycled through later versions of the tale and so became an integral part of the legend. The antiquaries of the sixteenth and seventeenth centuries looked for hard fact in the quicksand of fiction and found very little. John Leland, king's antiquary to Henry VIII, recorded the association of Robin Hood with Barnsdale and his burial at Kirklees. John Stow, the London tailor who became a prolific historian, editor and a zealous collector of manuscripts, simply repeated Major. His great literary rival, Richard Grafton, king's printer to Edward VI, claimed to have the advantage of an 'olde and aunciente pamphlet' recording Robin's life and references in the Exchequer rolls to the confiscation of his lands, but he too placed Robin in the reign of Richard I; his 'aunciente pamphlet' has not survived and his reference to the 'recordes in the Exchequer' is imprecise and has never been traced. An anonymous prose life of Robin, surviving in a manuscript in the Sloane collection in the British Library, was later treated as an independent authoritative account, but is really nothing more than a hotchpotch of the legend. It follows Major's dating; its only fresh contribution is to provide Robin with a birthplace – Locksley. Details of Robin's death also acquired a spurious accuracy. Thomas Gale, dean of York 1697–1702, left among his papers a record of an epitaph allegedly inscribed on Robin's grave. This recorded that he died on the 24 Kalends of December 1247. Unfortunately there is no such date in the Roman calendar, as Gale, who was a fine classical scholar, well knew, and the doubt which that induces is deepened by the record of a similar epitaph at the end of Martin Parker's *The True Tale of Robin Hood*, published in 1632; this states that Robin died on 4 December 1198. At Kirklees there was unquestionably a grave-slab. Grafton described this in his *Chronicle*; the antiquary William Camden referred to it in the fifth edition of his *Britannia* published in 1607; the Pontefract doctor, Tory pampleteer and antiquary, Nathaniel Johnston, made a drawing of it in 1665 and this appeared in Richard Gough's *Sepulchral Monuments of Great Britain* in 1786. The slab apparently carried the inscription, no longer legible in Gough's day: 'Here lie Roberd Hude, William Goldburgh, Thomas'.[4] William Goldburgh and a Thomas never figure in the legend. Nevertheless, the slab bore the name of Roberd Hude and that was enough to give it the appearance of authenticity. None of the early authorities, apart from Gale, Parker and the Stamford antiquary, Francis Peck, mentions an epitaph. A spurious inscription based on Gale's epitaph was erected in the nineteenth century when the slab was enclosed by iron railings. By then it was badly damaged. Labourers constructing the Yorkshire and Lancashire railway took fragments from it as a cure for toothache. Thus were the attentions of the twentieth-century tourist forestalled by the superstitions of the nineteenth-century labourer.

There was more in this than the mere addition of fanciful detail. It also embodied a new social bias. Leland described Robin as *nobilis* – a nobleman – and so also, apparently, did the prose life in the Sloane manuscript.[5] In 1598 the playwright Anthony Munday wrote two plays in which Robin appeared as Robert earl of Huntington, and it was in this guise that he figured in all versions of the epitaph. Gale's epitaph, couched in pseudo-antique English which betrays its spurious character, runs:

| | |
|---|---|
| *Hear undernead this laitl stean* | Here underneath this little stone |
| *Lais Robert earl of Huntington* | Lies Robert earl of Huntington |
| *Nea arcir ver as hei sae geud* | No archer was as he so good |
| *An pipl kauld im robin heud* | And people called him Robin Hood |
| *Sick utlaws as hi an is men* | Such outlaws as he and his men |
| *Vil England nivr si agen* | Will England never see again. |
| *Obiit 24 kal dekembris 1247.*[6] | |

Parker's epitaph, recorded over half a century earlier, was derived from the same tradition, but bears this writer's own particular moralizing stamp:

*Robert Earle of Huntington*
*Lies under this little stone.*
*No archer was like him so good:*
*His wildnesse named him Robbin Hood.*
*Full thirteene yeares, and something more,*
*These northerne parts he vexed sore.*
*Such out-lawes as he and his men*
*May England never know agen.*[7]

It remained in 1746 for Dr William Stukeley, Lincolnshire antiquary, doctor and parson, fellow of both the Royal Society and the Society of Antiquaries, to provide the fictitious earl with a spurious pedigree. For this he first misused and confused the information provided in William Dugdale's *Baronage* of 1675 – itself by no means full or accurate, although a great and fundamental work for its date – and then, of his own, added families and individuals which were entirely fictitious. He concocted a marriage between Gilbert de Gant and Rohaise, daughter of Richard fitz Gilbert, both great lords of the Norman settlement, which only occurred between their descendants, of the same name, two generations later. Among the children of this misplaced, misdated marriage he added a daughter, Maud, who was entirely fictitious. He

The grave-slab at Kirklees, drawn by Nathaniel Johnston, 1665.

then married the fictitious Maud to a fictitious husband, Ralph fitz
Ooth, after which not surprisingly, it was easy to discover a fictitious
family of fitz Ooth with Robert fitz Ooth 'commonly called Robin
Hood, pretended earl of Huntington' in the third generation.[8] Stukeley
could not even get the spurious date of Robin's death correct; he
converted 1247 into 1274. He also made the fitz Ooths lords of Kime in
Lincolnshire. This too was fictitious; the pedigree of the lords of Kime
is well established and leaves no room for such intrusion. 'Fitz Ooth'
itself seems redolent of antiquity. It is a strange name, otherwise
unknown. It may be that Stukeley had picked up some distant and
distorted echoes of William fitz Othuer or fitz Otuel, who lived in the
middle of the twelfth century and had claims to the lands of his maternal
grandfather, Eudo Dapifer, who was the real husband of Rohaise,
daughter of Richard fitz Gilbert. But this family had nothing to do with
Kime or the earldom of Huntingdon, least of all with Robin Hood. As a
wiser and more cautious antiquary, Thomas Hearne, commented in
another context, Stukeley was 'very fanciful'. His gimcrack contrap-
tion would scarcely deserve attention were it not still wheeled out from
time to time as a vehicle for bogus expositions of the legend.[8a] The
pedigree is false and the more general claim to nobility fictitious. In the
early ballads Robin was a yeoman, nothing more, nothing less.

43

This, in today's jargon, was mainstream. There were also minor rivulets of the tradition with their flotsam of corroborative detail, no more and no less convincing. Roger Dodsworth, one of the greatest figures of the antiquarian movement of the seventeenth century, noted:

Robert Locksley, born in Bradfield parish, in Hallamshire [S. Yorkshire], wounded his stepfather to death at plough: fled into the woods, and was relieved by his mother till he was discovered. Then he came to Clifton upon Calder, and came acquainted with Little John, that kept the kine; which said John is buried at Hathershead [Hathersage] in Derbyshire, where he hath a fair tomb-stone with an inscription. Mr Long saith that Fabyan saith, Little John was an earl Huntingdon. After he joined with Much, the Miller's son.[9]

These miscellaneous jottings scarcely suggest that Dodsworth was convinced. Others began to doubt more seriously. In 1765 Bishop Percy clearly appreciated that the accepted tradition was inconsistent with the early ballads:

The epitaph appears to me suspicious . . . the most ancient poems on Robin Hood make no mention of this earldom. He is expressly asserted to have been a yeoman in a very old legend in verse preserved in the archives of the public library at Cambridge in eight fyttes.[10]

In 1786 Gough was just as sceptical about the grave-slab:

The late Sir Samuel Armitage, owner of the premises, caused the ground under to be dug a yard deep, and found it had never been disturbed; so that it was probably brought from some other place, and by vulgar tradition ascribed to Robin Hood.[11]

Even so, the story which first surfaced in Major's *History* in 1521 was peculiarly buoyant. It reached its final form in 1795 in Joseph Ritson's *Robin Hood*. In this, as part of his introduction to the ballads, Ritson attempted a definitive life embodying the whole tradition stemming from Major. He began disingenuously:

It will scarcely be expected that one should be able to offer an authentic narrative of the life and transaction of this extraordinary personage. The times in which he lived, the mode of life he adopted, and the silence or loss of contemporary writers, are circumstances sufficiently favourable, indeed, to romance, but altogether inimical to historical truth. The reader must, therefore, be contented with such detail, however scanty or imperfect, as a zealous pursuit of the subject enables one to give; and which, though it may fail to satisfy, may possibly serve to amuse.[12]

This was an excuse rather than a warning, for Ritson then proceeded to retell the legend yet again, this time in the form of a 'life' which assembled almost all the work of the earlier antiquaries and ballad-mongers. Like others before and since, Ritson was loath to jettison unsubstantiated detail. He failed to appreciate that the prose life in the

Sloane manuscript was simply a rehash of the tradition. Treating it as an independent authority, he announced that 'Robin Hood was born at Locksley . . . in the reign of King Henry II, and about the year of Christ 1160'. He noted that Stukeley's pedigree was unsupported, that it had been condemned by one critic as 'quite jocose, an original indeed', but he nevertheless repeated it. He respectfully acknowledged Percy's criticism of the epitaph, but added that 'he could perceive nothing in it from whence one should be led to pronounce it spurious'; hence he pronounced that 'Robin died on the 18th November, 1247, being the 31st year of King Henry III and (if the date assigned to his birth be correct) about the 87th of his age'. [13] Ritson, it may be noted, was not the first or last student of Robin Hood to hide the insubstantial nature of his information behind the archaic quality of his language.

In fact the tradition he summed up was aboriginally ramshackle. The plethora of detail had overwhelmed the critical apparatus available for its sifting. Faced with a confusion of alleged fact and fiction, Ritson and his predecessors, with scarcely an exception, were at a loss to distinguish earlier evidence from later accretion, or historical record, however enigmatic, from poetic invention. They lacked method.

Method was provided, in 1852, by Joseph Hunter. Indeed, Hunter completely refashioned the whole question of Robin's possible identity. Born in 1783, the son of a Sheffield cutler, Hunter was educated locally and then trained at York for the ministry. From 1809 to 1833 he was a Presbyterian minister at Bath and during this period wrote two scholarly histories of Hallamshire (S. Yorkshire), 1819, and the deanery of Doncaster, 1828, 1831. Then, in 1833, he was appointed sub-commissioner of public records and from 1838 to his death in 1861 assistant keeper of the new Public Record Office. In this post he was to the fore in the work of editing and publishing the records of medieval government. His editions are still valued; some have never been replaced. As an antiquarian from South Yorkshire, Hunter could scarcely avoid the problem of Robin Hood. As an assistant keeper of public records, bringing new professional standards to antiquarian study, he could scarcely accept the pastiche left by Ritson. Instead he sought confirmation of the *Gest* and other early versions of the legend in the government records which his new post laid open to him.

Hunter established, first, that the circuit of 'Edward our comely king' through the royal forests of Yorkshire and Lancashire and thence to Nottingham, as described in the *Gest*, fitted only one known royal progress, namely that made by Edward II between April and November 1323; secondly, that subsequently to this journey, between 24 March and 22 November 1324, a Robyn or Robert Hood appeared in royal service as one of the porters of the Chamber; and thirdly, that a

Robert Hood with his wife Matilda figured in the court rolls of the manor of Wakefield in 1316 and 1317. So far he was carried by the facts. He then went on to argue that this Robert Hood of the Wakefield rolls was driven into outlawry as a contrariant, a supporter of Thomas earl of Lancaster, who was executed for his rebellion against Edward II after his defeat at the battle of Boroughbridge in 1322; that he made his peace when the king came to Nottingham in November 1323 and so entered the royal service where he appears as Robyn Hood, porter of the chamber; and that, wearying of his new role, he returned to his haunts in Barnsdale in 1324 and ceases to appear in the records of the chamber. Turning to another section of the legend he suggested a possible identity for the treacherous prioress of Kirklees: Elizabeth de Staynton, a daughter of a family of lesser gentry, tenants of the baronies of Tickhill and Pontefract, and he hinted at a faintly possible connection between them and Robert Hood. To sum up, he pointed to a Robert Hood, in the right place (for Wakefield is a mere ten miles from Barnsdale), of the right social status, for the porter of the king's chamber was listed among the *vadlets* or yeomen, at a time which apparently allows a reasonable interval for the development of the legend of the *Gest* and the other early tales in currency by the fifteenth century. The scheme seemed to fit some of the salient features of the *Gest*: the presence of the outlaws in Barnsdale, the visit of the king, Robin's journey to court and his subsequent return to the greenwood.

This identification has been widely accepted. Yet Hunter found no evidence that the Robert Hood of Wakefield and the Robyn Hood of the king's chamber were one and the same person, no evidence that Robert Hood was ever a contrariant or in any way involved in Thomas of Lancaster's defeat at Boroughbridge, no evidence that either he or the porter Robin was ever an outlaw or other than a law-abiding subject, and no evidence of a family relationship between either of them and Elizabeth de Staynton. His own comments were cautious:

This appears to me to be, *in all likelihood* the outline of his life; some parts of it, however, having a stronger claim on our belief than other parts. It is drawn from a comparison of the minstrel testimony with the testimony of records of different kinds, and lying in distant places. That I give full ample and implicit credence to every part of it, I do not care to affirm; but I cannot think that there can be so many correspondences between the ballad and the record without something of identity; and if we strike out the whole of what is built upon the foundation of the alleged relationship of the outlaw to the Prioress of Kirklees, it will still remain the most probable theory respecting the outlaws that they were soldiers escaped from the battle of Boroughbridge, and the proscription which followed.[14]

Even that modest summary exaggerates the strength of the case. Hunter set out to corroborate the *Gest* by record evidence. He discovered a Robert Hood and a Robyn Hood in two quite different contexts. To correlate them he could only call on the evidence of the *Gest* itself, which was just what he was seeking to confirm. The procedure was circular. The one hard fact in it was that the king's journey described in the *Gest* matched Edward II's progress of 1323. The rest was a hypothetical reconstruction. And it can be proved wrong.

In time, cautious hypothesis came to be treated as gospel truth. On Hunter's careful excavations a vast jerry-built structure was erected by later writers. In 1944 and again in 1952 the Yorkshire antiquary J. W. Walker maintained that Robert Hood of Wakefield did indeed serve in Thomas of Lancaster's army at Boroughbridge, that he was dis-possessed with other contrariants and that a plot of land on 'Bickhill' (Bitchhill), Wakefield, which he and his wife took up lease on in 1316 and which is described in 1357 and 1358 as the tenement 'formerly of Robert Hood', is to be identified with five stalls newly erected on Bitchhill for which the custodians of the contrariants' lands rendered account in 1322. All this was based on misunderstanding or misreading of the evidence. In 1316 Robert Hood was included in the muster of the army against Scotland; he had to pay 3*d*. for his failure to answer the summons. He paid nothing for a subsequent muster in 1317, and Walker therefore concluded, quite unwarrantably, that he must have served. He could equally well not have been summoned at all. But Walker ventured still further. There are no surviving court rolls covering the muster for the earl's army which fought at Boroughbridge in 1322. Yet he maintained that Robert Hood must once more have served. He referred to an order for a muster sent by the earl to his steward, Simon of Balderstone. He then went on:

Robert Hood was one of those who obeyed the summons, and took up service as an archer when called upon to do so by Simon de Balderstone, Steward of the manor of Wakefield, for his name does not appear among those tenants who were fined for not attending the muster. This is the last mention of Robert Hood's name in the Manor Court Rolls.[15]

It is not easy to make anything of this. Not only does the absence of Robert's name not prove that he served, but there is now no trace at all of any of this evidence,[16] and certainly no court roll for 1322. In any case it is difficult to understand how the non-appearance of Robert's name could constitute the 'last mention' of him.

The story of Robert's land on Bitchhill is more obviously erroneous. There is nothing to identify his plot measuring 30 ft by 16 ft, leased in 1316 with the five stalls mentioned in 1322. There is no warrant for Walker's translation of the five stalls into a 'dwelling house of five chambers' built by Robert; that is a tendentious error apparently based on an elementary misreading of the Latin record.[17] Moreover, Walker misinterpreted the so-called contrariants' roll. Certainly it begins with a long list of the tenements which contrariants had held of the manor of Wakefield, but this does not include the stalls on Bitchhill. On the contrary, the account for the stalls appears subsequently as part of the ordinary revenues of the town of Wakefield. There is nothing at all to suggest that the tenants of these stalls had been dispossessed. It is not even certain that they formed a single tenement; no tenant is named. To be blunt, Walker's additions to Hunter's case are a tissue of errors. Hunter guessed that Robert Hood might have been a contrariant. Walker claimed to have proved it. In fact the contrariants' roll strongly implies the opposite. It lists some 45 tenancies of the manor of Wakefield, some yielding as little as 6*d*. or 8*d*. for the half year between March and Michaelmas 1322. It names some 60 tenants who had been contrariants. Robert Hood is not among them.[18]

Both Hunter and Walker also tried to identify some of the minor characters of the cycle: Little John, Will Scarloke, Scathelocke or Scarlett, Much the Miller's son, Reynold Grenelef, a pseudonym adopted by Little John in his encounter with the sheriff, Roger of Doncaster and, from the later accretions to the legend, Maid Marian. Hunter suggested that Matilda, wife of Robert Hood of Wakefield, was the original Maid Marian, and Hunter's conjecture became Walker's fact:

[Robert Hood and his wife] changed their names from Robert and Matilda to Robin and Maid Marian after he was outlawed and went into the forest of Barnsdale.[19]

Walker also found a Roger of Doncaster, a chaplain, 'But whether he was the lover of the prioress of Kirklees it is impossible to say'.[20] This in turn acquired certainty. P. Valentine Harris, writing in 1973, commented:

Surely there would not be two Roger de Doncastres in Yorkshire at the same time. It is very doubtful if another could be found in England. Here then, it may safely be claimed is the very man mentioned in the ballad, living at one time within ten miles of Kirklees.[21]

In fact, Harris's evidence refers to at least two men called Roger of Doncaster, neither of whom was a knight, like the prioress's lover. Harris also found in the Wakefield court rolls and other sources three men called Richard de Legh or Richard of the Lee, two in Lancashire and one in South Yorkshire; a surname Withondes, but no Gilbert who might have become Gilbert of the White Hand; John le Nailer for Little

John; for Will Scarlett or Scathelocke, the surname Shacklock, but no William; and for Reynold Grenelef, at least three Reynolds, not called Grenelef, and several men, surnamed Greenwood or something similar, not called Reynold. Only Much the Miller's son, who combined a nickname with a common occupational name, defeated him. None of this carries any weight. It may be, as Mr Harris states, that 'the original names in ballads were often transformed out of all recognition', but, once that is allowed, identification becomes mere guesswork inspired by wishful thinking. Historians have evolved clear, straightforward procedures, involving the use of charters, court rolls, inquisitions and other materials, along with the known descent of estates, for the construction of genealogies and the identification of individuals. It is best to stick to them.

None of this has added anything significant to the case originally made by Hunter, and that case is nowhere near so convincing as even Hunter's own modest claim for it. Its apparent strength lies in a number of coincidences. A Robert Hood can be traced at Wakefield up to 1317; he then disappears. Edward II travelled north to Yorkshire, Lancashire and Nottingham between April and November 1323, and Robyn Hode appears as a porter of the king's chamber for the first time in March 1324. He remained in employment until November 1324, then he left the king's service and he too disappears. This seems to match the story of the *Gest* in a straightforward fashion.

Nevertheless, the evidence is by no means so simple. First, there is a gap in the surviving Wakefield court rolls from August 1317 to March 1323. After the interval the Robert Hood who figures not infrequently in the rolls between 1307 and 1317 no longer appears. The obvious conclusion would be that he had died. Whether so or not, nothing at all is known of this Robert Hood after 1317, that is for nearly six years before Edward II journeyed north in 1323. Secondly, the record of Robyn Hode, porter of the king's chamber, is even less satisfactory. Hunter appreciated that his argument turned on the appearance of Robyn Hode as a porter of the chamber only after Edward II visited Nottingham from 9 to 23 November 1323. He searched earlier accounts, encountered the difficulty that they failed to name individual porters, and admitted that 'this is not so satisfactory an evidence, of a negative kind, to prove that Hood was *not* in the king's household much before 24 March 1323–4, as it would have been had each one of the porters been named'.[22] In fact an earlier account does indeed survive, a fragment in poor condition which is nevertheless largely legible under ultraviolet light.[23] It is a day-book of the chamber for the period 14 April to 7 July 1323 and it reveals that on 27 June Robyn Hode received his wages along with the other porters of the king's chamber for the fourteen days from 5–18 June. In short, he was already in Edward's service before he visited Nottingham in November, and that fact is sufficient to bring the whole edifice which Hunter built tumbling down. To be sure, it is possible to attempt a reconstruction. It might, and no doubt will, be argued that the author of the *Gest*, or his source, got it slightly wrong and that Robin must have joined the king earlier in his journey north before he came to Nottingham. It nevertheless remains that this one reference destroys the coincidence of detail which made Hunter's argument seem so attractive. The final reference to Robyn Hode, porter of the chamber, drives the point further home. On 22 November 1324 he was paid off:

To Robyn Hod, formerly one of the porters, because he can no longer work, five shillings as a gift, by command.[24]

This was not the Robin Hood of the *Gest* who, pleading his desire to visit the (fictitious) chapel of St Mary Magdalen which he claimed to have founded in Barnsdale, left the court through boredom to return to the greenwood where he lived for twenty-two years before his fatal journey to Kirklees.

Hence to sum up: there remain two separate men, Robert Hood, tenant of the manor of Wakefield, and Robyn Hode, porter of the chamber; there is nothing to identify the two as one and the same person; there is nothing to suggest that the first was a contrariant, still less an outlaw; the second cannot have been the prototype of the Robin Hood of the *Gest* who encountered the king in Sherwood and returned with him to enter the royal service. Only the name connects either of them with the outlaw of legend. So much for the detail of Hunter's case.

Yet the name counts for something. Hunter may have missed a vital detail which undermined his argument, but he was almost certainly looking in the right place. At least it is clear that in Wakefield and its dependencies there were several families which bore the name Hood and used the Christian name Robert. In Robert Hood's own lifetime there was another Robert Hood, distinguished as Robert Hood of Newton, who first appears in the Wakefield court rolls in 1308; he or his son, also named Robert, died in 1341–2. They were preceded by Adam Hood who appears in the first surviving court roll of 1274 and lived until at least 1314. Walker believed that Adam was Robert Hood of Wakefield's father, but of that there is no proof. There was also a John Hood who first appears in 1313 and was still active in 1329. Yet another John Hood succeeded to Robert Hood of Newton in 1341–2. All these men were tenants of the manor of Wakefield itself or in the townships lying immediately to the west and north: Alverthorpe, Newton and Stanley. Further up the Calder valley at Sowerby there was yet another family of Hoods: a Richard already active in 1274 when he was at odds with the foresters of Sowerby Chase; his son John, who seems to have succeeded his father in 1296–7; and John's sons, both apparently called Robert, one of whom first appears in the court rolls in 1308, and who were both active from 1313. To cap it all there is also Robert Hood the Grave who was penalized in 1309 for breaking the lord of the manor's fold at Alverthorpe; he frequently appears simply as Robert the Grave; whether he should be identified with Robert Hood of Wakefield or Robert Hood of Newton is problematical.

The earliest surviving Wakefield court roll comes from 1274. Earlier information is much sparser. Yet it is certain that the Hoods were long-established tenants of the manor, for in 1202 John Hood and Ragnild his wife were parties to an agreement concerning land in Stanley Bottom, one of the Wakefield townships in which the Hoods still held land a century later. So the family had a continuous history in the Wakefield area from at least the beginning of the thirteenth century. They lived no more than a dozen miles from Barnsdale. The townships which were their home yielded some of the earliest 'Robin Hood' place names. In Stanley, in which Robert Hood leased land in 1315, 'Robin Hood Hill' was recorded in 1657, and either there or in Newton, immediately to the south, there lay 'Robinhood strete close', first recorded in 1650. There is a gap of three hundred years between the fourteenth-century family and the seventeenth-century place names. But the coincidence of family and place names in the vicinity of Barnsdale, the most realistic and detailed of all the locations of the legend, is unlikely to be accidental. Either the Hoods of Wakefield gave Robin to the world, or they absorbed the tale of the outlaw into their family traditions or their neighbours and descendants came to associate the two. Of these the last is the most likely.

However, the fourteenth-century Hoods of Wakefield are not the only possible candidates. To appreciate this it is first necessary to understand the difficulty of putting dates on Robin's supposed lifetime. It is particularly important not to be misled by the accretion of information from the late thirteenth century onwards. For example, at Wakefield the court rolls only survive from 1274, but by then the Hoods were long-established tenants of the manor. Any earlier generation of them could have included a Robert or two, any one of whom could have been *the* Robin. Hunter's notion of an original Robin Hood alive and active in the 1320s was always inconsistent with the earliest histories. All these placed Robin up to a century earlier: Wyntoun in 1283–5, Bower in 1266, Major in 1193–4. What weight should be attached to these traditions is debatable. All three writers came from Scotland. All three mentioned Little John along with Robin.

They may provide no more than variants of a single tradition engendered by the legend as it proliferated in Scotland in the course of the fifteenth century. But at least these men who were deliberately trying to place Robin in a historical context, writing in Wyntoun's case within a century of the battle of Boroughbridge of 1322, had no inkling that the outlaw might have belonged to the reign of Edward II. Something more is said of this in the Postscript.

Two pieces of evidence support such earlier dates. The first provides no more than background. In 1306 William de Lamberton, bishop of St Andrews, Robert Wishart, bishop of Glasgow, and Henry abbot of Scone were sent south as prisoners, seized by Edward I's men in Scotland. In their journey from Pontefract to Tickhill their guard was increased *propter Barnsdale*, 'on account of Barnsdale'.[25] So already in 1306 Barnsdale was known as an area of special danger to travellers. Of course a Robert Hood of Wakefield could subsequently have taken himself off to Barnsdale as the nearest known haunt of outlaws. But a Robin Hood of the reign of Edward II cannot have founded Barnsdale's reputation.

The second piece of evidence is more telling. 'Robinhood' appears as a surname or nickname before the end of the thirteenth century. The name Hood was not uncommon; men called Robert Hood appear frequently enough to preclude the snap identification of any one of them with the outlaw of the legend. But the combination 'Robinhood' is rare. Among the earliest examples, a Gilbert Robynhod, tenant of the Liberty of Leicester in Sussex, which was centred on the manor of Hungry Hatch in Fletching, is recorded in a tax roll of the county of 1296. A Katherine Robynhod is recorded in London in 1325. Another, a Robert Robynhoud, appears at West Harting, Sussex, in 1332 and yet another at Winchelsea, Sussex, in 1381. Katherine Robynhod's surname was almost certainly a patronymic, for she was probably the daughter of Robert Hood, a common councillor of London, who died in 1318 and gave his name to a London inn, the Robin Hood (*hostel Robin Hod*), in Vintry Ward, recorded in 1294. Something similar may well explain the Sussex examples; indeed they could all have originated as patronymics. But all these people, if indeed they were all children of men called Robert Hood, could have been called fitz Robert, or Robertson, or Robinson, or Hudson, or Hodson or just plain Hood. The combination of Christian name and surname which was used instead is most unusual. It is this exceptional formation of the name as well as its rarity which make it difficult to dissociate the surname 'Robinhood' from the tradition of the outlaw.[26] That means that the legend was already known in Sussex by 1296. Indeed, by then, as I shall show in the Postscript, it was widespread.

It is easy enough to imagine how the legend might have travelled down the Great North Road from Yorkshire to London. From Barnsdale to Sussex, in contrast, seems a far cry. Yet it was not so far in terms of feudal property. The Warenne earls of Surrey who were lords of Conisborough and Wakefield in South Yorkshire were also lords of the Rape of Lewes in Sussex. This link between Lewes and Wakefield went back to the grant of Wakefield to William de Warenne, second earl of Surrey, by Henry I, *c.*1106, and to William's grant of the church of Wakefield to Lewes priory shortly afterwards. It remained unbroken until John Warenne, the eighth earl, was compelled to surrender Wakefield to Thomas earl of Lancaster in 1318.[27] In the case of Gilbert Robynhod of 1296 there may have been a closer, more precise connection, for the Liberty of Leicester of which he was a tenant had been part of the honour of the earls of Leicester since the twelfth century.[28] In 1265 it passed with the other lands of Simon de Montfort's earldom to Edmund earl of Lancaster, and thence to his son Thomas. Edmund died in 1296. Thomas took homage from his tenants in 1297 and was instated in his lands in 1298. Six years earlier, in 1292, he had been betrothed to Alice de Lacy, heiress to the honours of Pontefract and Clitheroe. The two were married by 1294 when most of the Lacy inheritance was settled on them; they succeeded to this when Alice's father, Henry de Lacy, died in 1311. In 1296, therefore, the heir to the Liberty of Leicester in Sussex, where Gilbert Robynhod was a tenant, was married to the heiress to the honour of Pontefract, within the southern bounds of which lay Barnsdale. Now there were only four years between the betrothal of 1292 and the appearance of Gilbert Robynhod in Sussex in 1296. In that interval nothing is known of the movements of Alice de Lacy, and all that is known of Thomas of Lancaster is that he was abroad in Brabant in the Low Countries in 1292–3 and spent the early summer of the latter year journeying in southern England. But if the appearance of Gilbert Robynhod on a Lancastrian manor in Sussex in 1296 is no more than coincidence it is surely a very strange one. It invites speculation. Perhaps Gilbert Robynhod was in the household of Alice de Lacy. Perhaps he played or recited the story and hence acquired the name. Perhaps he was an established Sussex tenant, the son of a Robert Hood, who now acquired a new surname from the outlaw hero whose deeds were set in the family lands of the new lady of the manor. By some such process the legend infected Sussex. Whatever it was, it is likely to have been linked to the marriage of Lancaster and Lacy.

In this there is a hint that any original Robin Hood should be sought in the thirteenth rather than the fourteenth century, and indeed there is a possible candidate who was first brought to light by L. V. D. Owen in 1936. On 25 July 1225 and the following days, royal justices headed by

53

Robert de Lexinton held assizes at York. When the penalties were put in charge at the Exchequer at Michaelmas 1226 they included 32*s.* 6*d.* for the chattels of Robert Hod, fugitive. The account recurred in the following year when the name appears in a more colloquial form as *Hobbehod*. A marginal note to this entry indicates that the debt was due from the Liberty of St Peter's York; *Hobbehod* or Robert Hod must therefore have been a tenant of the archbishopric.[29] That is all that is known of him, for the plea roll which might have contained details of the charges against him has not survived. There is nothing to associate him with the Hoods of Wakefield; the nearest archiepiscopal lands lay some ten miles to the east, where the villages immediately to the north of the crossing of the Aire at Ferrybridge formed part of the great manor of Sherburn in Elmet. Only one thing is certain: Robert Hood had fled the jurisdiction of the court. He was an outlaw. He is the only possible original of Robin Hood, so far discovered, who is known to have been an outlaw.

There are other, less likely possibilities. There was a Robert Hood, servant of Alexander Nequam, abbot of Cirencester, who slew Ralph of Cirencester in the abbot's garden sometime between 1213 and 1216. Yet another Robin Hood lay in prison in 1354 awaiting trial for offences committed in the forest of Rockingham. The first is far removed from the traditional scene of Robin's activities. The second seems not to have enjoyed the appropriate success; in any case a prototype Robin still active in 1354 allows very little time for the development of the legend by 1377. Hence the choice really lies between Robert Hod, the Yorkshire outlaw of 1225, and some member of the Hood family of Wakefield and its neighbourhood. It might be settled if more were to be discovered about the outlaw of 1225, or if an outlaw called Robert could be traced among the Hoods of Wakefield or, neatest of all, if the outlaw of 1225 could be shown to have been a member of the Wakefield family. Without such additional evidence it is bound to be inconclusive. There is some further comment in the Postscript.

All this assumes that somewhere behind the legend there was a real Robin Hood. That had been challenged even while Ritson still held the field. In 1846 Ritson's 'life' was savaged as 'the barren production of a poor mind' by Thomas Wright, an enthusiastic editor and antiquary who helped to found the Camden Society, the Percy Society, of both of which he was the founding secretary, and the British Archaeological Association. Wright argued that Robin was entirely mythical; that his name was a mere corruption of 'Robin of the Wood', suitable for the mounds and stones which 'our peasantry always attributed to the fairies of their popular superstitions', and that he belonged 'with tolerable certainty among the personages of the early mythology of the

Teutonic peoples'.[30] Wright was the first editor of the political songs of medieval England. Rightly, he felt that Robin Hood was 'less a real person' than the kings, great noblemen and churchmen who figured in the songs, or the heroes of romance such as Hereward the Wake.[31] But he failed to prove that the legend of Robin was derived from the mythology of the Teutonic or any other people. His positive arguments, based largely on mythological elements in the May Games in which Robin also figured and on the characteristics of some Robin Hood place names, were fragile and were concerned with the outer growth rather than the inner core of the legend. He did not try to explain the earliest tales as myth. All he showed was that the legend, as it spread and developed, mixed with myth. Unconsciously, perhaps, he revealed the weakness of his own case. One of the companion essays in his collection of 1846 concerned the 'national fairy mythology of England'; it contains no reference at all to Robin Hood. In fact, Wright printed the essay on Robin alongside pieces on Hereward the Wake, Eustace the Monk and Fulk fitz Warin, all real men, all heroes of romance. That made a better fit.

None the less, Wright's work was important. He introduced a healthy scepticism into the identification of Robin Hood, and although the scepticism did not extend to his own mythological theories, he altered the rules of the game. Henceforth the identification of Robin would have to be more exact and painstaking if it were to seem convincing. These were the qualities which Hunter provided. He and Wright changed antiquarian guesswork into academic controversy. Their ideas could not coexist. Hunter rounded on

writers, who acting in the wild humour of the present age, which is to put everything that has passed into doubt, and turn the men of former days into myths, would represent the outlaw living in the woods as a mere creature of the imagination of men living in the depth of antiquity, so far back that we know neither when nor where, Hudkin because his name was Hood, and Robin Goodfellow, because his name was Robert, or as Mr. Wright chooses to represent the matter in more general terms, 'one among the personages of the early mythology of the Teutonic people.' Trusting to the plain sense of my countrymen, I dismiss these theorists to that limbo of vanity, there to live with all those who would make all remote history fable.[32]

But both sides in the argument were vulnerable. The great nineteenth-century editor of the ballads, F. J. Child, commented:

To detect a remarkable coincidence between the ballad and the record requires not only a theoretical prepossession, but an uncommon insensibility to the ludicrous. But taking things with entire seriousness, there is no correspondence between the ballad and the record other than this: that Robin Hood, who is in the King's service, leaves it: in the one instance deserting, and in the other being displaced.[33]

That did less than justice to Hunter's case. But Child believed that Robin Hood was 'absolutely a creation of the ballad-muse'.

The denial of Robin Hood's historical reality rests on two counts. The first, which associates Robin with sundry elfs and spirits of the forest, no longer merits serious attention. 'There can be little doubt', claimed Sir Sidney Lee, that 'the name originally belonged to an original forest-elf', that 'in its origin the name was probably a variant of "Hodekin", the title of a sprite or elf in Teutonic folk-lore'.[34] But there is every doubt for, although Hood was sometimes confused with a' Wood, its primary sense was simply 'Hood'. There is nothing therefore in the name to establish a link with Teutonic myth. Like Wright, Lee mustered the Robin Hood place names to support the argument, but these are not sources of the legend; they simply reflect its subsequent widespread popularity. Like Wright, Lee connected Robin with the May Games, but this link came after the legend had taken root. He pointed to possible connections with the benevolent woodland sprite, Robin Goodfellow, but these too, were later contaminations. Here and there the early stories drew on common literary conventions such as the greenwood theme. *Robin Hood and the Monk* opens (1–3):

| | |
|---|---|
| *In somer, when the shawes be sheyne,* | In summer, when the woods be bright |
| *And leves be large and long,* | And leaves be large and long |
| *Hit is full mery in feyre foreste* | It is very merry in the fair forest |
| *To here the foulys song:* | To hear the birds' song: |
| | |
| *To se the dere draw to the dale,* | To see the deer draw to the dale, |
| *And leve the hilles hee,* | And leave the hills high, |
| *And shadow hem in the leves grene,* | And shade themselves in the green leaves, |
| *Under the grene-wode tre.* | Under the greenwood tree. |
| | |
| *Hit befel on Whitsontide,* | It befell on Whitsuntide, |
| *Erly in a May mornyng,* | Early in the morning in May |
| *The son up feyre can shyne,* | The sun up fair did shine |
| *And the briddis mery can syng.*[35] | And the birds did sing. |

But it does not follow that Robin and his men have to be explained as mythical occupants of the forest. The early tales of Robin, indeed the cycle as a whole, are without myth and magic.

The second count is that Robin, although not mythical, is entirely fictional, that the ballads are a yeoman's substitute for the knightly Arthurian romances, and that, in bringing them together, the author of the *Gest* did for them what Sir Thomas Malory, perhaps within the same generation, was doing for the Arthurian cycle in his *Morte Darthur*. Against this there can be no complete counter. If Robin Hood or others in the legend cannot be identified, if even 'Edward our comely king' cannot be pinned down with certainty, then the tales may indeed be fictional.

This difficulty is not resolved by the content and form of the tales. They are realistic and down to earth. Robin is not set to fight mythical giants as is Fulk fitz Warin, a Welsh marcher baron of King John's time, who became a hero of romance. True, they contain some tall stories of outstanding valour with the sword or prodigious accuracy with the bow; characters adopt effective disguise with unnerving ease, and rescues are achieved in the most unlikely circumstances. But such imaginative excess scarcely goes beyond that of *Kinmont Willie*, for example, which tells of a real-life escapade in which the Scots rescued William Armstrong from Carlisle castle in 1596. Again, the geographic background is real and, for Barnsdale, exact in detail. Sometimes the distance from Barnsdale to Nottingham is covered at an impossible speed, but that arose from the conflation of two traditions which were originally distinct. In all these characteristics the earliest tales of Robin Hood are not far removed from the ballads recounting the incidents of border warfare: *Durham Field, The Battle of Otterburn* or *Chevy Chase*. True, the ballad-form imported great immediacy and realism to the subject-matter even when it was entirely fictional, and there are many ballads which are fiction and nothing more. Yet, when Robin Hood is translated into this make-believe world he seems uprooted. As the hero of *Erlinton*, a simple tale, first surviving in a version of *c.*1650, of a maid and her lover escaping to the greenwood, he is quite debilitated. There is no sheriff, nothing of the 'dun deer', and only a bare reference that Robin is 'an outlawe bolde'. Nothing remains of the original but the swordsmanship which enables him to kill one of the maid's brothers and wound the other.[36] The tales therefore have to remain in a group of ballads which cannot be related exactly to identifiable individuals and circumstances. These include one of the greatest of the shorter ballads, *Sir Patrick Spens*. They also include all the forest ballads: the whole of the Robin Hood cycle, the tale of *Adam Bell, Clim of the Clough and William of Cloudesley*, and, less realistic in tone, *Johnnie Cock* and *Robin and Gandelyn*. It may be that the heroes of these tales were too humble or the period in which they lived too early for the necessary information about them to survive in other sources.

There are further complications. Before the end of the fifteenth century Robin and his men had become familiar dramatic characters both in the May Games and other plays. The inevitable consequences were noted by Hunter:

We hear of this person and the other being the veritable Robin Hood and Little John, and houses are shown where they lived, and graves where they are interred; and some-times bows are exhibited, which are said to be Robin

Hood's bow. All these stories may safely be referred to this: that these are traditionary recollections, not of the veritable heroes themselves, but of persons who sustained those characters in the dramatic entertainments which were founded on this story, and who obtained a celebrity for the ability with which they performed their parts.[37]

Hunter was inclined to think that the attachment of Robin Hood to Locksley arose from this. It may also explain Little John's attribution to Hathersage (Derbyshire). Certainly his alleged surname Naylor seems to have been derived from the fact that his pretended longbow, which hung in Hathersage church as early as 1652, was marked with that name, possibly by a Colonel Naylor in 1715.

Play-acting was more serious than even Hunter allowed. In 1498 Roger Marshall, of Wednesbury, Staffordshire, adopted the name Robin Hood when he directed a gang of a hundred men in an allegedly lawless affray in Willenhall.[38] Something similar may lie behind the complaint made in a parliamentary petition of 1439 against misdoers in Derbyshire who behaved 'like it hadde be Robyn Hode and his *meynee* [company]'.[39] Such aliases were not uncommon. In 1469 malcontents took the field against the Yorkist government led in Northumberland by Robin of Redesdale (or Robin Mend-all), and in Yorkshire by Robin of Holderness, the one a pseudonym for Sir John Conyers, the other, if distinct, for Robert Hillyard of Winestead. In 1336 Adam of Ravensworth sent a threatening letter to Richard, parson of Huntington near York, under the title of 'Lionel, king of the rout of *raverners* [robbers],' and addressed his message from 'our castle of the wind in the Greenwood Tower in the first year of our reign'.[40] In the winter of 1231–2 another Yorkshireman, Sir Robert Thwing, led marauding bands in attacks on the property and persons of foreign clergy who enjoyed benefices in England under the title of William *Wither* (William the Avenger). The drift of this for Robin Hood is obvious. First, the legend could well embody the adventures of several distinct real outlaws all borrowing the name and adding to the fame of the original. This strengthens the claims of earlier and reduces the claims of later possible candidates. Secondly, some or all the names in the legend could be aliases. Little John, Scathelock or Scarlett, and Much the Miller's son fit that very well. Robin Hood alone seems authentic, but that name too could be an alias. If so, identification of an original outlaw is rendered nigh impossible.

One such alias, Friar Tuck, deserves closer attention. The name appears in two royal writs of 1417 and a further letter of 1429. The writs of 1417 record that a man called Friar Tuck had gathered around him a band of armed malefactors who had committed murders and robberies and threatened the peaceful existence of the men of Sussex and Surrey, and had entered the warrens and chases of the two counties to hunt without licence, burn the lodges of the foresters and warreners and so menace them in life and limb that they could no longer carry on the king's business. The writs went on to commission men to identify and arrest the friar and his associates. Little success was achieved, for he was still at large in 1429. By then it was known that his real name was Robert Stafford and that he was chaplain of Lindfield, Sussex.

In this there are two features of special interest. First, Lindfield was the parish immediately to the west of Fletching, where the surname Robynhod was first recorded in 1296. If it is correct to think of Fletching as a centre from which the legend spread in Sussex it is easy to see how it came to embrace Friar Tuck. Secondly, here if anywhere it is possible firmly to attach the origin of part of the legend to a real person. For the men who drafted the writs of 1417 had apparently never heard the name Friar Tuck before. One recorded that the malefactor had 'assumed the name of Frere Tuk newly so called in common parlance', the other that he had taken 'the unusual name, in common parlance, of Frere Tuk'. It could well be that Robert Stafford was the first and original Friar Tuck.

None the less, it is plain that the use of aliases creates great difficulties both of identification and in relating the legend to its originating historical circumstances. There is a possible line of escape. Hunter placed great weight on the king's encounter with Robin Hood. In effect he removed a piece from the jigsaw of the legend and tried to fit it into the jigsaw of known events. The piece he chose fitted quite well, and could perhaps be made to fit even better.[41] The same can be tried with other pieces – the abbot and the sheriff, for instance. Much the most elaborate attempt is that recently made by J. R. Maddicott in which, in the tale of Robin Hood and the knight, Thomas de Multon, abbot of St Mary's York from 1332 to 1359, is tentatively suggested as a pattern for the abbot of the story; Geoffrey le Scrope, chief justice of the king's bench from 1324 to 1338, for the justice; and for the sheriff, John de Oxenford, sheriff of Nottingham for most of the period 1334-9. Thomas de Multon can be shown to have lent money to townsfolk and landowners. Scrope was a Yorkshire landowner. During the 1330s the king's bench sat at York and, although there is nothing to establish any relationship between him and Multon, Maddicott concludes that 'it would be surprising if he were not retained by the Abbot'.[42] John de Oxenford was the son of an Oxford goldsmith and step-son of Stephen of Shoreditch, a royal administrator and ambassador. He was perhaps unpopular in Nottinghamshire as a townsman and a newcomer to the county. As sheriff he greatly abused the right of purveyance and took corn and stock, ostensibly for the king's need, without payment; later enquiries revealed that he took bribes and made unlawful levies. He failed to answer these charges, was outlawed as a result in 1341 and pardoned in 1342. During his shrievalty the Exchequer sat at York and hence Oxenford would have to travel through Yorkshire to present his accounts. The case for these identifications is of varying strength: thoroughly fragile for Scrope, not strong for Multon, more substantial for Oxenford. For Oxenford indeed it might be strengthened, for such a *parvenu* might well have become a local butt like the sheriff of *Robin Hood and the Potter*. The case gains further strength from the coincidence of the three.

The difficulty is that the method is in large measure arbitrary. The size, shape and fit of the jigsaw-piece is determined not by its place in the legend, but by the place into which it is pressed among known personalities and events in Yorkshire and Nottinghamshire in the 1330s and 1340s. Hence it seeks to date the original of the legend through its incidental rather than its essential features. It places considerable weight on the relationship between the abbot and the justice, yet this is only a minor theme confined to the scene of the repayment of the knight's debt; indeed, the justice appears in only eight of the sixty-one stanzas of the second fytte and nowhere else either in the rest of the *Gest* or the other early stories. Again, in this tale, the sheriff of Nottingham only appears once in the introductory linking stanza at the beginning of fytte four. The sheriff, like the justice, figures in the scene of the repayment of the debts, but he has no more than a casual mention and is not attached to Nottingham. The search for a sheriff of Nottingham who played some role in Yorkshire therefore depends on the remaining sections of the *Gest* and the other early tales, and it is quite uncertain that these were coeval with the story of the knight and the abbot of St Mary's. There is therefore no compelling need to plump for a sheriff of Nottingham who coincided with the proposed abbot and justice.

Some of these criticisms apply with equal force to other attempts which have been made to identify the sheriff. Two possibilities were put forward by the present writer in 1960: Philip Mark, sheriff of Nottinghamshire and Derbyshire from 1209 to 1224, and Brian de Lisle, chief forester of Nottinghamshire and Derbyshire from 1209 to 1217, chief justice of the forest from 1221 to 1224 and sheriff of Yorkshire in 1233–4. Either of these would coincide with Robert Hode, the Yorkshire outlaw of 1225. An even better proposal, made by Jeffrey Stafford, is Eustace of Lowdham, who was sheriff of Yorkshire from 29 April 1225 to 26 May 1226 and then deputy-sheriff until Michaelmas in that year. He was also a forest justice north of Trent in 1226 and in 1232–3 became sheriff of Nottinghamshire. It was Eustace who, as deputy-sheriff of Yorkshire, had to collect and account at the

Michaelmas Exchequer of 1226 for the penalties imposed by Robert de Lexinton, who sat in judgment on Robert Hode, and for the sale of the chattels of felons and outlaws. He is the only known sheriff from whom there may have been a tenuous link to the only known outlaw bearing the name of Robert Hood, and he later became sheriff of Nottingham. But all these suggestions depend, more or less, on the notion that the prototype of the legendary sheriff of Nottingham must be one who was also active in Yorkshire. This assumes that the *Gest* embodies a single, homogeneous and undifferentiated tale derived from interrelated historical circumstances. The structure and content of the *Gest* make this highly improbable. In all likelihood the Yorkshire and Nottinghamshire tales were originally distinct. A sheriff of Nottingham who impinged on Yorkshire may have helped to bring them together. But the identity of the prototype of the villainous sheriff of Nottingham, if indeed there was one, need not depend at all on his intervention in Yorkshire.

The whole matter of identifying individuals and incidents in the stories is put in perspective by genuinely historical ballads. *Kinmont Willie*, for example, is a heightened version of events in which the central incident of the rescue of William Armstrong, the sequence of events which preceded and followed it, the names of the participants on both the English and Scottish sides, and even the height of the water in the River Eden where it was forded by the Scots can all be corroborated from other sources. Literary exaggeration apart, the tale fits the facts throughout. This is not so with the legend of Robin Hood. Fragments can be made to fit, but the only substantial piece of evidence to do so is that first matched by Hunter: Edward II's northern progress. None of the rest gets beyond the guesswork or coincidence of name or circumstance. The early versions of the legend do not help. Tellers and listeners were free with the names of Robin and his men and with some of the villains of the story: Guy of Gisborne and Roger of Doncaster. But no one ever put a name to the abbot or to the sheriff or to the monk of *Robin Hood and the Monk* or even to the prioress of Kirklees. They are lay figures. They contributed to the legend as types, not as individuals.

# IV
# The Original Robin Hood

The stories of Robin Hood are a very mixed bag. It is now time to examine the mixture, to analyse the blend of fact and fiction and of original and borrowed material. This is an essential conclusion to the attempt to identify the outlaw, for the case must rest on the factual and original, not the fictional or derivative elements in the story. It is equally necessary as a preliminary to any discussion of the circumstances which shaped the legend, for both the remembrance of fact and the concoction of fiction reflect the concerns and tastes of the generations of tellers and listeners who fashioned the tales into the form in which they first survive.

The fiction is motley, derived from widely scattered sources. Some elements in it stem from the tales of real-life outlaw heroes. Some come from romantic literature which seems entirely fictional. Some are analogous to material in other stories which are roughly contemporaneous with the first versions of the Robin Hood legend, and in such instances it is far from clear whether the legend was the origin or the recipient of the shared material or whether it was dependent, along with the analogous story, on some common source.

Of these categories, the first, which links the legend with tales of earlier outlaws, is much the most important. There were three such: Hereward the Wake, Eustace the Monk and Fulk fitz Warin.

Of Hereward, who has become a national hero as leader of English resistance to the Norman conquerors, little need be said except that almost nothing certain is known of him. His turbulent career began before the Conquest of 1066, for it was recorded in the Domesday survey of 1086 that he had fled the land in the reign of Edward the Confessor. After 1066 he based himself on the Isle of Ely and in 1071 burned and looted Peterborough abbey. A year later William the Conqueror drove him from his stronghold in the Isle, where he had attracted others hostile to the Normans. He may subsequently have been reconciled with the king, and it is possible, but not certain, that he is one of the Herewards recorded in Domesday as a landholder in Lincolnshire and the Fenland in 1086. That is as far as fact and probability go. All other details come from legendary tales of his adventures which spread within the next century. The most important of these is the *De Gestis Herewardi Saxonis* (The Deeds of Hereward the Saxon), which survives in a compilation made by Robert of Swaffham, monk of Peterborough, in the middle of the thirteenth century. It is usually taken as a straightforward, if exaggerated and inaccurate account of English resistance to the Normans. In fact it is a peculiar and interesting literary amalgam which owes something to Norse saga and much to French epics of feudal resistance to an overlord, for Hereward's adventures started, not with a 'nationalist' rebellion against the invader, but earlier with his disinheritance by his father and Edward the Confessor.

Eustace the Monk was the son of a knightly house of the county of Boulogne. He entered a monastery but around 1190 abandoned it in order to avenge the murder of his father. He later became seneschal to the count, Renaud de Dammartin, but in 1203 fell foul of him and took to the woods as an outlaw. Thereafter he built up a reputation as a soldier of fortune and naval commander. He served in turn both King John of England and King Philip of France. He seized control of the island of Sark in 1205 and for the next decade organized piratical raids on shipping in the Channel, effectively dominating the passage at times. In 1217 he commanded a fleet bringing reinforcements to Prince Louis of France and his baronial supporters in England. He was defeated by the young Henry III's forces in a battle off Sandwich, Kent, on 24 August. His ships were taken and he was beheaded on the spot. His career was soon embellished in a romance, *Wistasse li Moine*, composed sometime after 1223 and surviving first in a manuscript written in or shortly after 1284. This is chiefly concerned with his feud with the count of Boulogne.

Fulk fitz Warin was a baron of the Welsh marches, born in the 1170s. On the death of his father in 1197 he took over a long-standing family claim to the barony and castle of Whittington, Shropshire. In 1200 the case went against him and he was outlawed; it is likely that he murdered the successful rival claimant. For the next three years he levied war against King John in the marches. He was pardoned in November 1203, recovered Whittington and remained in the king's peace until 1215 when he joined the baronial rebellion in support of Magna Carta. He was not reconciled until 1217. He recovered Whittington, of which he had been deprived during the rebellion, in 1223, and he lived on, increasingly venerable and appearing occasionally as a baronial spokesman, blind in his last years, to die in 1256–7. His deeds are the subject of a prose romance, *Fouke le Fitz Waryn*, first surviving in a compilation of a Hereford scribe of 1325–40. The prose version is based on an earlier verse romance, now lost, which was probably written in the late thirteenth century. The tale reviews the history of Fulk's claim to Whittington but is chiefly devoted to the three years between 1200 and 1203 when Fulk was an outlaw, engaged in a battle of wits with an enraged and vengeful King John.

The legends of these men contaminated the tale of Robin Hood. Two, Eustace and Fulk, live their life as outlaws in the forest, just as Robin does. Two, Hereward and Fulk, like Robin, are reconciled with the king. All show a remarkable prowess with arms. There is no one to resist them; they may be undermined by treachery or overpowered by numbers but, if so, they gain release through skilful ruse and the base stupidity of their captors. It is only in the last few lines of *Wistasse* that reality breaks in with the account of the hero's defeat and summary dispatch.

There is more to this than coincidence. Some of the analogous material must have been transmitted, by confusion of memory or literary borrowing, from one tale to another. All three heroes, in legend, are masters of disguise. Hereward, like Robin Hood, takes the disguise of a potter to make his way into King William's court and discover his plan of attack on Ely. His disguise is suspected, but not penetrated, until in the end he gives the game away when, like Little John in the *Gest*, he fights the kitchen staff while the king is out hunting. Eustace the Monk flits from one disguise to the next in bewildering fashion: monk, inn-keeper, charcoal-burner, prostitute. He too makes a brief appearance as a potter.

There are other, equally significant parallels. Just as the sheriff is decoyed into the woods, captured and then released by Robin in fytte three of the *Gest*, so is the count of Boulogne lured into the woods, captured and released by Eustace, and so does Fulk, disguised like Eustace on one occasion as a charcoal-burner, entice King John into an ambush by promising to show him a fine stag. The king, like the sheriff and the count, is captured; he swears to restore Fulk to estate and favour and is then allowed to go. Again, just as Little John takes service with the sheriff in the *Gest*, so one of Fulk's men, John de Rampaigne, enters the castle and service of his enemy, Maurice fitz Roger, in order to discover his intentions. Subsequently in the lavish, unlikely guise of an Ethiopian minstrel, he rescues one of Fulk's men from King John. Fulk robs the king's merchants, at the king's expense, and forces them to dine with him. Eustace, even more significantly, asks those whom he had waylaid what they carry with them. A merchant of Boulogne who honestly admits that he has 40*l*. 5*s*., is allowed to go in peace. The abbot of Jumièges, in contrast, is less direct. He admits to carrying no more than 4 marks; Eustace finds that his purse holds over 30; he returns four to the abbot who is sent on his way with the sentiment that he has lost the rest of his money just because he lied. This seems too close to the tale of Robin Hood, the knight and the abbot of St Mary's for the analogy to be accidental.

There is one other notable analogue, quite separate from these romances. In fytte seven of the *Gest* the king is only able to track down Robin by acting himself as a decoy. Disguised as an abbot he sets off into Sherwood, hoping and intending to be captured, and great play is made of his entertainment by Robin and of his subsequent revelation of his real identity. This theme of the king incognito is shared with the famous legend of King Alfred and the cakes which was interpolated into Asser's *Life of Alfred* in the twelfth century. Gerald of Wales, writing in 1216, also preserved a tale of King Henry II passing the night incognito at a Cistercian abbey after losing his company on a hunting expedition.

Taken as a whole, these analogues are numerous but limited in range. Only a few broad themes are shared between the romances and the Robin Hood stories: the greenwood, the honest outlaw, his ultimate reconciliation with authority. The rest is made up of bits and pieces, useful to string a tale together and to touch a familiar chord in the audience. Some notions of justice and injustice are shared; honour, trustworthiness, the keeping of oaths are set in sharp contrast to falsehood and treachery. But other themes important in the romances are not transmitted at all. The romantic hero seeks restitution. The grudge he bears is that the just claims of his family have been denied; he may even be dispossessed or disinherited. Hereward is an outlaw because he was rejected as heir by his father and King Edward; he is provoked to fight the Normans when his brother is slain and the family lands are seized; in his reconciliation with King William his lands are restored. Eustace the Monk is launched on his career by the murder of his father, killed in a dispute over a fief. In *Fouke* the family claim to Whittington informs the whole tale. In all three tales title to an inheritance plays a fundamental part. There is nothing of this in Robin Hood. Indeed, his presence in the greenwood as an outlaw is never explained and his restoration to royal favour is not accompanied by the satisfaction of any grievance. Robin moves in a different world from that of the dispossessed feudal landowner. Equally it is a world in which Saxon resistance to the Norman conquerors must have seemed out of place for none of that element in *Hereward* is used to embellish Robin's story.

Those who first told tales of Robin were not just copying in simple fashion. They were building up and spreading a new cycle of stories by calling on dramatic situations made familiar in earlier tales cast in a different poetic mould about other heroes set in a different social context. The ballads are not bred in simple fashion from the romances. Mutation has intervened. Yet there is one characteristic common to all the situations which the ballads share with the romances: in both they seem to be drawn from the fictional rather than the factual elements in the tales. There was nothing so universally useful as a tall story, nothing so adaptable as the stock dramatic tricks of disguise or the simple moral rule of tit for tat. These elements made up much of the common ground.

If in one direction some of the characteristics of the legend of Robin lead back to the historical romances of earlier outlaw heroes, in another they look to other stories coeval with the legend and even less certain in their factual content. All of them may be entirely fictional. Some certainly are.

The most important of these deals with Adam Bell, Clim of the Clough and William of Cloudesley who, like Robin and his men, are outlaws (4).

| | |
|---|---|
| *They were outlawed for venyson,* | They were outlawed for venison, |
| *These three yemen everechone.* | These three yeomen everyone. |

They are based not on Barnsdale, Sherwood and Nottingham, but on Inglewood in Cumberland and Carlisle. Their deeds are the subject of a lengthy poem of 170 stanzas which first survives in a printed fragment of 1536 and a fuller text of *c.*1560, but the first certain reference to these Cumbrian outlaws belongs to 1432[1] and there is no real doubt that their story is medieval in origin.

Like the *Gest* the tale is divided into fyttes. It is a simple yarn of yeoman outlaws living off the royal deer in the greenwood and successfully outwitting the sheriff, the justice and even the king himself. But it has some important elements in which Robin's tale does not share. William of Cloudesley has a devoted wife, Alice, and three sons. It is the desire to see his wife and family which leads him to visit Carlisle, where he is betrayed by an 'old wyfe' of the household whom he had befriended for charity. On hearing her information the sheriff and the justice muster the townsfolk. William's house is burned down about his head and, after a notable fight, he is seized. New gallows are erected for his execution on the morrow but a small boy flees to the forest to tell Adam and Clim of the disaster to their comrade. So ends fytte one.

In fytte two Adam and Clim gain entry to Carlisle by persuading the porter that they carry the king's writ and seal. They are admitted and then (65):

# ADAM BELL,

## CLIM of the CLOUGH,

### AND

## WILLIAM of CLOUDESLE.

Clim of the Clough.   Adam Bell.   William.

## LONDON,

Printed by *A. M.* for *W. Thackeray*, at the *Angel* in *Dnck-Lane*,

A frontispiece of the 1680s. Compare with that of the *True Tale of Robin Hood*, below, p. 175.

| | |
|---|---|
| *(They) called the porter to a councell,* | (They) called the porter to confer, |
| *(And) wronge hys necke in two,* | (And) wrung his neck in two, |
| *(And) kest hym in a depe dongeon,* | (And) cast him into a deep dungeon, |
| *(And) toke the keys ym fro.* | (And) took the keys from him. |

They string their bows and proceed to the market-place to find William of Cloudesley ready for execution. They shoot the justice and the sheriff, release their friend and fight their way out leaving all the town's officials and many others dead. The second fytte ends with them safely back in Inglewood where William is reunited with his wife and family.

In the third fytte the outlaws travel to London to seek the king's pardon for shooting his deer. The king will not give it but the queen asks it as a boon and it is granted. No sooner done than messengers arrive bearing news of the outlaws' doings in Carlisle (138–40):

| | |
|---|---|
| *The kyng opened the letter anone,* | The king opened the letter forthwith, |
| *Hym selfe he red it tho,* | Himself he read it then, |
| *And founde how these thre outlawes had slaine,* | And found how these three outlaws had slain |
| *Thre hundred men and mo.* | Three hundred men and more. |
| | |
| *Fyrst the justice and the sheryfe,* | First the justice and the sheriff, |
| *And the mayre of Caerlel towne;* | And the mayor of Carlisle town; |
| *Of all the constables and catchipolles* | Of all the constables and catchpoles |
| *Alyve were left not one.* | Alive were left not one. |
| | |
| *The baylyes and the bedlys both,* | The bailiffs and the beadles both, |
| *And the sergeauntes of the law,* | And the sergeants of the law, |
| *And forty fosters of the fe* | And forty foresters in fee |
| *These outlawes had y-slaw.* | These outlaws had slain. |

This report put the king off his food, but he has given them his pardon and nothing can be done (142):

| | |
|---|---|
| *When the kynge this letter had red,* | When the king this letter had read, |
| *In hys harte he syghed sore;* | In his heart he sighed sore; |
| *'Take up the table,' anone he bad,* | 'Take up the table,' he bade at once, |
| *'For I may eate no more'.* | 'For I can eat no more'. |

The scene then shifts to an archery contest in the butts. William of Cloudesley demonstrates his skill by splitting a hazel-wand at 400 paces and then, like William Tell, by cleaving an apple placed on his son's head. The king promptly makes him his bow-bearer and 'chefe rydere' of all the north country. The queen makes him a gentleman of clothing and of fee, his two comrades become yeomen of her chamber, and his wife is summoned to become her chief gentlewoman and governess of the nursery. The yeomen, no longer outlaws, blessed indeed with office and fee, find a bishop to confess their sins and all live happily ever afterwards.

The similarities between this story and the tales of Robin Hood are striking and obvious. Throw together Robin Hood's capture and rescue in *Robin Hood and the Monk* and the reconciliation with the king in fytte eight of the *Gest*, and the result comes very close to *Adam Bell*, even in some detail. Adam tries to dissuade William of Cloudesley from his visit to Carlisle just as Little John does with Robin Hood. The sheriff and justice in *Adam Bell* raise the hue and cry against the outlaws in Carlisle just as the sheriff does against Robin in Nottingham. Adam and Clim gain entry to Carlisle by using a writ which they present to an ignorant porter as bearing the king's seal. Little John inveigles himself into the king's good graces and comes to Nottingham carrying a genuine royal writ. Clim, like John, takes the keys from the porter, Clim to ensure escape from the town, John to get access to Robin's cell. The social contexts of the two stories are similar. Adam Bell and his friends are 'Yemen of the north countrey'. The poetic techniques are identical, with introductory and concluding references to the greenwood, and the springtide of May. Each poet addressed his audience: 'Lyth and lysten, gentylmen'.

The two tales of Adam and Robin remained closely associated from their origin in the Middle Ages on to the eighteenth century. The first reference to Adam Bell is in the return of members of parliament for Wiltshire in 1432. The clerk responsible for the return was given to literary flourishes. For the 1433 parliament he arranged the sureties of the members returned for the county and boroughs of Wiltshire so that the initials of the names, which were entirely fictional, formed an acrostic making up a benign prayer for the well-being of those representing the local communities at Westminster. In 1432 he attempted something similar, but less consistently. The first eight surnames, read vertically, may or may not be genuine, but what followed was plainly fictitious for they run: 'Adam, Belle, Clyme, Ocluw, Willyam, Cloudesle, Robyn, hode, Inne, Grenewode, Stode, Godeman, was, hee, lytel, Joon, Muchette, Millersson, Scathelok, Reynoldyn.'[2] Here, it should be noted, the Cumbrian outlaws take precedence over Robin Hood and his companions. At times there was some confusion between the two outlaw bands. Andrew de Wyntoun placed Robin in Inglewood as well as Barnsdale, and later, in broadsheets and chapbooks, identical illustrations were used for the two different tales. Indeed, in the iconography of Robin Hood, any frontispiece representing three men is likely to have been borrowed from the other tale for they usually stand for Adam, Clim and William. It is scarcely surprising that attempts were made to link the two legends. In *Robin Hood's Birth, Breeding, Valor and Marriage*, an unconvincing hotch-potch written probably no earlier than the seventeenth century and sur-

Parliamentary Return for Wiltshire, 1432, the acrostic in the right-hand column.

viving first in eighteenth-century versions, the pinder of Wakefield arranges a shooting match between the three Cumbrian outlaws and Robin Hood's father. The author of this piece had plainly set himself up as a kind of literary marriage bureau for he made Robin's mother a niece of Guy of Warwick and gave her a brother called Gamwell, by whom presumably he intended Gamelyn.

Robin soon predominated over Adam Bell and his friends. The tale of Adam was still printed in broadsheet and chapbook in the seventeenth century, but it never proliferated into many different versions as did Robin's legend. There are several possible explanations. The legendary centres of Robin's activities, in Barnsdale and Sherwood, lay on or near to the Great North Road, one of the main arteries of medieval England. Inglewood, on the other hand, was isolated. The legend of Robin drew heavily on the thirteenth-century romances. In *Adam Bell* in contrast there are none of the familiar analogues with *Wistasse li Moine* or *Fouke*. Instead, for William's cleaving the apple from his son's head, it drew on Icelandic saga. That this should appear in a story associated with the hinterland of Carlisle, with access to the Irish Sea and the Isles, is scarcely surprising. But it reinforces the impression that Adam Bell is more peripheral than Robin, not only geographically but also in its literary sources, social context and potential audience.

There were other, less important, forest tales. *Johnnie Cock* is a Northumbrian and Border story, collected by Percy, in which the hero goes hunting dressed in Lincoln green and falls asleep with his dogs after slaying a dun deer. An old palmer reports him to the foresters against whom Johnnie's mother has already warned her son (3):

| | |
|---|---|
| *'There are seven forsters at* <br>    *Pickeram Side,* <br> *At Pickeram where they dwell,* <br> *And for a drop of they heart's bluid* <br> *They wad ride the fords of hell.'* | 'There are seven foresters at <br>    Pickeram Side, <br> At Pickeram where they dwell, <br> And for a drop of your heart's blood <br> They would ride the fords of hell.' |

The foresters attack and wound him mortally. He shoots all but one who is left to bear news of his death to his mother. It is a brief story of some twenty stanzas, but has tragic, foreboding tones perhaps only matched in *Robin Hoode his Death*. *Robyn and Gandelyn* is an older more enigmatic fragment of 17 stanzas surviving in a manuscript collection of the mid-fifteenth century. It opens simply with Robyn and Gandelyn going to the woods to hunt deer. It is not until eventide that they find a herd. Robyn shoots the largest of them and then is himself shot and killed. The assailant proves to be Wrennok of Donne. After verbal interchanges Wrennok shoots at Gandelyn and misses. Gandelyn in reply pierces Wrennok through the heart. The circumstances throughout are obscure. It is not clear whether Wrennok is a forester or a private enemy. It is uncertain whether Robyn and Gandelyn are outlaws. The reiterated theme is simply that Gandelyn must avenge the death of his master, Robyn. There is nothing to identify this Robyn with Robin Hood or Gandelyn with Gamelyn of *The Tale of Gamelyn*. The setting is the forest, but no specific forest is named.

*The Tale of Gamelyn* is the last parallel of any importance. It survives as a long poem running to nearly 1,000 lines, composed in its present form about 1350. Gamelyn is the youngest of three sons who is maltreated and deprived of his rightful share of his patrimony by his evil and treacherous elder brother, John. Gamelyn reacts with vigour. He defeats his brother's champion wrestler and kills his porter. He flees to the forest to escape arrest by the sheriff and there he becomes **king of the outlaws**. Meanwhile, his eldest brother is made sheriff. Gamelyn then seeks more legal forms of redress in court. He is arrested but is bailed by his second brother, Ote. When Gamelyn later appears for trial he finds Ote is in fetters. Gamelyn frees him and then takes the justice's place on the bench and sits in judgment on both him and his brother. Good triumphs over evil (879–82):

| | |
|---|---|
| *The Iustice and the scherreve bothe honged hye,* | The justice and the sheriff both hanged high, |
| *To weyven with the ropes and with the winde drye.* | To swing with the ropes and with the wind to dry. |
| *And the twelve sisours (sorwe have that rekke!)* | And the twelve jurors (woe to those who care) |
| *Alle they were hanged faste by the nekke.* | All were hanged firmly by the neck. |

Gamelyn and Ote then seek pardon from the king. Ote is made a justice and Gamelyn achieves apotheosis as chief justice of the Free Forest.

There are parallels in this with Robin Hood. Gamelyn, like Robin, is an outlaw in the greenwood. Like Robin he makes his peace with and receives office from the king. Like Robin he expresses violent anti-monastic sentiments (491–2):

| | |
|---|---|
| *Cursed mot he worthe bothe fleisch and blood,* | Cursed may he be both flesh and blood, |
| *That ever do priour or abbot ony good.* | That ever does prior or abbot good. |

In *Gamelyn* a wrestling match plays an integral part in revealing the hero's strength and courage. In the *Gest* a wrestling match is interpolated incongruously at the end of fytte two as a means of delaying the knight's return to the greenwood.

Yet there are also important differences. *Gamelyn* is the more sophisticated piece of literature. Although it has some technical similarities with the *Gest* and with *Adam Bell* (at intervals the poet addressed his audience – 'Litheth and lesteneth and holdeth youre tonge'), it is a romance, not a ballad. It survives in some of the manuscripts of Chaucer. The poet may have considered it for the Canterbury Tales, perhaps as a Knight's Yeoman's Tale. Subsequently, Shakespeare drew on it for *As You Like It*. Moreover, Gamelyn and Robin move at different social levels. Gamelyn is of knightly family and is rewarded well beyond the expectations of mere yeomen such as Robin or Adam Bell. But the contrast lies not so much in Gamelyn's higher social status as in the feudal background to his tale. The plot is based on the division of an inheritance and on the wardship of the youngest son, Gamelyn, by his false and treacherous eldest brother. It is of great interest in that it carries over into the tales of outlawry of the later Middle Ages all the interest in rightful inheritance which is found in works like *Fouke le Fitz Waryn*. It preserves that part of the thirteenth-century tradition which the Robin Hood tales and *Adam Bell* never acquired. Perhaps for this reason Gamelyn focuses more sharply on the corruption of justice. In Robin's legend and *Adam Bell* the sheriff is simply the Law, the outlaws' natural enemy, and there is no need to explain their enmity. In *Gamelyn*, in contrast, the evil brother has become the sheriff, the justice has been suborned and the jurors have been bought. They connive in denying justice to a younger son and they must all hang. Only at one point does the *Gest* present a comparable picture of judicial corruption, in the scene where the justice supports the abbot of St Mary's rejection of the knight's plea for further delay on his mortgage. There, too, property was at stake. Nothing kindled a sense of injustice quite so effectively.

What conclusions are to be drawn from these varied analogues? There is no rule of thumb. Where they link Robin Hood with *Hereward, Wistasse* and *Fouke*, it seems inescapable that Robin is indebted to the earlier stories. Between the Robin Hood cycle and *Adam Bell*, in contrast, Robin could have been the source, or indeed they could have drawn from and given to each other, directly or indirectly. The significance of *Adam Bell* is not as a source for Robin Hood but as evidence that tales closely similar to those told of Robin were also told of other men in closely similar contexts. That puts the authenticity of both stories in doubt, but it does not utterly destroy it, for in an age when the king and his court emulated King Arthur and his knights and when genuine robbers took the name of Robin Hood and Friar Tuck, the possibility that outlaws might model their actions on legend cannot be ruled out. Yet doubt alone is enough, and it reduces the original and authentic element in the Robin Hood cycle to a small proportion of the total.

*Robin Hood and the Potter* is the most vulnerable to trial by analogue. The specific disguise had already been used in *Hereward* and *Wistasse*, and the luring of the sheriff into the forest is paralleled in both *Wistasse* and *Fouke*. *Robin Hood and the Monk* also rings hollow, for it runs too close to *Adam Bell*. In the *Gest*, fytte three, in which Little John takes service with the sheriff of Nottingham and then lures him into Sherwood, has to be classed as a tall story; there are too many similarities to it in both *Wistasse* and *Fouke*. The visit of the king in disguise to Sherwood is also suspect, for that was an old literary chestnut. The restoration of Robin to royal favour and his entry into royal service, on which Hunter built so much, is frail indeed for it has numerous parallels in *Hereward, Fouke, Adam Bell* and *Gamelyn*.

Some parts of the story are less easy to pin down. There is no general analogue to fyttes five and six of the *Gest* which tell of the sheriff of Nottingham's archery contest, the alliance of the outlaws with Sir Richard of the Lee and the rescue of Sir Richard and the slaying of the sheriff, but some of the detail of this section is reminiscent both of *Fouke* and *Adam Bell*.

Some parts of the story survive the test in whole or to a large degree. There is no obvious parallel to the tale of Robin Hood, the knight and the abbot of St Mary's, although one feature of it, Robin's test of a traveller's honesty through questions on the contents of his purse or baggage, is shared with *Wistasse*, and another, the wrestling match, has a more distant analogue in *Gamelyn*. Finally, there is no analogue to *Guy of Gisborne* or to *Robin Hoode his Death*.

It is improbable that all relevant analogues have survived. Hence there can be no certainty that those parts of the tale which lack obvious analogues are original. Even if they are, that is no guarantee of historical authenticity. It could well be that a real incident in which an outlaw gave aid to a knight in repaying a mortgage on land pledged to a monastery underlies the story of fyttes one, two and four of the *Gest*. But it is very doubtful whether real life was so nicely pointed as the tale. In *Wistasse* the confessions of resources, honest from the merchant, false from the abbot of Jumièges, are unrelated. In the *Gest* the honesty of the knight and the dissemblance of the monks are counterbalanced one against the other so that the monks' lie repays the knight's troth. That a real Robin recouped himself from monks of the monastery to which the land was pledged is possible. That the monks should appear on the very day appointed to the knight for repayment, and that they should come from St Mary's, thus rewarding Robin's devotion to the Virgin, presses coincidence altogether too far. Equally, an outlaw, even one called Robin Hood, may have died through treachery, even of a cousin who was a nun. Nevertheless, it would be surprising if much of *Robin Hoode his Death* were anything other than fiction.

However, the analogues provide only a very rough and ready test for the originality and authenticity of the tales of Robin Hood and, after making due allowance for all cautions and qualifications, one important point remains: on the whole, the stories based on Barnsdale and South Yorkshire, the tale of the knight and the abbot of St Mary's in fyttes one, two, and four of the *Gest, Guy of Gisborne* and *Robin Hoode his Death*, come through relatively unscathed; those which fail the test are based on Nottingham and Sherwood, fyttes three, seven and eight of the *Gest, Robin Hood and the Monk* and *Robin Hood and the Potter*. So the nearer Robin gets to Nottingham the less authentic he becomes. It is to Barnsdale and South Yorkshire that the greater part of the original tradition of Robin belongs. It is to Yorkshire too that the evidence of identification leads. And it is in Barnsdale that the tales are given their most detailed and exact locale.

These conclusions can be supported by an entirely different line of argument. Throughout the whole cycle, both in the original and derivative stories, the tales are presented to the listener in a realistic fashion which calls on everyday experience. If the weft of the fabric is spun from a mixture of legend and the doings of real outlaws, the warp is made up of themes and topics with which the audience would be familiar: archery, hunting and poaching, the iniquities of the sheriff and the like. These themes in turn are susceptible to a very rough and ready chronological examination: rough and ready because the warp, like the weft, is a mixture; the older threads were overlain by newer strands as the audience's interests and circumstances changed from one generation to the next. Such changes rarely lead to precise dates, and it was probably easier to bring in new themes than to jettison old; so the method yields probabilities, not certainties.

Even so, one striking coincidence is apparent. The analogues to the tale of Robin Hood, the knight and the abbot of St Mary's are few and incidental. The main theme of the story, the knight's debt by mortgage to the abbot and its repayment, the consequent loan from Robin and its repayment, is to all appearance original; there is certainly nothing similar in any of the obvious sources on which the legend called. It is also a theme which fits more easily into the circumstances of the thirteenth than the fourteenth century, for the Statute of Mortmain (*de viris religiosis*) of 1279 forbade alienation of feudal estates to the church or to churchmen by gift, sale or mortgage. Thereafter, in effect, it required a royal licence or dispensation. This might be obtained quite easily, but no such move was envisaged by the abbot of the *Gest*. Quite apart from the statute, the *Gest's* picture of the abbot as the hard-hearted mortgagee would be more readily and widely understood in a period when such monastic investment was at its height. By the end of the thirteenth century many houses had run into severe financial difficulties and were themselves heavily in debt; they were in no position to take up mortgages.

This seems reasonably firm ground. Some attempt has been made to circumvent it by suggesting that the knight's mortgage was arranged with the abbot as an individual,[3] but even if this were so the prohibition of the statute would still stand for the abbot plainly intended that the knight should lose his land. Moreover, this is not what the story is getting at. The abbot was acting, not just for himself, but for his house.

True, in fytte one the knight confesses that he has pledged his lands (54):

| | |
|---|---|
| *To a ryche abbot here besyde* | To a rich abbot here nearby |
| *Of Seynt Mari Abbey.* | To St Mary's Abbey. |

But in the second fytte the abbot explains the arrangement to the convent and it is plain that it is a matter for discussion between him, the prior and the cellarer. Indeed the prior objects (90):

| | |
|---|---|
| *'It were grete pyte', sayd the pryoure,* | 'It were a great pity', said the prior, |
| *'So to have his londe;* | 'So to have his lands; |
| *And ye be so lyght of your consyence* | If you are so easy with your conscience |
| *Ye do to hym moch wronge';* | You do to him much wrong'; |

only to be met with the abbot's retort (91):

| | |
|---|---|
| *'Thou arte ever in my berde'.* | 'Thou art ever in my beard'. |

It is difficult to see how the prior could hinder the abbot in a purely private matter, and indeed the cellarer puts the matter beyond doubt (92):

| | |
|---|---|
| *'He is dede or hanged', sayd the monke,* | 'He is dead or hanged', said the monk, |
| *'By God that bought me dere,* | 'By God that bought me dear, |
| *And we shall have to spende in this place* | And we shall have to spend in this place |
| *Foure hondred pounde by yere.'* | Four hundred pounds a year.' |

By 'we' the cellarer plainly meant the convent. Hence in fytte four it is through the cellarer, not the abbot, that the debt is repaid, and indeed he acts not merely for the abbey, but for St Mary, in whose name Robin's loan to the knight had been secured. Robin's devotion to the Virgin and the dedication of the abbey are both integral to the story. This is a well-wrought tale of right triumphing over evil conceived for an audience which was familiar with the reputation which some monastic houses had attracted to their order and was sympathetic to the plight of knightly landowners who got enmeshed.

Already, however, this particular complaint against the monks is embedded in more general anti-monastic sentiment. It is plain in all these tales that Robin reveres the Virgin Mother. In *Robin Hood and the Monk* his devotion is used to set the framework of the plot and even brings him to the edge of disaster. But it only does so because he is betrayed by a 'great headed monk', who suffers the proper penalty at the hands of Little John. The monk is the real villain of the tale, treacherous and untrustworthy. In *Robyn Hoode his Death* it is Robin's cousin, the worldly prioress. In some of the later stories the attack is broadened by casting bishops as Robin's enemies or victims. A friar, in contrast, becomes one of the leading figures of the band. Hence the sentiments which the tales express are not limited to those financial activities of monasteries that were at their most prominent in the thirteenth century. They also draw on a more general hostility to the monastic order characteristic of the later fourteenth century and, in that they leave room for a mendicant to become one of the heroes, do so in partisan fashion.

It may be that these more general sentiments helped to preserve the tales of the abbot of St Mary's as the miserly, monastic mortgagee. Even so, it is the one theme in the story where the balance of probability clearly favours an earlier rather than a later date of origin. In other cases the evidence is less certain. The difficulty is that it was easier to generate than to forget a grievance; and some grievances were enduring and widely shared.

Hostility to the sheriff is expressed in so deep-rooted but so generalized a fashion throughout the legend that it is difficult to pin down chronologically. It could embody the mistrust of local government which led county landowners in the thirteenth century to demand that sheriffs should be elected by the shire court. It could equally well express a more general discontent with shrieval corruption which ran through from the twelfth century to the later Middle Ages. There is nothing in the story in any way coeval with the demand for the control of local office by local men as expressed in *The Song of Lewes*, written after Simon de Montfort's victory over Henry III in 1264. Equally, there is nothing in it which smacks at all of the abuses of purveyance which, in the fourteenth century, could be laid against the reputation of John of Oxenford, one of the many who have been advanced as the legendary sheriff of Nottingham. There is a timeless quality in the villainous sheriff. He is as evergreen as the forest in which he was condemned to his unavailing pursuit of the outlaw hero.

The attitudes expressed in the legend towards the forest and its deer are more suggestive chronologically. The forest of Robin Hood, as of Adam Bell and Gamelyn, is the royal forest, the deer slain are the king's deer, and in the *Gest* it is the state of his forest which brings King Edward north to seek the outlaw band. Now, while it is true that the royal forest remained a source of grievance throughout the Middle Ages, this was an area where the crown was on the retreat by the beginning of the fourteenth century. Edward I formally surrendered many of the forest areas in dispute with local communities in the forest ordinance of 1306. General circuits by the forest justices became less frequent; there was none in Sherwood, for example, between 1286 and the last of such visitations in 1334, when the justices recorded offences committed by men long since dead. Forests were being eroded from within by enclosure of land for cultivation. In Sherwood Edward I converted such 'assarts' into ordinary leaseholds which no longer shared rights of common within the forest, so that by the end of his reign a map of it would have been speckled with small estates no longer subject to the forest law. Meanwhile great landowners tried to absorb areas of forest which the crown had been forced to abandon. Among the lords against whom the first-known complaints were made by the men of Lancashire and Westmorland in 1225 were William de Warenne, lord of Wakefield and John de Lacy, lord of Pontefract and Clitheroe. As the thirteenth century advanced private chases were increasingly protected and private parks proliferated. At Wakefield in the early fourteenth century the Warennes had established two parks, the 'old' and the 'new'. There was also a 'great wood' where the trees and pasture were protected. At the head of the Calder valley they maintained the chase or forest of Sowerby which extended to the bounds of their lands on the watershed of the Pennines. At Sowerby Richard Hood was at loggerheads with the foresters in 1274–5. At Wakefield between 1308 and 1317 Robert Hood, like other tenants of the manor, made regular payments for fire-wood from the earl's woods.

Such preserves provoked widespread opposition. In 1302 a commission of *oyer and terminer* was issued to try persons who had entered the park, chases and warrens of the earl of Warenne at Wakefield with a multitude of armed men, while the earl was in Scotland fighting in the king's service, and had hunted there, carrying away deer, hares, rabbits and partridges, and had also taken fish from his fishery at Sandal. Between February 1322 and July 1324, a period whence the affairs of the forest penetrated the story of the *Gest*, there were fifteen commissions of *oyer and terminer* occasioned by raids on the royal forests and attacks on the king's foresters, a total which includes the parks of Queen Isabella and the forests, chases and parks which came to the crown with the forfeiture of Thomas earl of Lancaster. During the same period there were thirty-four similar commissions occasioned by attacks on chases, parks and warrens of other landowners, the great majority of them concerning parks. Forests and parks, royal and private, were all under attack. Yet in the tales of Robin Hood there is nothing even to suggest that such private preserves existed. They mention one park, 'Plumpton park', and that is a royal one. It will be argued later that the affairs of one particular private forest, that of Thomas of Lancaster, obtruded into the story, but that came into royal hands after the earl's defeat at Boroughbridge in 1322. This instance apart, the tales seem to reflect an earlier rather than a later stage in the interplay of royal and aristocratic interests in the forest law. The royal forest is their sole target. Private preserves, which enjoyed their greatest extension later, are ignored.

Another element in the story, the expert archery, has been thought to point to a later rather than an earlier date and also to a plebeian milieu.[4] This has not proved convincing. It is natural enough to move from the tales of Robin's prowess to the victories achieved by the bowmen of England and Wales at Crécy (1346), Poitiers (1356) and Agincourt (1415), but the longbow was recognized as a highly penetrative long-range weapon centuries before. According to Gerald of Wales, writing at the end of the twelfth century, an arrow could pin a knight to his mount through both mail and saddle or penetrate an oak door a palm's width thick. The men of Gwent were already famed as archers in the twelfth century as were the archers of the Kentish weald in the civil wars of 1216–7 and 1264–5. In the legal records of the early thirteenth century the bow figures as a common household article, and one frequently used by robbers and in cases of assault. Outstanding accuracy might be alleged, even shooting out the light. Some historians have been misled by a semantic confusion. Almost inevitably the longbow has been contrasted with the 'short bow', which is alleged to have preceded it as the conventional weapon of the twelfth and thirteenth centuries. But the longbow was so described to distinguish it, not from a short, but from the crossbow. There were short bows. There were short men. Women also used the bow, and then, as now, children played with bows and arrows. But the short bow as a category of weapon and a necessary precursor of the longbow was invented by the military historian, Sir Charles Oman, in the nineteenth century. In the century after the Norman Conquest there may have been changes in the technique of bowmanship. The illustrations

An archer redrawn from the Bayeux Tapestry.

The Battle of Sandwich: archers shoot bags of lime on the left, Eustace the Monk is beheaded on the right. After Matthew Paris, *c.*1250.

of the Bayeux tapestry present the archers of Hastings drawing their bows to the chest rather than to the ear in classic longbow style, but the bows of the archers depicted in the margins of the tapestry are clearly longbows in size. Whether any weight can be placed on such artistic conventions is problematical. Matthew Paris in contrast, in the middle of the thirteenth century, included archers with characteristic longbow actions in his drawings of the battles of Bouvines (1214) and Sandwich (1217). Robin Hood could have shot with a similar weapon and in similar fashion in Matthew's lifetime.

The sheriff, the forest and the archery are dominant themes in the story which reflected the enduring interests of the listeners: hence the difficulty of dating them. Also scattered throughout the tales are other allusions to everyday experience which are equally difficult to date. For example, when Robin first entertains the indebted knight, the impoverished condition of his guest leads him to wonder whether he was 'made a knyght of force', that is, compelled to take up knighthood. This reference to distraint of knighthood by the crown would strike a chord in the listener as early as the 1240s. It would be equally familiar more than a century later. Some allusions, on the other hand, are more likely to be derived from the fourteenth than the thirteenth century. In the *Gest* the justice has clearly been retained by the abbot – 'I am holde with the abbot . . . Both with cloth and fee'; the sheriff of Nottingham offers to retain Reynold Grenelef, alias Little John, at a fee of 20 marks a year; and Little John promises the same fee to the cook if he will join Robin and his band. In *Robin Hood and the Monk* Little John receives a fee of £20 and becomes yeoman of the crown. All this was possible in the thirteenth century, but it was much more likely a century later when the permanent relationships of feudal tenure were decomposing into the more evanescent associations of 'bastard feudalism': livery, maintenance, the retinue and the money fee. But these instances are not many. They are not even consistent, for an earlier age seems to be reflected in *Guy of Gisborne* where Guy might have had a knight's fee for slaying Robin had he so wished. And they are incidental to the main themes of the stories: seasonal top dressing applied to keep them fertile.

In some respects the complexion of the ballads belongs entirely to the later Middle Ages. The author of the *Gest* addresses his audience as 'gentlemen'. Robin and his men are yeomen; so is Guy of Gisborne. Along with 'knight' and an occasional 'squire' and 'husbandman' these are the terms of social status on which the tales rely. 'Knight' apart, terms based on tenurial definitions, characteristic of the earlier Middle Ages, are entirely absent; there are no freemen or villeins, still less any sokemen or cottars; there is not even a franklin, a term which enjoyed some temporary importance in the later fourteenth century as the old social definitions declined. Hence the social categories of Robin's world belong to the early fifteenth century. For this there may be a simple explanation. The stories are in English. There is no evidence at all that Robin's deeds were told in any other language, Latin, Anglo-Norman or French. The new words went with the new literary language.

England: places and the roads from London to the North.

# V

# The Physical Setting

In the surviving stories Robin Hood and his men roam through two different localities: Barnsdale in South Yorkshire and Sherwood in Nottinghamshire. In some tales their adventures are confined exclusively to one or other of these settings. In others, Barnsdale, Sherwood and Nottingham are all confounded; each locality contaminates the other, so that the sheriff of Nottingham intrudes into Barnsdale, where he had no business to be, and both he and the outlaws move from Barnsdale to Sherwood at a speed beyond the fleetest of horses. The tales also draw names and perhaps some incidents from a third locality, centred on the uplands of north-east Lancashire and West Yorkshire between Lancaster and the upper valley of the Ribble.

Of these locations the legendary Barnsdale is by far the most detailed and realistic. In fytte one of the *Gest*, Robin, as he stands in Barnsdale, addresses Little John thus (18):

| | |
|---|---|
| 'And walke up to the Saylis, | 'And walk up to Sayles, |
| And so to Watlinge Stret(e), | And so to Watling Street; |
| And wayte after some unkuth gest, | And watch for some unknown guest |
| Up chaunce ye may them mete.' | On the chance you may them meet.' |

These place names are not in doubt. Watling Street, the ancient name of the Roman road from London to Wroxeter, the modern A5, was also applied to the section of the Great North Road which ran from Ferrybridge, through Wentbridge and Barnsdale to Doncaster. Sayles, as Hunter showed, was a tenancy of the honour of Pontefract, and the name, as Dobson and Taylor pointed out, still survives in Sayles Plantation. From Sayles Plantation it was still possible, prior to the construction of the modern viaduct over the valley of Went, to observe all traffic crossing Wentbridge, and from Sayles it was easy to intercept south-bound travellers in the high rolling country which they had to cross once they had ascended the winding road up the valley-side of the Went. For Robin and his men the setting was ideal, and this is registered in the legend: all the travellers whom he intercepts are travelling south. Modern traffic and the viaduct apart, the scene is still almost as it is described in the *Gest* and as it survives in the medieval place names.

Almost, but not quite, for there have been some slight changes which were already under way when the *Gest* took its present form.

First, 'Barnsdale' is not used very precisely. The Ordnance Survey attached it to the upland area lying athwart the Great North Road some two miles south-east of Wentbridge. Barnsdale Bar, where the North Road forks from the old Roman road to Castleford, is at the southern boundary of this area. This was accepted local usage in 1806–7, when the inhabitants of the neighbourhood of Pontefract petitioned for a turnpike from Barnsdale to Leeds via Pontefract. It was probably ancient.

In Jeffery's map of 1771–2 the area is labelled 'Barnsdale Moor', and Leland in the sixteenth century seems to have applied the term to the whole of the upland area lying to the south of Ferrybridge. The natural feature to which Barnsdale was first applied, the original 'Beorn's valley', was probably the shallow valley of the Skell, to the south of Barnsdale Bar, which runs south-eastwards through Skelbrooke and Skellow to join Hampole Dyke and ultimately to flow into the Don below Doncaster. But in the *Gest* it has another connotation, for there can be no doubt that when Little John stood at Sayles and 'loked into Bernysdale', he was looking at Wentbridge lying in the deeply cut valley of the Went. So the legend has Barnsdale three miles north of its true location and this may account for the more generalized sense which the word enjoyed by Leland's day.

Secondly, 'Watling Street' and the main line of the road north have also shifted. The old Roman road, Roman Ridge, ran from Barnsdale Bar past Pontefract to ford the Aire just below the inflow of the Calder at Castleford. There was a better crossing at Ferry Fryston, four miles downstream and two miles north-east of Pontefract, and the construction of a bridge there before the end of the twelfth century gave rise to the modern name Ferrybridge. In the course of the thirteenth century the whole route shifted to a new line direct from Barnsdale Bar to Ferrybridge which followed a Magnesian limestone escarpment and avoided the low lying heavy claylands in the flood plain of the Aire. This route forked just north of Ferrybridge, one road leading to Tadcaster and York, the other rejoining Roman Ridge seven miles further north at Aberford. One consequence of the change was that 'Watling Street' was transferred to the newer route. It was applied to the old line in the thirteenth century, but to the newer line by 1433. Another was that Wentbridge developed as a staging post complete with inns and a hospital. In 1339 the fellows of Merton College,

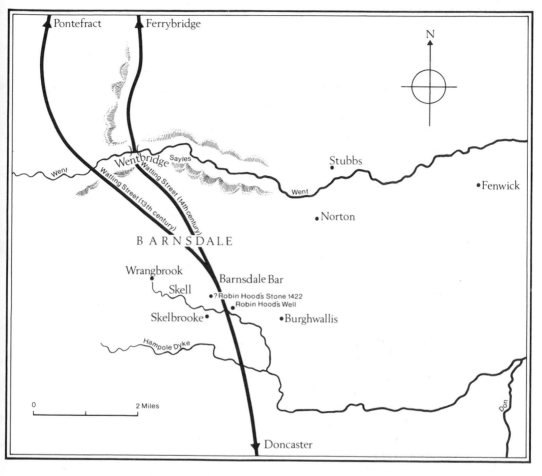

Barnsdale and its environs.

Oxford, stayed there on their way north to attend to their Northumbrian manors. By the early seventeenth century there were at least four inns, one of which acquired an evil reputation; its landlord was deprived of his licence for harbouring footpads and ne'er-do-wells. It is this newer route which provides the locale for Robin Hood's activities, and the earliest tales may reflect an early stage in these developments. True, in the story of the knight and the abbot of St Mary's the Great North Road has already got the name of Watling Street, but there is no direct mention of Wentbridge.[1] Indeed there is no hint either here or in any other of the early tales that travellers might have stayed there. Doncaster or Blyth were where both the knight and the monks expected to lodge when Robin's men waylaid them.

On Jeffery's map of 1771–2 Barnsdale is shown as heathland with unfenced roads. In his time the park of Skelbrooke was enclosed. There may also have been a warren, for Barnsdale Warren survives as a place name on its southern boundary. But there was no forest or chase. This is not a matter in which local inhabitants or officials would be casual for these terms had a technical sense: 'forest' designated an area subject to the forest law. And the forest law was never in force here, whether under the Lacys, the earls of Lancaster or the crown. Indeed there was no royal forest in the immediate neighbourhood. The nearest were Knaresborough to the north and Sherwood to the south.[2] Barnsdale derived its later reputation as a forest from the legend. This had already occurred by the sixteenth century for Leland wrote that he had seen 'the wooddi and famose forest of Barnsdale, where they say Robyn Hudde lyvid like an outlaw'.[3]

The author of the tale of the knight and the abbot knew better. His Barnsdale is certainly not a royal forest. True, his story embraces the generalized greenwood theme, for Little John greets the knight (25):

| | |
|---|---|
| *'Welcom be thou to grene wode,* | 'Welcome are you to greenwood, |
| *Hende knyght and fre;'* | Courteous knight and free;' |

Robin and the knight dine off the 'noumbles of the dere' and Little John tells the monks that his master is a 'yemen of the forest'. But the story has nothing of raiding the king's deer. Much else is also missing. Robin's men are armed with bows, but there are no feats of archery; indeed not a single arrow is let fly; the threat is sufficient to put the monks' retinue to flight. A sheriff makes but a cursory appearance as a weak-kneed supporter of the abbot; he has no status as the chief villain of the plot. The sheriff of Nottingham only intrudes in the poet's introductory verses and the linking verse at the beginning of fytte four. The monk asserts that Robin is 'a strong thefe' (221):

| | |
|---|---|
| *'Of hym herd I never good'*, | 'Of him I never heard good', |

but he is not declared an outlaw. On the whole the story fits the setting remarkably closely. Robin simply waylays travellers. He cloaks his robbery by compelling them to accept his invitation to dinner and then requiring them to pay for it. That dramatic conceit could well have been a practical ruse. How in the circumstances could his guests complain of robbery? The scene could have been re-enacted many times in Barnsdale in the Middle Ages.

The early Barnsdale stories were not concerned with the forest and did not draw on forest themes to any marked degree. But they were infected by them. In fyttes one, two and four of the *Gest* the infection is very mild. In *Guy of Gisborne*, on the other hand, it has taken a deeper hold. In *Guy* Robin and his band are still firmly placed in Barnsdale. It is also clear that Barnsdale is quite separate from the greenwood in which

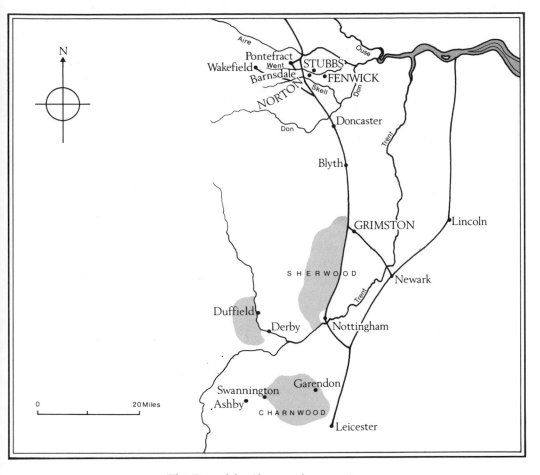

The Barnsdale–Sherwood connection.

Robin and Guy have their encounter. But the sheriff who pursues Robin's band and captures Little John in Barnsdale is firmly identified as the sheriff of Nottingham, and it is to Nottingham that he attempts to flee before Little John's arrow transfixes him. Here, in contrast to the tale of the knight and the abbot, archery plays a large part. Here too it is plain that Robin and his men are outlaws. Their strife with the sheriff underlies the whole story.

The most obvious source of this infection was Sherwood. There is no objection to supposing that a criminal band based on Barnsdale could also have been active elsewhere. The charges brought by those who turned king's evidence in the courts and agreed to act as 'approvers' suggest that individual criminals, far from confining their activities to a single locality, ranged far and wide over several counties. Robin, by contrast, did not stray far. Kirklees, the legendary site of his grave, was a mere twenty miles west of Barnsdale. The northern tip of Sherwood, near Thoresby, lay less than thirty miles to the south, and Nottingham twenty miles beyond that. The whole area could easily be traversed in a single day; King John managed it when he travelled from Rothwell, some ten miles north-west of Barnsdale, to Nottingham on 9 September 1213. The difficulty in imagining that the Robin Hood of Barnsdale and the Robin Hood of Sherwood were one and the same person and that the surviving tales constitute one single cycle does not lie therefore in the geography, but in the manifest patchwork used by the compiler of the *Gest* to stitch together two sets of stories which were distinct not only in geographic setting, but also in subject-matter, and to the confusions of time and place to which this led. In the *Gest* Little John is sent off with the knight to Wyresdale at the end of fytte one and is with him there at the beginning of fytte two. In fytte three in contrast, he is suddenly transported without explanation to the archery contest at Nottingham, and by fytte four he is back in Barnsdale. Confusion is worse confounded in some of the other tales. In *Robin Hood and the Potter* Little John encounters the potter at Wentbridge, but Robin, in the potter's guise, beguiles the sheriff in Nottingham and it is to Nottingham that the sheriff returns at the end of the tale. In *Guy of Gisborne* the sheriff who captures Little John in Barnsdale is the sheriff of Nottingham; it is to Barnsdale that Robin returns to rescue John, but it is to Nottingham that the sheriff flees before John's arrow cleaves his heart.

*Robin Hood and the Monk* is the only tale to retain the Nottinghamshire end of the legend uncontaminated by other locations. But its setting is vague. Robin is in the greenwood which is soon identified as 'mery Scherwode'. He decides to worship in Nottingham and goes to St Mary's church. Here knowledge that the chief church of Nottingham was dedicated to St Mary may have blended with Robin's devotion to the Virgin Mother, most clearly portrayed in the *Gest*. Thereafter the piece reveals that Nottingham is a walled town with a gaol and a sheriff, but that is all. Little John apparently knows every path in Sherwood – 'the pathes he knew ilkone' – but he fails to impart any fragment of his knowledge to the audience. None of the forest townships is mentioned, none of the roads and none of the monasteries. Sherwood differs from the idealized greenwood only in its name. The other tales centred on Sherwood and Nottingham do no better. They have the name of the forest, or the name of the town, or the office of the sheriff, or even all three, but that is all. This stands in sharp contrast to the remarkable detail and the accurate representation of Barnsdale in the tale of the knight in fyttes one, two and four of the *Gest*. Barnsdale seems real. Sherwood is somewhat like the 'wood near Athens' of *A Midsummer Night's Dream*.[3a]

88

1 Little John's view of Wentbridge, seen from Sayles, half a mile away, the bridge itself now partly obscured by buildings in the centre middle distance

2 Wentbridge from the south-west. The Great North Road winds south from top left to middle right on the near side of the triangular cornfield. Sayles, whence it was easy to intercept southbound travellers, lies just beyond the southern end of the modern viaduct which carries the new trunk road. The viaduct reveals the deeply cut nature of the Went valley at this point

3 *Right* Pontefract castle before its demolition in 1648. The centre of the Lacy estates in Yorkshire and of the power of Thomas earl of Lancaster, Pontefract was the hub of the feudal complex within which the legend of Robin Hood developed. Thomas of Lancaster was tried and condemned for treason in the castle hall and was beheaded outside the castle walls in 1322

4 *Below right* Wakefield in 1722 seen from the south across the Calder valley. Hoods held property here and in the surrounding villages in the thirteenth and fourteenth centuries. In the foreground is Sandal castle, seat of the Earls Warenne in the thirteenth century, destroyed like Pontefract in 1648

5 *Below* A longbowman in action. A heavily symbolic fifteenth-century representation of the poet John Gower aiming his shafts of satire at the world. The bow is not an exclusively plebeian weapon

6 The appeal of the archery in the Robin Hood tales was wide-reaching, as it was a skill shared by all social classes. Hunting with the bow was even thought to be a proper pursuit for a lady. This picture is a good representation of longbow action and the barbed broadhead of the hunting arrow. From a fourteenth-century manuscript

7 Nottingham seen from the banks of the Trent to the south, late eighteenth century. The seventeenth-century mansion which replaced the castle is on the castle rock to the left; St Mary's church, the scene of Robin's betrayal by the monk, is in the old English borough to the right

8 The gatehouse of Nottingham castle, the only remnant of the medieval castle. The foundations and arch are of the fourteenth century, but the whole is very heavily reconstructed

9 Practice or competition at the butts. Whichever it is, an occasion, as with Robin, for showing off, and the figure proudly demonstrating the garland is hooded. From the Luttrell Psalter. *c.* 1340

10, 11 *Far left* Scenes in Sherwood. Remnants of the old forest west of Ollerton. The Major Oak (*top left*) lies half a mile north of Edwinstowe. Its age is difficult to estimate, but it is not thought to be older than the sixteenth century. Now one of the centres of Robin Hood tourist commerce, this part of Sherwood owes its prominence and all its supposed detailed associations with the legend to the romantic interest in Robin which developed in the nineteenth century

12 *Left* A hooded longbowman at rest. Note the broad-head hunting arrow in his right hand. The projecting arrow follows the conventional portrayal of arrows in the belt. From a spandrel in the north aisle of Beverley Minster, *c.* 1340

13 *Above* Probably the King and Robin Hood, each with his long bow; the archer hooded. A misericord at St Mary's, Beverley; Ripon school of carvers, *c.* 1450

14 *Below* A hunting party. Hounds figure frequently in illustration and are mentioned in legislative and other official action against poaching but, except in *Robin Hood and the Curtal Friar*, play no part in the legend. From Queen Mary's Psalter, early fourteenth century

15 Lee in Wyresdale, the hamlet seen from the south-east across the Wyre. The most likely legendary home of the knight whom Robin befriended

16 The road from Pontefract to Colne and Clitheroe, looking west above Stanbury to the pass into Lancashire, a feudal highway linking the Yorkshire and Lancastrian estates of the Lacy family and the earls of Lancaster, along which elements of the legend must have been transmitted

Nevertheless, the Sherwood stories are important to the legend as a whole. They introduce the sheriff of Nottingham as Robin's chief enemy; they are the chief source of the tales of archery and one of the main sources for the poaching of the king's deer. Sherwood was already well known as a haunt of robbers by the end of the twelfth century. The confirmation of the hereditary forestership to Ralph fitz Stephen and his wife, granted by John Count of Mortain, the future king, between 1189 and 1194, allowed them the chattels of all robbers and poachers taken within the forest bounds. Moreover, between 1266 and 1272 Nottinghamshire and the neighbouring counties of Derbyshire and Leicestershire were the centre of a guerilla campaign, led by one Roger Godberd, which ultimately required royal intervention.

Roger Godberd was a tenant of Robert de Ferrers, earl of Derby, in Swannington, Leicestershire, on the western bounds of the forest of Charnwood. He was a member of the garrison of Nottingham castle in 1264, but apparently joined the party of Simon de Montfort, earl of Leicester, in the Barons' War of 1264–5. He came to the peace in December 1266. But not for long. Already before his submission, in September and October, he had descended on Garendon abbey and forced the abbot and monks to surrender land which they had leased from him and hand back bonds for money he owed to them, and it is likely that early in 1267 he went into open rebellion. At all events in March 1267 the king wrote to Roger Leyburn, constable of Nottingham and justice of the forest north of Trent, expressing his concern at the robberies in Nottinghamshire which had become so serious as to threaten the town itself, and instructing Leyburn that the townsfolk were to be allowed timber for constructing barricades and repairing pallisades. In April Leyburn led his garrison out to fight the 'enemies of the lord King' in Duffield Frith in southern Derbyshire, and in September he took a similar expedition into Charnwood. In these two actions he suffered fatal casualties and lost horses worth £54. Now so far Roger Godberd had not been mentioned either in the king's letters or Leyburn's accounts. However, five years later, in February 1272, the king announced that Roger had been captured by Reginald de Grey of Codnor, one of the robber's old comrades-in-arms in the Nottingham garrison of 1264, who had undertaken the task as a special commission in return for the payment of 100 marks which was levied on the three counties of Nottinghamshire, Derbyshire and Leicestershire. The royal letters give a graphic description of local conditions:

Through outlaws, robbers, thieves and malefactors, mounted and on foot . . . wandering by day and night, so many and great homicides and robberies were done that no one with a small company could pass through those parts without

97

being taken and killed or spoiled of his goods . . . and no religious or other person could pass without being taken and spoiled of his goods.

Godberd was now clearly identified as 'leader and captain of the male-factors'. Reginald de Grey later reported that he had pursued him 'from the county of Nottingham to the county of Derby and from the county of Derby to the county of Hereford, where at length he had seized him as a felon of the lord king'. Godberd pleaded that all had been pardoned by the King as done in time of war. He was sent to Newgate for trial in 1276, after which he leaves no record.

At first sight this has little to do with the tale of Robin Hood. Indeed, its relevance has been exaggerated as a result of a simple error: when the accounts for Leyburn's expeditions were first discovered 'Charnwood' was misread as 'Sherwood', and that has been repeated in all subsequent discussion. It would be easy to dismiss it as no more than general background, typical of many areas of the country in the troubled years which followed the Barons' War, but for one fact. After Godberd's capture it was alleged that he and his gang had been protected and 'received' by Richard Foliot, and Foliot was a local knight of some prominence. He had negotiated on the barons' side in their quarrel with Henry III and acted for a time as a Montfortian sheriff of Nottingham. But from January 1264 he sided with the king, served in the royal army in the siege of Kenilworth in 1266, and assisted subsequently in restoring order in Nottinghamshire, Derbyshire and Yorkshire. He was well rewarded: in 1263 with the gift of six hinds and a hart from Sherwood to stock his park at Grimston, in 1264 with permission to fortify and crenellate his residence there, and in 1268 with the grant of the right to hold a market and fair in his neighbouring manor of Wellow. By 1271 there were signs that he might have criminal connections for in October he was given power of safe conduct for one Walter of Ewyas who, more than two years earlier, had been pardoned for a homicide at the instance of Prince Edward. In February 1272 Walter of Ewyas was associated with Godberd, and Richard Foliot was now accused of sheltering both them and other malefactors. The sheriff of Yorkshire seized his lands in Yorkshire and came to take his castle at Fenwick. Richard forestalled a siege by surrendering both the castle and his son, Edmund, as sureties that he would give himself up as a prisoner at York on an agreed date. But his influence and connections still counted for something. He appeared before the king and council at Westminster and was able to find guarantors – many of them knights of the old Montfortian party – for his good behaviour. On that, the matter was referred to the king's bench, and Richard recovered his lands in Yorkshire pending judgment. So the story is told in instructions sent to the sheriff of Yorkshire on 17 February, six days after the king had announced the capture of Godberd.

It is immediately apparent that there is a parallel here with some of the material in fyttes five and six of the *Gest*. Robin Hood found refuge with Sir Richard at the Lee: Richard Foliot, if the charges were correct, harboured Roger Godberd. In the legend Sir Richard successfully held his castle against the sheriff; in real life Foliot had to surrender his. Each incident involves a knightly patron of the outlaws and his castle. That may be no more than coincidence. More important is the fact that Foliot's lands included not only Grimston and Wellow on the eastern bounds of Sherwood, but also Fenwick, Stubbs and Norton, which lay in the valley of the Went a mere six miles below Wentbridge. Richard held these lands as a tenant of the Lacys of Pontefract. From his castle at Fenwick, of a spring evening, he would see the sun go down over Barnsdale, no more than five miles away. With this in mind it is easy to appreciate how tales about outlaws in Barnsdale and outlaws in Sherwood came to be conflated.

Roger Godberd was no flash in the pan, and his was not the only tale which may have been carried north from Nottinghamshire into Yorkshire. The enforcement of the forest law in Sherwood continued to provoke violence. In 1287 a jury of foresters reported to the forest justices that on 7 July 1277:

John de Lascelles, then Steward of the Forest, came to Salterford and there found Robert the Monk and Robert of Alfreton with bows and arrows; and he seized them and took them to Blidworth to hold them in custody until the morrow. And later that night twenty men armed with bows and arrows came to where the aforesaid men were under arrest, broke down the entrance to the buildings, sorely beat a certain Gilbert, page of the aforesaid John the Steward, who was keeping guard over the men, and released them from custody. Later all the aforesaid men attacked the chamber where the said John de Lascelles lay and broke the doors and windows of the said chamber. In which matter an enquiry was made by foresters, verderers, regarders and other officials of the forest. They state on oath that Lawrence and John, sons of Thomas Chaworth, John of Stansfield, John of Huckelawe (who has died), Richard de Riboeuf, William and Robert, sons of Ranulph de Bolemere, all men of the aforesaid Thomas Chaworth, John de Mereok, Thomas Archer of Wortley, Robert Monk, Robert of Alfreton and John Pilat, men of Ralph of Eccleshall, and Roger of Shipley, entered the forest with the intent to commit offences against the venison and all the aforesaid did the aforesaid deed.

Not much could be done when the case came up before the justices ten years after the event. Many of those charged were local. The Chaworths were Nottinghamshire gentry. Eight of the culprits were now in Yorkshire. Three of these, along with Thomas Chaworth and two others, later appeared before the court and were convicted, imprisoned and then released on bail. The other five could not be traced.

These incidents illustrate the real stories in which Nottinghamshire and Yorkshire shared. They illustrate how similar material in the tales of Robin Hood may have come to be woven into one and the same legend. But they do not establish when. To answer this it is best to turn to the third locality of the stories, northern Lancashire and Bowland.

This third locality is no more than an occasional contaminant of the other two. In fytte two of the *Gest* the knight returns home to 'Verysdale'. For that the obvious rendering is Wyresdale to the west of the Forest of Bowland. In fytte five the knight is identified, admittedly very artificially, as Sir Richard at the Lee. Several identifications are possible for the place names which might be rendered thus, but indeed in Wyresdale, where the road from Bowland to Lancaster crosses the Wyre, there stands the hamlet of Lee. Quite apart from that, Wyresdale was part of the forest of Lancashire and a family of Legh or La Legh, was involved in the administration of the forest, including Wyresdale; none of them, however, was called Richard. There are other, fainter hints. In the *Gest* the knight's troubles originate with his son (53):

| | |
|---|---|
| *'He slewe a knyght of Lancaster* | 'He slew a knight of Lancaster |
| *And a squyer bolde.'* | And a squire bold.' |

In *Guy of Gisborne* the villain takes his name from a village but ten miles from Wyresdale to the east of Bowland forest. Admittedly knights of Lancaster could be killed anywhere, even by a member of a family whose home was in Wyresdale, and Guy of Gisborne could roam far and wide. Other tales of Guy, quite independent of the legend of Robin Hood, may have been in circulation in north-western England for at the beginning of the sixteenth century the Scottish poet, William Dunbar, mentioned him along with Adam Bell and his comrades without any reference to Robin Hood. But it is likely that the names were preserved in Robin's story because they struck a chord in the audience. At least the inclusion of all these names becomes comprehensible if it is accepted that somehow places, persons and incidents from this area filtered into the mainstream of the legend.

Fytte seven of the *Gest* turns this surmise into a strong probability. Here 'Edward our comely king' comes to Nottingham, where he remains for half a year or more until his ultimate encounter and reconciliation with Robin in Sherwood. However, he is concerned about the condition of the royal forests and this takes shape in a different location (357–8):

| | |
|---|---|
| *All the passe of Lancasshyre* | All the way through Lancashire |
| *He went both ferre and nere,* | He went both far and near, |
| *Tyll he came to Plomton Parke;* | Till he came to Plumpton Park; |
| *He faylyd many of his dere.* | He missed many of his deer. |

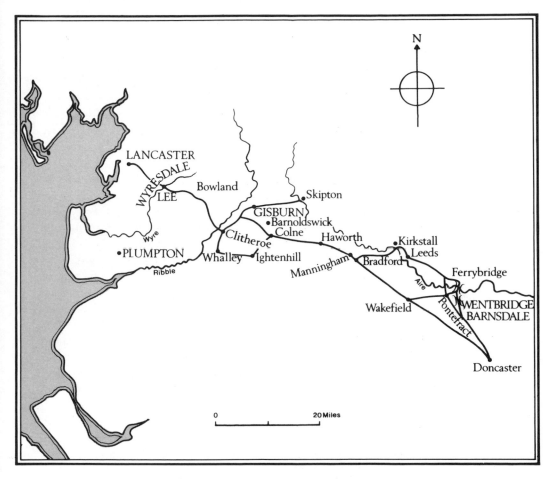

The Pontefract–Clitheroe connection.

| | |
|---|---|
| *There our kynge was wont to se* | There our king was used to seeing |
| *Herdes many one,* | Herds many a one, |
| *He coud unneth fynde one dere,* | Now he could scarcely find one deer, |
| *That bare ony good horne.* | That bore any good horn. |

Childs, following Camden, placed Plumpton Park in Cumberland. Hunter, tentatively followed by Dobson and Taylor, identified it as a well-known park in the forest of Knaresborough. Much better sense is made of the passage if it is identified as Plumpton Wood in the Fylde district of Lancashire. Plumpton Wood was within the forest of Lancaster adjacent to the king's demesne wood of Myerscough. Whatever the weight of this suggestion it is clear that 'Edward our comely king' was particularly concerned with the state of the forest in Lancashire. So also was Edward II during his northern visitation of 1322–3.

Thomas earl of Lancaster was executed on 22 March 1322. His death and the defeat of his retainers and supporters was a signal for widespread disturbances originating partly in factional squabbles and acts of vengeance, partly in the opportunities offered by the political vacuum left by the earl's death. In Lancashire the forest was one of the chief targets. On 16 May, when he was at York, Edward II ordered an inquiry by men of both Yorkshire and Lancashire into the malefactors 'who broke into our chases at Bowland in the county of York and at Pendle, Trawdon, Rossendale, Accrington and Haddlesden in the county of Lancashire with force and arms and without any licence and permission hunted and took the game and carried them away and committed other outrages'. A Scottish invasion prevented further action in 1322, but in July 1323 the investigations were renewed. In September Edward himself travelled from North Yorkshire to Skipton and then to the manor of Ightenhill, near Burnley, where he stayed from 4 to 13 October. Meanwhile, on 20 August special commissioners sat at Clitheroe to receive evidence on the disturbances. Proceedings before the king were opened against the offenders at Wigan on 22 October when Edward lay at the neighbouring manor of Upholland. Case after case was presented of the pillage of the king's deer. Those charged ranged from Sir Roger Leyburn and Sir Robert Holand, late steward of the earl, down to simple tenants. The raids had occurred in all parts of the forest. The demesne lands of the dead earl had also been pillaged. Ten years later his executors claimed that stock had been seized by force of arms to the value of £1,500 and other goods and chattels to the value of £10,000. It was not all the work of Lancashire men. William Dautre kidnapped Gilbert de la Legh, the stock manager of the park of Ightenhill, and held him prisoner at Holbeck, near Leeds, until ransomed for £20. Nicholas Mauleverer, constable of Skipton castle led a raiding party from Craven and Airedale and stripped the stud farm of Ightenhill of stock and cattle worth £200. The breakdown was serious and there was nothing quite on the same scale elsewhere. In March 1323 the king ordered investigations into raids which were said to have taken place in his forests in Staffordshire and southern Derbyshire. There was trouble in the forest of Pickering which had now reverted from the earl of Lancaster to the crown; the king ordered the arrest of numerous offenders when he stayed at Pickering in August. At Knaresborough the parks were invaded, the deer plundered and one of the foresters was killed, but the king was not apparently alerted to that until June 1324 after he had returned south. Further he showed no particular concern in these years for Sherwood. But like 'Edward our comely king' he ended his northern progress at Nottingham.

It seems likely that Edward II's response to the attack on the forests of Lancashire underlay the story of 'Edward our comely king' in fytte seven of the *Gest*. Here, more than anywhere else, the legend approximates to known historical events. It is no more than an approximation, for the legend simply embodies the knowledge that the king was called Edward, that he was concerned with the condition of his forests and that this was particularly serious in Lancashire. Thereafter it preserves place names which can only have come from that county, Wyresdale, Lancaster and possibly Lee. It is the presence of the place names and the story of the king's journey together which makes a common origin in Lancashire seem probable.

There is no difficulty at all in understanding how names and incidents occurring in Lancashire seeped into a legend centred on South Yorkshire. The honour of Clitheroe, like Pontefract, belonged to the Lacys. From the early days of the twelfth century they also held Bowland. All the chases of Blackburnshire which were raided in 1322–3 had belonged to them; so also had the stud and park at Ightenhill. Wyresdale was part of the honour of Lancaster, demesne of the crown until granted to Edmund, second son of Henry III, in 1267. The whole area came into a single hand on the death of Henry de Lacy in 1311, when the Lacy estates came by marriage to Thomas earl of Lancaster, Edmund's son.

Within the Lacy lands there were long-established links between the Yorkshire and Lancashire properties. The priory of St John which Robert de Lacy founded at Pontefract in 1090 was endowed with a tithe of the demesne of Clitheroe, the castle chapel and the church of St Mary Magdalene at Clitheroe, and the churches of Slaidburn, Whalley, Colne and Burnley. The Cistercian monastery established at Kirkstall in 1152 was first founded five years earlier by Henry de Lacy at Barnoldswick, five miles north of Colne, which the Lacys had won from the Bigod family. The monks of Kirkstall established a grange at Accrington. They surrendered their estates in Blackburnshire to Henry de Lacy in 1287 in return for an annual rent, but they still drew one mark annually from the revenues of Clitheroe for the upkeep of the abbot's dress, and the light which burned before the host at the altar in the abbey church was paid for by an annual charge of half a mark on these same revenues. The monks of Kirkstall also held an acre of land and buildings at Wentbridge immediately to the west of the bridge, which Robert de Lacy gave them *c*.1180. The monks' interests, through their dependence on the Lacys, spanned the whole of the area on which the legend of Robin Hood drew for its names and locations, except for Sherwood.

Administratively Clitheroe and Pontefract were separate but closely interrelated units. It was from Bowland, administered through Clitheroe, for example, that venison was supplied to Pontefract.

Geographically they were contiguous, for the honour of Pontefract extended westward through Leeds, Bradford and Haworth until it marched with the lands of the honour of Clitheroe above Colne. They were held together by a medieval road which ran through Leeds, over the Aire at Kirkstall bridge to Bradford, thence via Manningham to Haworth, thence due west where it reached a height of over 1,100 ft before descending to Colne. Here it branched southwards for Ightenhill, which by the fourteenth century was emerging as the administrative centre of the honour of Clitheroe, northward for Barnoldswick or round Pendle Hill for Clitheroe. Except for short sections in Bradford and at Downham on the north side of Pendle it was independent of the old Roman roads. In the Middle Ages it was the main road up Airedale.[4]

A traveller who took this road never left the Lacy lordship. It is no surprise therefore to find the stock manager of Ightenhill carried away prisoner to Holbeck, half way between Kirkstall and Leeds in 1322–3. His was not an exceptional journey. Indeed, it was so common and so essential to the administration of the Lacy lands that it was embodied in customary manorial services. At Bradford in 1341 John Riens, villein, held his land in bondage for services which included carrying 'the lord's victuals with one horse and one man from Bradford to Haworth and from Haworth to Colne and thence to Ightenhill, receiving 4*d.* as wages at each township'; fifteen villeins in Manningham, Bradford, held their land on similar terms. At Stanbury which lay on the road from Haworth to Colne below the steading later renowned as Wuthering Heights, villein tenants had to carry the lord's victuals eight leagues from Haworth to Colne and thence to Ightenhill. At Manningham, Thomas of Northorp, a freeman, held his land

by service of presenting himself every year at the feast of St. Martin at the manor court of Bradford, prepared to go with the lord as far as Blackburnshire for the space of 40 days with one lance and one dog to take the wild boar, receiving from the lord, daily 1*d* for himself and ½*d* for the dog and also of going with the lord's receiver or bailiff, as safe-conduct of the lord's money to Pontefract, at his own charges, as often as he shall be forewarned.[5]

Roger of Manningham held his land in Horton, another member of the manor of Bradford, by rendering similar services. There is no need to look further for men who might have transmitted names and events from the environs of Blackburnshire to Pontefract.

If any weight at all is attached to the preceding arguments it follows that some of the detail of the journey of 'Edward our comely king' cannot have been embodied in the tale of Robin Hood until after 1323. It could perhaps have absorbed the theme of the king incognito at any time and developed it as an encounter between the king and Robin, but the specific itinerary given the king, his special concern with the condition of the forests, especially those of Lancashire, and perhaps also his name, Edward, must in all probability have been derived from the events of 1322–3. It also follows, of course, that news of other incidents and personal or place names might have been carried eastwards over the Pennines at other times. If so, it is likely that Wyresdale and Lee (if indeed the Lee of the *Gest* lay in Wyresdale) came into the tradition after 1311 when Thomas of Lancaster succeeded to the honour of Clitheroe. Wyresdale soon became administratively dependent on Clitheroe. In 1322 it was included in the contrariants' roll for the honour.

It is tempting to press the argument a little further in two directions. Firstly, the implication that the Sherwood and Barnsdale stories had already come together before the Lancashire element intruded is attractive and indeed probable. The names and incidents attributable with varying degrees of certainty to Lancashire are widely distributed in the *Gest*. The killing of the knight of Lancaster is mentioned in fytte one; Wyresdale occurs in fytte two; Sir Richard at the Lee is introduced in fytte five; the king's journey, the reference to the 'passe' of Lancashire and to Plumpton Park are all in fytte seven. It should be noted that when Sir Richard at the Lee is introduced in fytte five, he is immediately identified with the knight of fytte one who is placed in Wyresdale in fytte two. This perhaps suggests that the themes of fyttes two and five were already associated. Secondly, although the obvious route for this material is from Clitheroe to Pontefract and Barnsdale, there is an additional possibility. After completing his circuit in Lancashire in 1323 Edward II went to Nottingham where he stayed from 9 to 23 November. Some stories of events in Lancashire could have spread from there. Robyn Hode, porter of the chamber, was already in the royal service. What attraction his name had to the folk of Nottingham, and what Robyn Hode the porter may have contributed to the tale of Robin Hood the outlaw can only be guessed.

This Lancashire material provides a chronological framework in which some of the development of the legend may be set. It also illustrates how material might be garbled as it was embodied in such a tale. Above all, if the Lancashire contribution is allowed, the structure of the Lacy estates leads straight to the problem of how such tales were generated and transmitted. It is unlikely that men like Thomas of Northorp and Roger of Manningham went without any kind of entertainment in their intervals of rest as they accompanied their lord in hunting the wild boar in the chases of Blackburnshire or helped his steward to carry his money to Pontefract. The contamination of the Robin Hood legend by Lancashire material indicates what some of that entertainment may well have been. It may be no accident that a present-day traveller on the road they followed will, if he travels from Bradford to Haworth on a clear day, be able to look across Airedale to Rivock Edge, which is known locally as Robin Hood's Point. Two miles west of Haworth, at Stanbury, he will pass Robin Hood's Well, and if west of Colne he follows the route to Clitheroe up Pendle Water, he will pass close to yet another Robin Hood's Well above Roughlee. But these names are not recorded before the nineteenth century.

So far the discussion has turned simply on the development of the legend. But development and dissemination went together. Places, persons and incidents came into the story from Lancashire, Craven, Sherwood and Nottingham as Robin's fame spread outwards from Barnsdale. The written versions of the tales simply catch this process at particular points in time like a series of photographic stills. They embody the development of the tales well enough; indeed they are almost the only guide to what the mixture contained when they were written, but they shed no more than side-lights on their dissemination. For this, more direct evidence is found in 'Robin Hood' place names.

These place names can only be used tentatively. What interval separated the acceptance of a name from its first appearance in record is an open guess. It may have been long in some cases, short in others; the mere appearance of a name in writing is a mere accident in its history. Hence the record of surviving names is bound to be an uncertain guide to real usage, and this is compounded by the fact that the survey of the necessary names is incomplete. Some counties have received more detailed treatment than others. Place names have been more fully studied than field names. In most counties major sources of information are still untapped. It is not only possible, but likely, that new Robin Hood place names will turn up. It is very probable, however, that the known place names are a representative sample.

That said, one conclusion is reasonably certain. With very few possible exceptions, the Robin Hood place names illustrate the spread of the legend, not the doings of the outlaw. There is no evidence at all that Robin Hood ever took ship in his 'bay', or sat in his several 'chairs', or leapt his 'leaps', or hid in his 'cave', or used his 'stables', or drank from his many 'wells', or shot in his widely scattered 'butts'. There are two obvious causes of the proliferation of such names. The first was psychological: those who told or listened to the stories tried to add to their realism by transferring the hero's name to familiar places in the immediate locality. The second was commercial: innkeepers and others could attract custom by claiming that 'Robin Hood was here'.

One possible exception is the name which at present stands as the earliest of them all – the 'Stone of Robert Hode' mentioned in a deed of

Little John's cottage, Hathersage, *c.*1832, from Walker's
*True History of Robin Hood*.

1422 copied into the cartulary of Monk Bretton priory.[6] Walker
jumped to the conclusion that this was on the site of Robin Hood's Well
which still stands on the east side of the Great North Road a mile south
of Barnsdale Bar, and he has been followed by all subsequent writers.
But this is thoroughly at odds with the topographical details of the
deed. The stone must have been much nearer to Barnsdale Bar and to
the west, not the east of the Road, for it was sited in the fields of
Sleep Hill abutting the ings of Skelbrooke between that village and
Wrangbrook.[7] At all events, here was a boundary stone or guidepost,
less than a mile south-west of Barnsdale Bar, which in 1422 carried the
same name as the local outlaw hero. That is as far as the case can be
pressed.

The environs of Barnsdale and Wakefield yield other names. Robin
Hood's Well, to the east of the Great North Road, was so named by
1622. In Stanley and Newton, near Wakefield, where Robert Hode had
held land in the early fourteenth century, Robinhoodstrete Close and
Robin Hood's Hill were so named by the middle of the seventeenth
century. By that date the legend and the associated names had been
carried far and wide. To the west it had been transmitted beyond
Ecclesfield, four miles north of Sheffield, where Robin Hood's Bower
was recorded in 1637, to Derbyshire where Little John's Grave was
already sited at Hathersage by the middle of the seventeenth century.
To the north Robin Hood's Stone was recorded near Whitby in 1540. A
few miles further south Robin Hood's Bay first appeared in 1544, and at

York part of the city wall bore Robin's name in 1622. Long before this the legend was well known in Scotland. Some hint of the route it took is provided by the appearance of Robin Hood Buttes as early as 1598 near Brampton, Cumberland, on one of the western roads over the border. To the south none of the Robin Hood place names in Sherwood can be traced before 1700, but at Nottingham itself Robynhode Closse was known by 1485, Robin Hood's Well by 1500 and Robin Hood's Acre by 1624–5. Here the story took root strongly and at a comparatively early date. South of Nottinghamshire four Robin Hood Courts are recorded in London before the end of the seventeenth century, and other names appear prior to 1700 in Berkshire, Essex, Surrey and Gloucestershire.

Occasionally this can be set in a rough chronological framework. The tower on the city wall at York which appears as Robin Hood's Tower in 1622 was called Frost Tower in 1485. It has been suggested very plausibly by Dobson and Taylor that it was Henry VIII who named Robin Hood's Walk in Richmond Park, Surrey. In Gloucestershire Robin Hood's Hill appears in the seventeenth century on a manor held by a family called Robins in the sixteenth century. Robin Hood Cross, three miles west of Hathersage, still appears merely as Robin Crosse, both in 1319 and 1640. All these examples suggest that the names began to spread fast in the sixteenth and seventeenth centuries. That may well be so. The tales were now in print and increasingly accessible to more numerous readers. But other evidence indicates that they were widespread earlier. In south–eastern England Robinhood surnames were widely scattered before the end of the thirteenth century. In Scotland Wyntoun knew of Robin Hood and Little John by 1420. The clerk of the sheriff of Wiltshire knew of Robin's tale in 1432. *Robin Hood and the Potter* of *c.* 1500 is written in a Midlands dialect. One of a collection of Welsh songs put together by the end of the fifteenth century carried the note:

*Robin Hwd ai kant.*[8]    Robin Hood sang it.

The legend was not only well developed but also widely known at the time from which it first survives. The audience was already widespread. It was therefore likely to be diverse.

# VI
## The Audience

Who listened to the tales and why? What was the social complexion of the audience and what was its interest in Robin's story? These seemingly obvious and straightforward questions have proved complex and controversial. They have been the main bone of contention in the debate about Robin's alleged social role and they also trespass on a much older controversy about the origin and nature of ballads. Yet some of the answers are plain enough in the stories themselves.

The surviving versions are of tales which must have been recited to the audience:

> *Lythe and listin, gentilmen,*  
> *That be of frebore blode.*  
> *I shale you tel of a gode yeman,*  
> *His name was Robyn Hode.*

> Give ear and listen, gentlemen,  
> Who are of freeborn blood.  
> I shall tell you of a good yeoman,  
> His name was Robin Hood.

So begins the first fytte of the *Gest*. Similar addresses preface fyttes three and six. The second stanza of *Robin Hood and the Potter* may differ in its social context, but it is identical in purpose:

> *Herkens, god yemen,*  
> *Comley, corteys, and god,*  
> *On of the best that yever bare bowe,*  
> *Hes name was Roben Hode.*

> Harken, good yeomen,  
> Comely, courteous, and good,  
> One of the best that ever bore a bow,  
> His name was Robin Hood.

At stanza 30, with Robin now disguised as the potter and on his way to Nottingham, there is a variant form of address marking a division in the poem:

> *Her es more, and affter ys to saye,*  
> *The best ys beheynde.*

> Here is more, to be related later,  
> The best is yet to come.

*Guy of Gisborne* gives no hint of an opening address, but in this tale some of the early verses which might have contained it are missing. *Robin Hood and the Monk* also lacks one, but its final verse is equally revealing:

| | |
|---|---|
| *Thus endys the talkyng of the munke* | Thus ends the telling of the monk |
| *And Robyn Hode i-wysse;* | And Robin Hood, in truth; |
| *God that is ever a crowned kyng,* | God who is ever crowned king, |
| *Bryng us all to his blisse!* | Bring us all to his bliss! |

There is a similar invocation, which may also hint at the immediate reward awaited by the performer, at the end of fytte four of the *Gest*:

| | |
|---|---|
| *God, that syt in heven hye* | God who sits in heaven high |
| *Graunte us well to fare.* | Grant us well to fare. |

*Adam Bell* provides good collateral evidence. It too has the familiar address (5):

| | |
|---|---|
| *Now lith and lysten, gentylmen,* | Hark and listen gentlemen, and those |
| *And that of myrthes loveth to here:* | Who love to hear of pleasant tales: |

Each of the first two fyttes announces that another is yet to come – 'another is for to saye', 'another I shall you tell' – and the whole poem ends with an invocation:

| | |
|---|---|
| *Thus endeth the lyves of these good yemen,* | Thus ends the tale of these good yeomen, |
| *God sende them eternall blysse,* | God send them eternal bliss, |
| *And all that with hande-bowe shoteth,* | And that all who with the hand-bow shoot, |
| *That of heven they may never mysse!* | Heaven may never miss! |

All this seems to put the matter beyond serious doubt. The tales were 'talkyngs'. They were said or told to listeners addressed as gentlemen or yeomen. The longer poems are divided into fyttes to allow both tellers and listeners an interval. They are an entertainment. There must therefore have been entertainers and an audience capable of sustaining them, in short patrons with resources in numbers and wealth. To describe Robin Hood tales as 'yeoman minstrelsy' has become an accepted convention, but the words leave much to be defined. If they are intended to mean that the *Gest*, as it stands, was composed initially for performance in a yeoman's household, they pass beyond reasonable conjecture. Minstrels of such attainment surely sought larger audiences and better pay. They looked to patronage of the crown, the aristocracy and the landed gentry. It is among their retainers and dependents, gathered together in circumstances which allowed for entertainment, that the original audience of the tales of Robin Hood must first be sought.

This conclusion is controversial, highly so if read without its qualifications. It takes a firm standpoint on the relative originality of the different elements in the legend, 'originality' embodying both independent authenticity and chronological priority. Reasons have already been given for thinking that the tale of the knight in fyttes one, two and four of the *Gest* is both original and early. Conversely *Robin Hood and the Potter* is plainly derivative. The first is more knightly in atmosphere, the second more plebeian. On the surface it would appear that the plebeian is an offshoot from the original, more knightly strain. But that does not allow for the possibility that the tales originated in oral tradition which can only be assayed through the surviving written versions. It might be claimed that there were rustic versions of the tales, passed on by word of mouth, which may have been drawn on in one direction by minstrels for public performance in a hall and in another by yeoman households in which local legends were preserved. But this is guesswork. It certainly does not create ground for thinking that the surviving written versions are atypical of the legend as a whole. One thing is certain: by the date from which the written versions first survive the story already had a diverse social appeal, to knights, to yeomen and to husbandmen. Certainly by 1500, probably by 1400, perhaps even earlier, there was not just one set of circumstances in which the tales were told, but several. So was one more important than the others in the origination of the story? Was there an aboriginal audience and a setting in which the tale first took shape?

A flood of light is thrown on the entertainment available in a feudal household at the beginning of the fourteenth century by the records of the arrangements made for the knighting of Edward of Caernarvon, the future Edward II, at Whitsuntide 1306. This was a great public occasion in which Edward I awarded knightly arms at his own expense to all those who wished to receive knighthood at the hands of the young prince. It was attended by many nobles and by a host of minstrels who provided varied entertainment and received payment from the king's wardrobe. The minstrels made up a diverse profession, varying from permanent members of the king's household, established men of substance who enjoyed the status of squire, down to casual entertainers who counted minstrelsy simply as an occasional service which they might provide from time to time. Some were musicians with command of harp or psaltery; others were acrobats or fencers; others again performed a primary function as heralds or messengers. On this occasion the company was reinforced by a large number who came in the trains of the nobles they served and were often simply identified by their master's name. Thomas earl of Lancaster had his vielle player there, along with two trumpeters. His wife Alice de Lacy was accompanied by her harper and her waferer. Their neighbour in south Yorkshire, the Earl Warenne, had Geoffrey his harper with him; the Countess Warenne also had her harper. There were many others, not all from such elevated households. The North was represented not only by those in the company of Lancaster and Warenne, but also by Adam of Clitheroe, the king's harper, Robert of Scarborough, Mayhew of the North and others.

It is likely that this was too grand a gathering to have been entertained with tales of Robin Hood. Whether some of the minstrels present knew them is a different matter. Here minstrels were employed in as large and formal an occasion as English royalty could provide short of a coronation; and the entertainment would be devised accordingly. There were many lesser occasions, royal, aristocratic or local and ad hoc, and for some of these some information about the entertainment survives. The undignified surrender of Henry III's brother, Richard of Cornwall, at the battle of Lewes in 1264 was celebrated in a poem which must have been recited or declaimed to a gathering of the supporters of the victorious Simon de Montfort, and that within a few months of the battle, for Simon was killed at Evesham in 1265. Probably very shortly after the great feast of 1306 an English audience, perhaps a muster or a garrison in Scotland, was regaled with the tale of the defeat of the Scots at Methven in June of that year and of the execution in September of Simon Fraser. These tales like those of Robin Hood open with an address to the audience: 'Sitteth alle stille ant herketh to me' or 'Listen, lordings, a new song I will begin'. Sometimes, too, even the king may have put up with a cruder brand of entertainment than that provided by the polished performers of his household. When Edward II lay at Whorlton castle, Yorkshire, in September 1322, he listened to Agnes the Redhaired and Alice of Whorlton who sang tales of Simon de Montfort and other songs. Still this seemingly local talent may have been quite good. Agnes and Alice were given 4s. for their performance, which was considerably more than some of the minstrels got in London in 1306.

By Edward II's reign there was the first of many signs that the profession was getting out of hand. In an ordinance of 1315 it was maintained that indolent persons, pretending minstrelsy, were seeking hospitality and pay, and it was laid down that no one except a professed minstrel should seek food or drink in the houses of prelates, earls or barons, that no more than three or four 'minstrels of honour' should seek to provide entertainment and gain reward in any one day, and that no minstrel should visit the household of those below the rank of baron except by invitation and then only in the expectation of food and drink and such payment as the housekeeper might offer. Two years later, in 1317, a woman dressed as a minstrel invaded the royal Whitsun banquet in Westminster Hall and insulted the king by leaving a manifesto critical of his government. The usher let her in because minstrels had never been forbidden the king's presence.

Now it is beyond question that the surviving information on minstrelsy and the minstrel's relation to his audience may amount to a distortion. Necessarily, it reveals more about royal entertainment than aristocratic, more about aristocratic than knightly, and more about the entertainment of the knight than of the yeoman and simple rustic. Even so, it is plain from arguments advanced in earlier chapters of this book that the household servitors and retinues of nobleman and knight played a part in the formation and dissemination of the legend of Robin Hood. First, one of the early Robin Hood surnames occurs in Sussex. The lords of Wakefield were also lords of Lewes, and the lord of the Liberty of Leicester in Sussex, where the name appears, was also lord of Lancaster; Thomas of Lancaster was husband to the heiress of the honour of Pontefract which included Barnsdale and the surrounding townships. All these had minstrels in their households in 1306. Secondly, places and incidents from Blackburnshire and Wyresdale appear in stories centred on Barnsdale and Sherwood. The Lacys were lords both of Barnsdale and Blackburnshire; in 1311 these lands came to Thomas earl of Lancaster, who was also lord of Wyresdale. These two geographic correlations are quite distinct, yet each leads to the same conclusion. Thirdly, similar arguments can be deduced to explain the amalgamation of the two geographic foci of Barnsdale and Sherwood. Fourthly, the legend inherited a great deal from thirteenth-century romances. There can be no realistic explanation of its origin which does not include access to *Fouke le Fitz Waryn, Wistasse li Moine* and *Hereward the Wake*. At some stage near the origin of Robin's story these tales and his overlapped and intermingled. It is this, above all, which tells against any notion that the legend was all put together in lowly circumstances, for *Fouke* and *Wistasse* are set in a context which is baronial and knightly. There can be no doubt at all that they were aimed at a knightly audience. And they are in Latin, Anglo-Norman or French. Their influence is apparent to varying degrees across almost the whole range of the early stories: *Guy of Gisborne* and *Robyn Hoode his Death* alone are completely free of it; and it is remarkable that it pervades *Robin Hood and the Potter*, but only contributes in small matters to the tale of the knight. The more plebeian story inherited much, the more knightly very little.

It is not surprising then that part of the legend is patently knightly in atmosphere. The tale of the knight cannot have made real sense except to an audience familiar with the relationship between the knightly debtor and the monastic mortgagee and sympathetic towards the knight in his plight. And the sympathy would have to have been strongly felt: the knight is in debt because he has had to buy his son off a charge of homicide. Nevertheless, his cause is just; he is one of the heroes of the tale. It is the abbot and his cronies, who try to profit from the knight's misfortune, who are the villains. Yet all the abbot does is to advance money against security and require, admittedly somewhat zestfully, repayment on the nail.

No other part of the legend fits so easily into a knightly background. Indeed, the tale of the knight is the only part concerned with a particular social class. The rest is more general in its appeal, for all sections of the community hated the restrictions of the royal forest law, and individuals from all ranks had cause, on various occasions, for resisting the authority of the sheriff.

The romances, such as *Fouke* and *Wistasse*, and the surviving tales of Robin, are not alike in all respects. The most obvious difference is linguistic. The romances survive in Latin, French or Anglo-Norman; there was also an English version of *Fouke*, now lost, which was available to Leland in the sixteenth century. The Robin Hood tales are in English and there is no evidence that they were ever composed in, or put into French. The increased use of English made room for a rapid expansion of the audience beyond the limits of the French-speaking aristocracy and gentry, but it also marked a change in the linguistic habits of this upper class. The song on Richard of Cornwall was already in English in 1264. So was the celebration of the execution of Simon Fraser in 1306. English was becoming a vehicle, but not yet the only vehicle, for this particular type of entertainment. Some indication of the progress of the vernacular is given by the attempt of the University of Oxford to check it by a decree of 1322 insisting that students should converse in French and Latin. But its advance could not be stayed. A parliamentary statute of 1362 laid down that henceforth pleadings in the courts were to be in English, not French, which was no longer intelligible to many litigants; and twenty years later the change was neatly summed up in a famous passage by John of Trevisa, sometime fellow of the Queen's College, Oxford, who entered the service of Thomas, Lord Berkeley, as chaplain and vicar of Berkeley, and enjoyed a considerable reputation for his English translations of Latin works:

Gentlemen's children are taught to speak French from the time they are rocked in their cradle and can speak and play with a child's brooch; and countryfolk wish to liken themselves to gentlemen and try with great diligence to speak French, in order to be more thought of.
This method was much used before the first plague [the Black Death, 1348–9], and is since somewhat changed. For John Cornwall, a master of grammar, changed the teaching in grammar school and the construing of French, into English; and Richard Pencrych learned that method of teaching from him, and other men from Pencrych; so that now, the year of our Lord, a thousand three hundred fourscore and five, of the second of King Richard after the conquest ninth (1385), in all the grammar schools of England children leave French and

construe and learn in English, and have thereby advantage on the one side and disadvantage on another. The advantage is that they learn their grammar in less time than children were wont to do; the disadvantage is that now children of the grammar school know no more French than their left heel knows; and that is harm for them if they cross the sea and travel in foreign lands, and in many other circumstances. Also gentlemen have now largely ceased teaching their children French.[1]

The tales of Robin Hood are first mentioned in 1377. It has been argued that the increasingly numerous references thereafter compared with the apparent blank earlier indicates that they were derived from incidents in the near past. This ignores the effect of linguistic change. Under the new syllabus described by John of Trevisa, pupils were suddenly cut off from the old literary culture in French and Anglo-Norman. Where it was not translated into English it became foreign. The result was to create a cultural desert which was rapidly filled by the extraordinary blossoming of English as a literary language from the middle of the fourteenth century. The change encouraged a revival in the old alliterative English style. It made room for Chaucer's genius. It accompanied an almost explosive development both in literary form and subject-matter. This could well explain Robin's first appearance as a literary figure in 1377. His tale must have been told more often to more eager audiences. Oral traditions must have been precipitated more frequently and persistently as written versions.

However, within this new literary vigour the stories played a relatively lowly role in both social and literary terms. Knightly romance and classical legend were both refurbished by Chaucer. The Arthurian epic was rewritten in several versions culminating in the next century in the great *Morte Darthur* of Sir Thomas Malory. By the side of these achievements the tales of Robin are, in modern jargon, distinctly 'pop'. Not even the praise of ballad enthusiasts can pass them off as great literature. They lack depth, subtlety and command of words. In their allusions they are unsophisticated and uninventive. Yet they conform to some kind of pattern. They are built on a structure which is almost entirely narrative. They rely on a short four-line stanza and the simplest of rhymes, usually in the second and fourth line, more rarely in the form ABAB. This finished ballad form of the sixteenth century, according to recent literary opinion, was not simply a derivative of folksong, but an amalgam of folksong and minstrelsy. And working its way through to the finished product was the influence of the thirteenth-century French *lai* and *carole*. Hence the form of the tales, like some of the subject-matter, can be traced back to a French connection. This was not simply blown by the wind. Minstrels travelled. Among those present at Edward I's great feast in 1306 there were probably at least six who came from France, Artois or Flanders, and among the English minstrels several had visited France or the Low Countries.

The argument here impinges on the prolonged dispute between those who believe that the ballads were an expression of communal tradition and those who hold that they originated as individual compositions, as the work of minstrels. In so far as this has been resolved, it has been along the line that ballads were initially composed by individuals but were preserved and developed as a tradition by communal repetition. This assumes, very reasonably, an interplay between invention and repetition and between more professional as against more amateur performance, in which the production of written versions, which established a canon, marked a crucial stage. But much also has come to depend, less reasonably, on a somewhat scholastic definition of balladry. Some have been ready to exclude the Robin Hood cycle in whole or in part from the genre. Some have excluded the *Gest* as an epic, while retaining its component stories and the other tales. This is to impose the strict definitions derived from the finished ballad of the sixteenth century on an earlier period when both form and content were less precise. And it is not a matter of literary form alone.

In the sixteenth century, ballads were sold in the streets and sung in the taverns. But on their route to that social destination they had been told in more lordly circumstances. Between 1450 and 1452 the duke of Norfolk's garrison at Framlingham castle (Suffolk) achieved some notoriety, even in the unruly circumstances of the mid-fifteenth century, for its riotous conduct. One of the duke's squires, Charles Nowell, commanded an armed gang which was alleged to have committed sundry acts of violence; Nowell himself assaulted John Paston outside Norwich cathedral and thereby achieved a niche in the Paston letters. In the end they were indicted by a jury made up of knights and gentlemen of the opposing faction who alleged that Nowell, Sir William Ashton and others of the garrison had published 'writings and ballads', claiming that King Henry had sold his realm to the king of France and urging the people to rebel and call in Richard duke of York to accept the crown. These 'ballads' were not folk-songs.

Yet, in the case of Robin Hood, it was not simply in language and poetic form that the tales broke away from the romances. There was also a change in social emphasis. The tale of the knight may be about the predicament of a knight, but it is also about a yeoman – Robin himself. The minstrel of the *Gest* may address his audience as gentlemen, but it is plain that the heroes of the tales are yeomen; so also are Guy of Gisborne and Adam Bell and his colleagues. And this is no mere superficial feature of the tales. Robin and his fellows, like Adam Bell and his friends, are not simply yeomen, but 'good yeomen'. They represent 'yeomanly' behaviour. They comment on the social conduct of a yeoman, the standards of 'good yeomanry'. So, if in one direction Robin's legend cannot be cut off from the knightly romances of the thirteenth century, in another it found its own setting in the society of yeomen. The clarification of the term 'yeoman' is perhaps the most important stage of all in defining the audience of these tales.

Definition is not easy, for three changes were taking place at the same time. First, English words were coming into use for French or Latin terms which hitherto had defined social class. Secondly, terms which had been based on tenure and legal status were being supplemented or replaced by terms indicating general social standing or economic function. Thirdly, the social structure to which these terms were applied was itself changing, though probably less rapidly and certainly less dramatically than the changes in terminology, taken at their face value, might suggest. Some words survived with their sense unimpaired. 'Knight' meant much the same in the fifteenth as in the later thirteenth century; it was simply used more frequently in place of the Latin *miles* or the French *chevalier*. Some words lost their original importance to the extent of passing out of everyday vocabulary. 'Villein' vanished with villein services and legal status. 'Churl', the Old English *ceorl*, retained a literary usage. 'Sergeant' or *serviens*, which had described a general category of feudal tenure, acquired a number of specialized meanings.

The new terms which crept in were of diverse origin. Some, such as 'gentleman', arose first in local society and staked a claim to birth and breeding. Some, such as 'husbandman', were general occupational terms which had been used earlier as English forms of the French or Latin terms defining status. Some originated in the household or at least enjoyed a dual history within the feudal household and without. Probably the first of these to achieve an exact sense was 'squire' or 'esquire', which in the course of the fourteenth century came to denote the social rank immediately below the knight; an esquire was of gentle birth and used a coat of arms which came in the second half of the century to be recognized by the heralds. One of the earliest whose arms are known was Geoffrey Chaucer. However, the claim to gentle birth which lay behind the blazon, categorized only a comparatively small upper band of the middling free landowners below the rank of knight. In the early fourteenth century this whole group was described in Latin as *valetti*, in French *valets*. *Valetti*, along with knights, attended parliament as county representatives in the first half of the fourteenth century. One English term for them in the late fourteenth century was 'franklin'. As such, they were men of substance; Chaucer's franklin had not only sat in parliament but also held office as sheriff. However, this term did not stick. By the early fifteenth century it had been largely superseded by two others: 'gentleman', which was applied to men of breeding, or used by those who claimed breeding, who were not of armigerous standing; and 'yeoman'.

These changes were hastened towards a conclusion by the Statute of Additions of 1413 which required plaintiffs in personal actions to describe the standing of their opponents exactly in the writ initiating an action. By the middle of the fifteenth century local society fell, in descending order, into knights, squires, gentlemen, yeomen and husbandmen, with franklins still making occasional, but less frequent appearances. Only the first two, knight and squire, had distinguishing qualifications. The gentleman, particularly, was sometimes simply he who claimed to be a gentleman, or lived like a gentleman, perhaps especially one who got into debt like a gentleman. The qualification of knightly arms apart, the borderlines were indistinct or movable. Squires were sometimes described as gentlemen. It was possible and not uncommon to describe one and the same person as 'gentleman' or 'yeoman' or perhaps 'franklin'. John Otter of Warwickshire is recorded as a gentleman in 1455, an esquire in 1468 and a yeoman in 1470. There were similar variations lower down the social scale. William and Richard Tomlinson, accused of murder in Nottinghamshire in 1497, are described as yeomen by the coroner's jury, but husbandmen by the victim's brother. They were said to have no goods or chattels. Roger Prentyse, who abjured the realm at Newark in 1507 for the killing of John Bradshaw, a fuller, is described variously as a weaver and a yeoman. Letters patent of 1510, pardoning William Forman, of Nottinghamshire, of murder, describe him as 'yeoman or husbandman'. Few of these can have changed status. Occasionally it may have been in doubt. But the main explanation of these variations must be that both in local government and private transactions these terms might be used casually or to suit the needs of the moment. Sometimes in legal actions the requirements of the Statute of Additions were met by giving a litigant a series of aliases which covered a range of status and occupation.

The king's government took a more ordered view. The Statute of Additions provoked a number of judicial judgments over the next thirty years which linked the status of gentleman with service in the royal or a superior feudal household. Sumptuary legislation propounded a strict hierarchy. The well-known ordinance of 1363 restricted grooms and husbandmen to 26s. for their whole cloth, yeomen and craftsmen to 40s., esquires and gentlemen of less than £100 landed income to 70s., esquires and gentlemen of 200 marks income to 76s. 8d., and so on. There were also recurrent moves to restrict certain positions to men of birth. In 1445, for example, knights of the shire attending parliament were to be drawn from knights, 'noteable squires' and 'gentlemen of birth' and not from those who stood in the 'degree of Yoman and bynethe'. Where such lines were drawn depended on the office under consideration. Gentlemen and yeomen were not always sundered. Under Henry VIII, for example, it was laid down that local constables were to be selected from substantial gentlemen or yeomen. But, wherever they were drawn, these sharp distinctions reflected policies and wishful thinking rather than the relationships of local life. Unintentionally, they illustrate the social mobility and ad hoc terminology which they sought to contain and define.

In the fifteenth and sixteenth centuries men took widely differing views on the yeoman's standing. Sir John Fortescue, chief justice of the King's Bench under Henry VI, wrote in the late 1460s that 'there are various *valetti* in that country [England] who can spend more than £100 a year'.[2] In the next century the statesman and scholar, Sir Thomas Smith, equated the yeoman with the forty-shilling freeholder. Bishop Latimer, in contrast, identified him with a farmer or leaseholder with some few pounds annual income. In short he could be a prosperous landholder who, if he was socially ambitious, might have pretensions to gentility and achieve recognition as a gentleman. At the other end of the social scale he would not be easy to distinguish from the general ruck of the rural population from which his family might recently have emerged. Those who listened to the tales of Robin Hood could place their yeomen anywhere within this range. That no doubt broadened their appeal.

However, that is to explore only one sense of the word 'yeoman'. There is another which places it in a different context. In the early fourteenth century the French *valet* and Latin *valettus* were used in official records to denote officers in both royal and feudal households. These men enjoyed lower status than the knights, but they were by no means menial; they were fed and liveried and were often drawn from gentle families. In the early fourteenth century the *valetti* included the esquires, but as the esquires came rapidly to be defined precisely as armigerous, *valet* and *valetti* came to be translated into English as 'yeomen'. This process was probably well advanced when the words were equated in a parliamentary petition of 1363. In the next century the ordinances of the royal household specify the number and quality of the yeomen of the crown. Today the yeomen of the guard still watch over the Tower of London.

This official or household usage was the original sense of both *valet* and yeoman. It may well be that it spread outwards to describe a broad social rank in the countryside partly because government officials viewed local society in terms of the hierarchy within which they themselves lived and worked – hence *valetti* and yeomen came to constitute the next social rank below knights and squires just as they did at court and in noble and knightly households – and partly because it brought a certain social cachet. It may well be that freeholders, appreciating the social differentiation taking place higher up the social scale in the emergence of a clearly defined body of esquires and a less formal array of gentlemen, preferred the terms which described the next rank in the household hierarchy to the totally neutral 'franklin'. A yeoman had standing.

Hence from its origin the word 'yeoman' had a dual sense. It could describe either a freeholder of some substance or a household official of some status. Sir John Fortescue was familiar with both senses. He envisaged *valetti* who could spend £100 a year. But he also regarded £5 a year 'of fee or rent' as a 'fayre lyvinge for a yeoman'.[3] In the first instance he was writing of local landowners, in the second of the king's officers. There was no contradiction.

The household or official yeoman was as diverse as the yeoman landholder. In the royal household the yeomen constituted a long-established hierarchy of their own, with precisely defined duties, fees and allowances. According to the *Black Book* of 1472, the yeomen of the chamber were to:

make beddes, to bere or hold torches, to sett bourdes [tables], to apparayle all chambres, and suche othyr servyce as the chaumbrelayn or usshers of chambre comaund or assigne; to attende the chambre, to wache [do guard duty for] the king by course; to go messagez.

The twenty-four yeomen of the crown were in effect the royal body-guard. They were to be:

most semely persones, clenely and strongest archers, honest of condicions and of behavoure, bold men, chosen and tryed out of every lordes house in Ynglond for theyre cunyng and vertew. Therof one to be yoman of the robes, another to be yoman of the wardrobe of beddis in houshold; thes ij [two] in sartaynte ete in the kinges chaumbre dayly, other ij be yomen usshers of chaumbre etyng there also; another to be yoman of the stole, if hit plese the king, anothyr to be yoman of the armory; another to be yoman of the bowes for the king; another yoman to kepe the kinges bookes; another to kepe his dogges for the bowe; or another to kepe his best [beast]; and except the first iiij [four] persones the remnaunt may to the hall as the ussher [shall determine]; and thus they may be put to busines. Also hit accordith that they be chosen men of manhoode, shotyng, and specially of vertuose condicions.[4]

These men in real life were intended to have many of the qualities which legend attributed to Robin Hood.

Another witness brings Robin and the 'official' yeoman even closer together. Chaucer himself was a yeoman of the king's chamber in 1367

A woodcut used by Richard Pynson for Chaucer's yeoman, 1491, and in
the Chepman and Myllar Prints for Robin Hood, 1508.

before he achieved the status of squire. When he came to describe the
knight's yeoman in the Prologue to the Canterbury Tales he knew what
he was talking about:

*And he was clad in cote and hood of grene;*
*A sheef of pecock-arwes brighte and kene*
*Under his belt he bar ful thriftily;*
*Wel coude he dresse his takel yemanly:*
*His arwes drouped noght with fetheres lowe,*
*And in his hand he bar a mighty bowe.*
*A not-heed hadde he, with a broun visage.*
*Of wodecraft wel coude he al the usage.*
*Upon his arm he bar a gay bracer,*
*And by his syde a swerd and bokeler,*
*And on that other syde a gay daggere,*
*Harneised wel, and sharp as point of spere;*
*A Cristofre on his brest of silver shene.*
**An horn he bar, the bawdrik was of grene;**
*A forster was he, soothly, as I gesse.*[5]

And he was clad in coat and hood of green;
A sheaf of peacock arrows bright and keen
Under his belt he bore full carefully.
Well could he dress his tackle yeomanly:
His arrows drooped not with feathers low,
And in his hand he bore a mighty bow.
**A cropped head had he with a brown face.**
Of woodcraft well knew he all the usage.
Upon his arm he bore a gay bracer,
And by his side a sword and buckler,
And on the other side a gay dagger,
Harnessed well, and sharp as point of spear;
A Christopher on his breast of silver sheen.
A horn he bore, the baldric was of green;
A forester was he, truly, as I guess.

121

That comes very close to descriptions of Robin Hood. The yeoman's arrows even share their peacock flights with the arrows presented by the knight of the *Gest* to Robin rather than the usual more effective goose. Some certainly appreciated the parallel. Richard Pynson's edition of 1491 of the Canterbury Tales and the version of the *Gest* printed in the Chapman and Myllar Prints of 1508 used the same woodcut as an illustration of the knight's yeoman and of Robin. The multiple use of illustrations was not uncommon. These two invited it.

The yeomen of the household of the fifteenth century were the successors to the *valetti* of the beginning of the fourteenth century. Robert Hode and the other porters of the chamber of Edward II were *valetti*. Likewise the yeomen of the bow of 1472 had been preceded by the archers who carried the king's bow in the twelfth century. The structure became more complex as time passed; official terms were changed; but the framework was ancient. Neither in the fifteenth century nor earlier were these officers restricted to the household. Yeomen of the chamber did indeed carry messages. So also did John Paston's yeoman. In the fifteenth century yeomen of the crown were used as envoys and as special agents sent to execute royal instructions or to inquire into matters touching the king. Their responsibility for the king's bow and bow-dogs involved them closely in the affairs of the forest. They were sent out in pairs or singly under Edward II to take the king's venison in the royal forests. They could look forward to honourable retirement in some forest office, like Robert de Maulay, king's yeoman, who was made steward of Sherwood for life in 1334 as a reward for his service 'in dwelling continually at the King's side'. This association of yeomen with the forest was of long standing. One of the earliest occurrences of the word is in the twelfth-century text, the *Pseudo-Cnut de Foresta*, where the 'yongermen' appear as under-foresters drawn from the *mediocres homines*, the middling ranks of freemen. Robin Hood and his men are 'yeomen of the forest' (*Gest*, 222, 377). Robin's most famous accoutrements, his bow and arrows and his horn, were the recognized tools and insignia of the local foresters which distinguished them from other bailiffs, and which appeared as the characteristic embellishment of their tombs.

As with the yeoman landowner, 'middling' allowed for a wide range. According to the *Black Book*, the squires of the royal household were allowed wages for one clerk, two *valetti*, two grooms and two pages. The *valetti*, or yeomen, were allowed £2 per annum, the same as the clerk, twice as much as the grooms and four times as much as the pages. The yeomen of the crown in contrast received 3*d.* a day and other allowances. In the context of the court the yeoman was subordinate. Against his 3*d.* per day should be set the squire's daily allowance of

7½d., and there was much in court protocol to distinguish the two. Nevertheless, once he moved outside the hierarchical world of the court, the yeoman enjoyed all the prestige of a royal aide-de-camp. Yeomen could even be in positions of command. When, in 1411, a settlement was arranged between William, Lord Ros and Robert Tirwhit, justice of the king's bench, attendance was required from all the 'knyghtes and esquiers and yomen that had ledynge of men' in Tirwhit's party. And the barriers between the various household grades were not impenetrable. Chaucer was first a yeoman, then a squire. William Akes, yeoman of the horse in Henry Percy's household in 1620, had become gentleman of the horse by 1622. The distinctions sometimes marked stages in a career.

Which kind of yeoman – landholder, household officer or official – did Robin Hood's audience imagine him to be? Probably it did not matter. Yeoman service was not menial. Yeoman officers came from landed families; if not landed themselves they would have expectations. Between the official and the landholding yeoman, contemporaries would see no dichotomy. But the question matters very much to the historian. One interpretation of the legend, advanced by Dobson and Taylor, is that it expressed the increasing self-confidence of a rising class of yeoman landowners. Another might be that, in its finished form, it reflected the circumstances of the feudal household of the fourteenth and fifteenth centuries. Between the two views there is a real choice to be made.

The choice does not turn on class. The dual sense of the word demonstrates that, as a social rank, the yeoman landholder and the yeoman officer were equated. It turns on the circumstances in which the tales took root and spread. The mark which these circumstances impressed on the first surviving tales is unmistakably that of the feudal household and of the patterns of service and dependence characteristic of the 'bastard' feudalism of fourteenth- and fifteenth-century England: of retainers sustained by annual fees and identified by grant of livery, who made up the retinues of the great and lesser lords, 'embraced' their quarrels and, in return for loyal service, were in their turn 'maintained' and supported by their lords in their own local disputes in county society or the courts of law. In the *Gest* the sheriff tells the king that the knight 'maintains' the outlaws and undermines the authority of royal government (324):

| | |
|---|---|
| '*He wyll avowe that he hath done,* | 'He will avow what he has done, |
| *To mayntene the outlawes stronge;* | To maintain the outlaws strong; |
| *He wyll be lorde, and set you at* | He will be lord, and set you at |
| *nought,* | nought, |
| *In all the northe londe.*' | In all the northern land.' |

Robin leads a *meinie* or retinue, every man of which wears his livery (229–30):

| | |
|---|---|
| *Seven score of wyght yemen* | Seven score stout yeomen |
| *Came pryckynge on a rowe.* | Came spurring in a row. |
| | |
| *And everych of them a good mantell* | Every one of them in a good cloak |
| *Of scarlet and of raye;* | Of scarlet and striped cloth; |

Like the yeomen of Justice Tirwhit in 1411 he has 'ledynge' of men. The king of the *Gest* also plays his part. For their journey from Sherwood into Nottingham he has the whole company dress in Lincoln green, the sight of which spreads panic among the townsfolk – 'Come Robyn Hode to the towne'. Service, livery as the mark of service, and the fee as the reward for service recur in the tales in widely diverse contexts. The justice in the *Gest* is 'holde with the abbot . . . both with cloth and fee'. At the royal court Robin spends 'an hondred pounde and all his mennes fee'; his dwindling resources are marked by the reduction of his company so that in the end only Little John and Scathelock remain. Little John's adventures are perhaps the most revealing of all. First Robin lends him to the knight as his knave (81):

| | |
|---|---|
| *'In a yeman's stede he may the* | 'He may stand for you in a yeoman's |
| *stande,* | stead, |
| *If thou greate nede have'.* | If you have great need of one'. |

Then, in the guise of Reynolde Grenelef, he is offered a fee of 20 marks by the sheriff, but he must first leave the service of the knight, and the sheriff allows him twelve months in which to serve out his time. Once in the sheriff's household he quarrels with the steward, the butler and the cook over his daily allowance of food. He wants to eat in his lord's absence and they refuse to accept this breach of etiquette (164):

| | |
|---|---|
| *'I make myn avowe to God', saide the* | 'I make my vow to God', said the |
| *coke,* | cook, |
| *'Thou arte a shrewede hynde* | 'You're a villain of a servant |
| *In ani hous for to dwel,* | To dwell in any house |
| *For to aske thus to dyne'.* | And thus to ask to dine'. |

He resolves the subsequent fight with the cook by offering him a place in Robin's company, neatly matching the sheriff's rate of pay (170–1):

| | |
|---|---|
| *'And two times in the yere thy clothinge* | 'And twice in the year thy clothing |
| *Chaunged shulde be;* | Changed shall be; |
| | |
| *And every yere of Robyn Hode* | And every year from Robin Hood |
| *Twenty merke to thy fe.'* | Twenty marks for thy fee.' |

When charged with treachery by the sheriff, Little John, by contrast, maintains that he has not received the allowance due to him (190):

| | |
|---|---|
| *'I make myn avowe to God', sayde Litell Johnn,* | 'I make my vow to God', said Little John, |
| *'Mayster, ye be to blame;* | 'Master, you are to blame; |
| *I was mysserved of my dynere* | I was misserved of my dinner |
| *Whan I was with you at home.'* | When I was with you at home.' |

That loyalty should turn upon a dinner is only comprehensible in such a household setting.

Yet another feature of the tales was strongly reinforced from the same context of the feudal household. Only once in the early tales is Robin described as 'gentle',[6] but time and again he is said to be courteous. He and Little John sometimes act with pointed courtesy, even though the potter lectures the outlaws on 'courteous' behaviour. It is easy today to assume that this was intended to do no more than contrast the behaviour of the outlaws with the boorishness and treachery of their enemies. But in the fifteenth century the context of the word was much more precise. It referred the audience to matters which were the subject of a rapidly expanding body of literature concerned with social behaviour and especially with behaviour in service, at court or in circumstances where men rubbed up against others of both superior and inferior rank. These books ranged from *The Boke of Noblesse* to John Russell's *Book of Carving and Nurture*, which explained the household duties of butler, pantler and carver, and to several versions of a *Book of Curtesye*, the best known of which is William Caxton's, printed in 1477–8. These were educational books, social training for pupils; much of Caxton's work is concerned with how the pupil should conduct himself in conversation and in general deportment. They owed their popularity to the progression of the mannered society downward from the gentle class and outward from gentle households to merchants, townsfolk, and yeomen in the countryside. But the source of the conventions in the feudal household was unmistakable; the origin of 'courtesy' was at court, with the knightly class and in the romances of courtly literature. In the *Chanson de Roland*, Oliver is *curteis*; the Gawain of *Gawain and the Green Knight* is the epitome of courtesy. One of the crucial dramatic conventions of the *Gest*, Robin's refusal to dine until he has welcomed an unexpected guest, parallels the behaviour of King Arthur who will not dine until some adventure has occurred.

On these social standards both Robin Hood and Little John are well informed. Each 'coud his curtesie', clearly revealed in the first encounter with the knight (24, 29):

| | |
|---|---|
| *Litell Johnn was full curteyes,* | Little John was very courteous, |
| *And sette hym on his kne:* | And knelt on his knee: |
| *'Welcom be ye, gentyll knyght,* | 'Welcome are you, courteous knight, |
| *Welcom ar ye to me.'* | Welcome are you to me.' |

| | |
|---|---|
| . . . *They brought hym to the* | . . . They brought him to the |
| *lodge-dore;* | lodge-door, |
| *Whan Robyn hym gan see,* | And when Robin saw him, |
| *Full curtesly dyd of his hode* | He doffed his hood very courteously |
| *And sette hym on his knee.* | And knelt on his knee. |

Similar formalities recur when Little John, still in the sheriff's service, encounters his master in the forest, when the knight returns to the forest, and when Robin encounters the king in the guise of the abbot. The real abbot on the other hand is discourteous (115):

| | |
|---|---|
| *To suffre a knyght to knele so longe,* | To suffer a knight to kneel so long, |
| *Thou canst no curteysye.* | Thou knowest no courtesy. |

So too, is the sheriff's butler; he refuses Little John's claim to his allowance of food. The contrasting standards are revealed most clearly of all in Robin's encounter with the monks (226–7):

| | |
|---|---|
| *Robyn dyde adowne his hode,* | Robin doffed his hood, |
| *The monke whan that he se;* | When the monk he did see; |
| *The monke was not so curteyse,* | The monk was not so courteous, |
| *His hode then let he be.* | His hood he let be. |
| | |
| *'He is a chorle, mayster, by dere* | 'He is a churl, master, by dear |
| *worthy God',* | worthy God', |
| *Than sayd Lytell Johan:* | Then said Little John: |
| *'Thereof no force', sayd Robyn,* | 'Thereof no matter', said Robin, |
| *'For curteysy can he none.'* | 'For courtesy knows he none.' |

The churlish monk may not have known the rules of courtesy, but the outlaws and their friends did, so much so that they were ingrained in their pattern of behaviour. The feasting, the exchange of gifts, the reception of guests are all settings for and manifestations of this one quality.

One final characteristic of the early tales smacks of the household and of service: none of the outlaws has a family. Much is a Miller's son, but there is nothing of the Miller. The treacherous prioress of Kirklees, Robin's near-of-kin or cousin, is the only relative in the whole cycle. There are no parents, no wives and no children. Apart from the prioress, women scarcely figure at all. The knight's wife makes a brief appearance in the *Gest*. There is the mysterious witch-like figure who 'bans' Robin Hood in *Robyn Hoode his Death*. The only woman with any appreciable role is the sheriff's wife in *Robin Hood and the Potter*. She raises a distant, distorted echo of courtly love for she treats Robin, as the potter, courteously, and he responds with a gift of a gold ring on his departure and the promise of a white palfrey as he dispatches her discomfited husband home from the forest. All this is linked to one other important feature: no family, no land. The knight's lands, pledged to the abbot of St Mary's, are the only property with which the tales are concerned. Robin's ultimate reward is not an estate, but a position at the king's court. His highest social ambition is service in the royal household. The only conceivable alternative is not rural life, even that of a man of substance, but the greenwood.

The view that a new class of yeomen established itself in the English countryside between the Black Death of 1348–9 and the end of the fifteenth century and came to constitute the chief market for the tales of yeoman valour of which Robin was prime example, has its own inherent difficulties. It is by no means certain that English rural society was more diversified in the fifteenth than in the thirteenth century; it is unclear how far yeomen were a product of real social change, how far a feature of new social terminology which did no more than apply new labels to old status. But even if these problems are proved insubstantial or simply bypassed, one dilemma remains. The emergence of the yeoman class, if that is what it was, is traditionally linked to the break-up of the manorial economy of midland and eastern England. Hence 'yeomanly' economic independence and self-confidence were rooted in soil far removed from the haunts of Robin Hood. Moreover, widespread though the ballad became in printed form, it was in the north and especially on the Scottish border and beyond that it survived longest and achieved its finest expression in the tales of Anglo–Scottish warfare and of the marauding and cattle-stealing endemic in an ill-governed part of the land: *The Battle of Otterburn, Flodden, Johnie Armstrong, Rookhope Ryde, Kinmont Willie* and the tales of the northern rising of 1569. It was in the north, too, that the conditions typical of feudal households and feudal service and the 'lack of governance' of late medieval England were prolonged into the sixteenth and seventeenth centuries. The eponymous hero of *Johnie Armstrong*, hanged by James V of Scotland in 1530, was 'a doubtit man, and as good a chieftain as ever was upon the borders. . . . And albeit he was a loose living man, and sustained the number of twenty-four well-horsed able gentlemen with him, yet he never molested no Scotsman'.[7] The Armstrongs, with their border keeps and raiding parties, were but one manifestation of this society. The northern earls, the heads of the great affinities of Percy and Neville, could still raise their men in rebellion in 1569. The marquess of Newcastle was still able to muster his white-coated tenantry to be cut down by Oliver Cromwell's troopers at Marston Moor in 1644, and still after 1660 Lady Anne Clifford could perpetuate the remnants of feudal lordship in her stately progresses and the building and reconstruction of her castles and towers from Appleby to Barden. This was the society which was a fitting subject for the ballad tales. It is a long way from the settled existence of the yeoman of midland England.

Once it is allowed that the tales of Robin Hood were nurtured among the officers, the retinue, the servants and the hangers-on who constituted and surrounded the feudal household, it becomes relatively easy to understand how the legend spread so far and took root so fast. The great estates were scattered. Households and retinues were itinerant. Household servants – yeomen – rode far about the business of their lords. Moreover, the household was not an enclosed world. Around the core of the permanent offices and servants with their annual fees and livery, there were men hired ad hoc, as the need arose, and temporary servants, tenants performing annual services, visitors and their servants, entertainers and scroungers looking for crumbs from the table. In the northern counties especially, households were reinforced by men who owed personal service as 'riders', escorts, messengers, huntsmen and the like, under the ancient tenures whereby they held their land. In examining the geographic spread of the legend some importance has already been attached to the example of Thomas of Northorp and Roger of Manningham, free-tenants of the manor of Bradford, who held their lands by rendering forty days' service as huntsmen in their lord's company in Blackburnshire.[8] When on such duty these men would count as yeomen; they received the appropriate fee. But Roger of Manningham also held two-thirds of the lordship of Haworth as the sixteenth part of a knight's fief, for which he paid rent and owed suit of court at Bradford. Thomas of Northorp also held additional parcels of land. In one of these, a holding of 1½ acres in Manningham, he was the partner of John Riens, and Riens was a bondsman whose servile duties were taken as a pattern for the whole of Bradford and Manningham. Thomas of Northorp and Roger of Manningham, in short, not only bestrode the road from Blackburnshire to Pontefract, but also spanned the whole range of social status and feudal service from knight down to villein within which the tales of Robin Hood came to circulate. There can have been few better placed to carry an infection.

They and their like were by no means the only carriers. So far the activity of minstrels has been considered solely in the context of the household. The justification for that lies in the deep impressions which that context left on the earliest surviving versions of the legend. But minstrelsy was not restricted to professionals in permanent household employment, although the king's government tried to have it so. In 1469 Edward IV incorporated the royal minstrels as a guild, with power to investigate the credentials of all those who claimed to be minstrels, and laid down that:

17 Travelling minstrels played a crucial part in the transmission of the legend. One of a group of fourteenth-century carvings of minstrels in Beverley Minster, an indication of the prestige of the Beverley Guild of Minstrels, the most famous and well established of all the northern groups

The tales were nurtured among the officers, retinue and hangers-on of the feudal household, reflecting many of its traditions. From there, they spread rapidly outwards: servants often had to travel on their masters' business and minstrels toured between household, market-place and tavern

18, 19 *Above* From the kitchen to the feast: the cook prepares a meal for his lord, not for the other servants. That was why Little John's demand for food in the absence of his new master, the sheriff, led to a quarrel with the cook. From the Luttrell Psalter, *c.* 1340

20-22 Minstrels provided a major source of entertainment both in public places and in the household. Entertainment could merely be a background to conversation at table, hence the minstrel's need to call for quiet before beginning his tale. Varied forms of entertainment are illustrated here – bagpipe, drum, guitar, vielle and (*right*) harp. From Queen Mary's Psalter, early fourteenth century

23 Inns were a focal point in travel, crime and entertainment in the Middle Ages. Here, the tales which had begun in more lordly circumstances, reached – and were influenced by – the whole social spectrum. The ale-stake with sheaf or fronds at the end is an indication of a brew ready for the official conners or tasters. A man in hermit's dress tries the hostess's brew. From a fourteenth-century manuscript

25-28 *Below* Social distinction in dress in fifteenth-century England, from the Ellesmere manuscript of Chaucer's Canterbury Tales. *From left to right*, the squire, the franklin, the knight and the canon's yeoman. The last is the only known painting of a fifteenth-century yeoman. The knight's yeoman has no tale and hence, regrettably, is not illustrated. As in Chaucer's Tales, the franklin and yeoman are clearly distinguished in age and dress. Both the squire (following Chaucer's text) and the yeoman are depicted as young men

24 A tinker, seen off by a dog. An ill-reputed fellow traveller of minstrels and criminals, and one of Robin's opponents in the later ballads of combat. From the Luttrell Psalter, *c.* 1340

29 *Left* The association of Robin Hood with the
May Games did not develop until the late
fifteenth century. Tollett's window,
designed for Betley Old Hall in 1621, is one of
the earliest illustrations of the May Games and
the morris dance. The queen of May (*bottom
centre*) and the friar (*bottom right*) are the only
figures identified with Robin Hood.
Participants took to fancy dress, so some of the
motley, especially the fifteenth-century style of
the queen, is earlier than the date of
composition

30 *Right* Robin Hood, Castle Green,
Nottingham. An essay in social realism by
James Woodford, 1949. The City Council
regularly, but unavailingly, make provision for
the replacement of the arrow which is missing,
as usual, in this photograph. The moral of the
robber robbed is unintended

31 *Below left* Little John's supposed grave,
Hathersage, nearly 14 foot long. In the
seventeenth century his home was traditionally
set in Hathersage and in the nineteenth century
the grave became a tourist attraction. The
attribution is as firmly embedded as the
modern headstone and railings, but the genuine
legend has nothing of it

32 *Below right* Robin Hood's Well, the arched
shelter by John Vanbrugh. First mentioned in
the seventeenth century, the well is the site
most likely to be linked directly with the
original outlaw. A well-known halting place
up to the nineteenth century, the well is now
largely ignored by tourists who pass within a
few yards of it on the neighbouring trunk road

33 The romantic view of Robin Hood was a nineteenth-century invention: Daniel Maclise, *Robin Hood and His Merry Men*, 1839/45

'no minstrel of our kingdom, although he may be sufficiently learned in this art or occupation, shall in any way exercise this art or occupation within our kingdom henceforth unless he be a member of the gild or fraternity . . . and has contributed to it with his fellow brethren'.

But in an age of ineffective legislation this was among the least effective regulations. The preamble gave the game away, for the king recorded, on the complaint of his minstrels, that:

some rough peasants and craftsmen of various mysteries of our realm of England have pretended to be minstrels, of whom some carry our letters, not issued by us, pretending to be our own minstrels: and so . . . under colour of the art or occupation of minstrels they fraudulently collect and receive great sums of money from our lieges. And although they are not intelligent or expert in that art or occupation, and are occupied in various arts and activities on week-days . . . on feast-days they travel from place to place, and take all the profits on which our aforesaid minstrels . . . who are learned and instructed on this art and occupation, and versed in no other work, occupation, or mystery, ought to live.[9]

Anyone, in short, who had a repertoire and could attract an audience might perform as a minstrel. They were the 'pop' singers of medieval England.

Like 'pop' singers, minstrels went on tour. This is not immediately apparent from the records of the households which retained them, for these are concerned with their fees, livery and other internal costs. The full picture is only revealed in the records of those institutions and households which were largely dependent for their entertainment on such visiting companies. The bursar's accounts for Fountains abbey in the late 1450s include the following:

to a blind minstrel, 6d.; to the players of Topcliffe, 4d.; to the minstrel of William de Plumpton, 8d.; to the boy bishop of Ripon, 3s.; to a fool from Byland, 4d.; players from Thirsk, 4d.; to the minstrel of the Earl of Northumberland, 8d.; to a story-teller (*fabulator*) whose name was unknown, 6d.; to the minstrels of Beverley, 16d.; to the minstrels of Lord Arundel, 16d.; of Lord Beaumont; of Lord fitz Hugh; to a herald of Lord Northumberland, 3s. 4d.; to the king's minstrels, in part, 3s. 4d.; to the story-teller (*fabulator*) of the Earl of Salisbury, 12d.; to the players of the Earl of Westmorland, 2d.; to the boy bishop of York, 6s. 8d.; . . . to the players of Ripon, 2d.; to a fool called Solomon (who came again) 4d.[10]

The accounts of the obedientaries of Selby abbey tell a similar story, although here the visitors were usually described as players or actors (*histriones*). In 1479–80 the monks received visits from the players of Sir John Conyers, Sir James Tyrell, Lord Scrope, the duke of Gloucester, the earl of Northumberland, and, on two occasions, of the king, and this quite apart from the visits of players whose origin is not stated. At Selby in this year such payments were made on eleven occasions and, fragmentary though the accounts are, they suggest that this was not unusual.

This evidence from Fountains and Selby is of varied interest. First, it demonstrates that in the second half of the fifteenth century minstrels or players were maintained in at least twenty baronial or knightly house-holds in northern England, their masters ranging from Richard duke of Gloucester, and the earls of Northumberland and Westmorland, down to Sir John Conyers, Sir James Harrington and William Plumpton. Secondly, at the level at which the great abbeys aimed, visiting entertainers still came largely from such households: 8 of the 13 visits recorded at Fountains, 22 of the 48 visits recorded at Selby up to *c.* 1496. Thirdly, at both abbeys, some entertainers came from less lordly, more miscellaneous circumstances. Both houses received visits from the minstrels of Beverley. At Fountains payments were made to players from Topcliffe and from Thirsk, and to boy-bishops from Ripon and York. At Selby visiting entertainers came from the bishop of Carlisle, and from St Mary's, York; some or all of these may well have been choristers. Finally, at Selby at any rate, the evidence suggests that, as time passed, more and more groups of minstrels and entertainers were operating without a base in an aristocratic household. The strongly aristocratic flavour suggested by the payments made up to 1500 con-trasts sharply with those of the next thirty years up to 1532. Of the thirty-four payments made in this second period only six were to groups which claimed aristocratic patronage. An equal number went to municipal groups, three to minstrels of York and one each to groups from Doncaster, Howden and Leeds.

This should probably be taken as no more than a change in emphasis. It would certainly be wrong to imagine that all minstrelsy was originally aristocratic or that at some point it became entirely bourgeois or rural. At Chester the minstrels probably originated in the early thirteenth century; at Tutbury they were certainly established by 1380: both groups owed their privileges to aristocratic patronage. At Beverley, the town guild of minstrels was already famous by the fourteenth century; its work is commemorated in the splendid label-mould carvings in the north aisle of the nave of the minster. It later claimed ancient jurisdiction over all minstrels between Trent and Tweed. There were many local variations. At Durham the earliest payment recorded in the accounts of the cathedral priory is to a minstrel of the king of Scotland; here a large proportion of the payments in the fourteenth century were to entertainers under royal or aristocratic patronage, but the monks also drew on groups from Newcastle. At Maxstoke (Warwickshire) in the early fifteenth century the canons were entertained by the players of the local aristocracy, the Earl Ferrers, Lord

Clinton and Lord Stafford, but most of the visiting troupes came from Coventry, Rugeley and other local towns. There were no hard and fast social distinctions separating aristocratic from municipal troupes. The accounts of Sir John Howard from 1465 to 1483 record that the greater part of his entertainment was provided by local groups from Coggeshall, Hadleigh, Thorington and elsewhere. Conversely the accounts of Shrewsbury corporation of 1574 include the payment of £8 10s. 8d. to 'the players of noblemen and others, and bear-wards of noblemen, and minstrels of noblemen, this yere'. That was two years after minstrels and fencers, with bear-wards and other wandering entertainers not under aristocratic patronage, had been included as vagabonds in the first Elizabethan Vagrancy Act of 1572.

That condemnation was not new. From the Fourth Lateran Council of 1215 onwards the clergy were forbidden such entertainments. But canonical condemnation was aimed at the lower end of the profession. Some years before the Fourth Lateran Council Master Thomas, rector of Chobham (Surrey) and sub-dean of Salisbury, established a veritable hierarchy of minstrelsy in his penitential. At the top, those who recited the deeds of princes and the lives of saints were acceptable. The rest, from those who sang wanton songs, or spread satire and scandal, down to those who performed lewd dances, were damnable. Minstrels, in short, were a mixed bag, embracing the king's minstrels who counted as squires and lived as gentlemen, the minstrels of honour of Edward II's ordinance of 1315, who had an established position in a household, and also the wandering players whose lot is summed up in the words of Sir Edwin Chambers:

To tramp long miles in wind and rain, to stand wet to the skin and hungry and footsore, making the slow bourgeois laugh while the heart was bitter within; such must have been the daily fate of many amongst the humbler minstrels at least. And at the end to die like a dog in a ditch, under the ban of the Church and with the prospect of eternal damnation before the soul.[11]

There were more dangerous aspects to the trade and perhaps even worse fates. Minstrelsy was the classic cover for the spy. The intentions behind the Scottish raid into northern England which ended at the battle of Otterburn in August 1388 were discovered and made known to the English by heralds and minstrels sent by the earl of Northumberland to infiltrate the preliminary Scottish conference at Aberdeen. The Scots gained knowledge of the English plan of defence from a captured English spy.

The artistic repertoire of these men has to be pieced together in haphazard fashion from incidental references. The most complete account of the range of a single performer comes from the late sixteenth century when minstrelsy was already taking on an antiquarian hue. In July 1575 Queen Elizabeth I was a guest of Robert earl of Leicester, at his castle of Kenilworth. The entertainment provided was described by a witness, Robert Langham, writing to a friend in London. On Hock Tuesday it included a pageant presented by the men of Coventry based on the massacre of St Bride's Day 1002 and the subsequent war between English and Danes. The director, chief actor and organizing genius was a certain Captain Cox, who aroused Langham's interest. He was 'by profession a mason, and that right skilfull', but he was also 'very cunning in fens and hardy as Gawin'; with another fencing master, he opened the play 'flourishing with his tonsword'. He was also a minstrel story-teller – 'great oversight hath he in matters of storie'. Langham listed thirty-four items 'with many moe then I rehearz here: I beleeve hee have them all at his fingers ends'. They included 'King Arthur's book', *Hugh of Bordeaux*, *Bevis of Hampton*, *Sir Gawain and the Green Knight*, *Sir Eglamoor*, and *The Four Sons of Aymon*; and ballads ranging from *Robin Hood* and *Adam Bell* to *The King and the Tanner*, the *Nut Brown Maid* and the *Wife Wrapped in Wether's Skin*. But this was not all; for Langham described Cox's library:

Then in Philosophy both morall and naturall, I think he be as naturally overseen: beside poetrie and Astronomie, and oother hid sciences, as I may gesse by the omberty [abundance] of his books.

The titles listed were popular items: *The Shepherds Calendar, The Ship of Foules*, a book of riddles and the like. Langham also noted a collection of

ballets and songs all auncient: As *Broom on hill. So woe is me begon, Troly la, Over a whinny Meg. Hey ding a ding. Bony lass upon a green. My bony or gave me a bek. By a bank as I lay*: and a hundred more, he hath fair wrapt up in Parchment and bound with a whipcord.

The collection was completed by 'Allmanaks of antiquitae'. Langham summed up:

I dare say hee hath as fair a library for thees sciences, and as many goodly monuments both in prose and poetry and at afternoons can talk as much without book, as ony Inholder betwixt Brainford and Bagshot, what degree soever he be.

Even this did not tell the full extent of Cox's capacities. He was also 'in the field a good Marshall at musters: of very great credite and trust in the toun heer'. Nay more, he was chosen Aleconner 'many a yaere', and his judgment of a cup of 'Nippitate' (strong ale) was taken 'above the best in the parish, be his nose near so red'.[12]

Captain Cox was near the upper end of the range: he entertained the queen. At the lower end the tales of Robin Hood probably ended in simple tales, proverbs and doggerel – the 'rhymes' of Langland's Sloth.

Minstrels performed not only in the royal court and in aristocratic households, but in the great monasteries, in the market-place, and in the inns where they mingled with other travellers. Occasion was found not only in the entertainments of nobles and gentlemen but also in the festivals of the church, in fairs and markets, in occasional gatherings in the wayside inns as men halted for a night's rest or simply sought shelter from the rain which fell on rich and poor alike. Minstrels who were story-tellers worked with fencers, jugglers and bear-wards and also alongside choristers and the participants in miracle plays. Some, such as Cox, must have played a multiple role. On the road the professional was marked by his dress and his musical instruments, but at an entertainment there was no sharp distinction between the professional and the amateur. At a feast each guest might be required to perform. In the tale of Hereward the Wake, Hereward himself took over the harp, played and sang with his companions; he did better than the professional household minstrel. In like fashion, a tale could take shape in sophisticated or popular versions. Hereward was the subject of a Latin prose-work, half saga, half romance. In addition 'the country folk extolled him and the women and girls used to sing of him in their dances'.[13]

Such diversity is already apparent in the earliest references to Robin Hood. He was known to Langland, a poor clerk in minor orders living in London during much of the composition of *Piers Plowman*. He was almost certainly known to the royal squire, Geoffrey Chaucer, for in *Troilus and Criseyde* of *c.*1382 he wrote:

| | |
|---|---|
| . . . *swich maner folk, I gesse,* | . . . such like folk, I guess, |
| *Defamen love as nothing of him knowe;* | Defame love but nothing of him know; |
| *They speken, but they bente never his bowe.*[14] | They talk, but never bent his bow. |

This is of common stock with a proverb of Robin Hood which appears in several fifteenth-century versions, some of them variants of *Troilus*, which runs:

| | |
|---|---|
| *And many men speken of Robyn Hood,* | And many talk of Robin Hood, |
| *And shotte nevere in his bowe.*[15] | And never shot his bow. |

By the beginning of the fifteenth century Robin was certainly known in ecclesiastical circles, for this jingle appears in a vernacular sermon composed *c.*1410 by Hugh Legat, monk of St Albans. At about the same time a fragment of verse, otherwise unknown, was scribbled in a Lincoln cathedral manuscript:

*Robyn hod in scherewod stod, hodud and hathud and hosut and schod*
*Four and thuynti arowus he bar in hits hondus.*[16]

Robin Hood in Sherwood stood, hooded and hatted and hosed and shod
Four and twenty arrows he bore in his hands.

And in *Dives and Pauper*, a homily which is possibly the work of a
Franciscan friar, the author complained of those who would rather
'heryn a tale or a song of robyn hode or of sum rubaudry than to heryn
messe or matynes'.

Only a little later did Robin begin to appear in administrative
records. In 1429 a judge in the Court of Common Pleas quoted the
phrase 'Robin Hode in Barnesdale stode'; the sheriff's clerk in Wiltshire
knew of Robin and his men along with Adam Bell and his companions
in 1432; in 1439 a petition presented by a Derbyshire jury to parliament
likened the criminal Piers Venables to 'Robyn Hode and his meyne'.
By this time the Scottish chroniclers Wyntoun, writing from 1408 to
1420, and Bower, writing in the 1440s, also knew of him. Wyntoun
was a canon of St Andrew's, and prior of St Serf's Inch in Loch Leven;
Bower was probably abbot of Incholm. Thereafter references to Robin
come thick and fast. In 1473 Sir John Paston, in a famous letter to his
brother, complained that a servant called Kothye Plattyng was on the
point of deserting him:

I have kepyd hym thys iij [three] yere to pleye Seynt Jorge and Robynhod and
the shryff off Notyngham, and now when I wolde have good horse he is goon
into Bernysdale, and I wythowt a kepere [am without a keeper].[17]

But if Sir John knew of Robin so also did the ploughmen of *How the
Plowman Learned His Pater Noster*, who:

| | |
|---|---|
| *Eche had two busshelles of whete that was gode.* | Each had two bushels of wheat that was good. |
| *They songe goynge home warde a gest of Robyn Hode.*[18] | They sang going homewards a gest of Robin Hood. |

In social order and status the audience had become almost universal:
poets, monks, friars, chroniclers, judges, juries, administrators, gentlemen and ploughmen: they all knew something of the tale or were
thought to do so by their contemporaries.

The early stories reflect this diversity, most obviously the tales of
personal combat and of prowess with the bow. The archery must have
aroused many different responses in widely varied circumstances. The
supremacy of the English longbow on the battlefields of France has
long been linked with the establishment of a class of yeomen in the
English countryside, and certainly the recruitment of archers would
have been impossible without an abundant social source. But the

association of the bow with the country yeoman is very loose and inexact. As has already been shown, the longbow was already a familiar weapon at the beginning of the thirteenth century,[19] two hundred years before men began to apply the word 'yeoman' to a rural class. Moreover, the archers of Crécy, Poitiers and Agincourt were paid troops, and many of them were not English but Welsh. Off the battlefield the bow was used by all classes. *The Master of Game* (c. 1410), of Edward duke of York, who was killed at Agincourt in 1415, describes the procedure followed when the king hunted with the bow. *The Art of Hunting* of William Twici, huntsman to Edward II, mentions similar methods of hunting. The twelfth-century *Constitutio Domus Regis* refers to the archers who carried the king's bow. In the twelfth century one great noble, Richard fitz Gilbert of Clare, who died in 1176, was nicknamed 'Strongbow'; his lands lay in Gwent, whence came the archers noted by Gerald of Wales. The bow was affected by ladies; illustrations of their prowess as archers are common enough in manuscript illumination of the fourteenth and fifteenth centuries. If anything, the bow became more fashionable as time passed. Henry VIII prided himself on his skill. In his treatise on education, *The Governour* of 1531, Sir Thomas Elyot recommended archery as a gentlemanly exercise. At Middleton, Lancashire, in a window in the church of St Leonard which commemorated the English victory at Flodden of 1513, an artist saw nothing incongruous in representing Sir Richard Assheton and his company, Sir Richard with a quiver on his back and the rest, some of whom bore the names of armigerous families, each with quiver and bow. So Robin Hood did not blunder when, on releasing Sir Richard at the Lee, he at once placed a bow in his hand, nor was it inappropriate that Robin and the king engaged in a shooting match as they rode from Sherwood into Nottingham.

Expert archery would therefore be appreciated within a very wide social range. But within this there was also a narrower frame of reference. The *Black Book* required that the king's yeomen should be 'strongest archers, chosen men of . . . shooting', selected from lords' households throughout the realm. *The Master of Game* described the duties of one of these, the yeoman of the king's bow. In the twelfth-century *Constitutio Domus Regis*, the forerunners of these men, the archers who carried the king's bow, received 5d. a day – a rate of pay equalled among the hunting staff by the huntsman and exceeded only by the knight-huntsman. Good shooting meant good prospects. Good archers might expect established and respectable household employment. This is what Little John's skill achieved with the sheriff and Robin Hood's reputation with the king. William of Cloudesley and his friends attained the same goal.

Ⲟⲣⲁⲧⲉ ⲡⲣⲟ ⲃⲟⲛⲟ ⲥⲧⲁⲧⲩ Ⲣⲓⲥⲝⲁⲣⲇⲓ Ⲁⲗⲗⲝⲉⲧⲟⲛ ⲉⲧ ⲉⲟⲣⲩⲙ ⲗⲁⲛⲥ ⲉⲛⲉⲩⲧⲣⲁ ⲉⲓⲉⲣⲓ ⲉⲉ-

Window commemorating Flodden Field, 1513, St Leonard's, Middleton, Lancashire.

However, the household is not the only specific background. The two archery contests in the *Gest* and the contest in *The Potter* are all held at Nottingham. On the second occasion in the *Gest*, in which Robin takes part, and again in *The Potter*, the contest is specifically located in the butts. The shooting is described in graphic detail. In *The Potter* in particular there is much play with Robin's selection of the bow offered to him which he regards as 'right weak gear'. In all three instances Robin and Little John slit the wand or 'prick' which was the centre of the target. Similar details recur in the friendly match which the outlaws hold in the presence of the king in Sherwood and in the contest between Robin and Guy of Gisborne. All this would no doubt be familiar to household archers. In *The Potter*, indeed, the match is introduced as a wager in the gossip of the sheriff's men, and they and Robin, in the guise of the potter, are the only contestants. But it must also have been familiar to all those who had shot or watched shooting in the butts. The bow was a national weapon. In the Assize of Arms of 1242 the possession of sword, bow, arrows and knife was enjoined on all free men who held land worth £2 to £5 a year or chattels valued between £6 and £13 6s. 8d. In 1363 Edward III instructed that archery practice was

cerunt quorũ nõina et imagines ut fupra oftenduntur anno dñi mcccccv

to be compulsory on feast days and Sundays, and in 1465 Edward IV
required that butts would be maintained in every township for regular
practice on festivals. These are but three examples of numerous
administrative measures which were continued into the sixteenth
century in vain attempts to preserve archery from the advance of
firearms on the one hand and on the other from the attraction of sports
which were condemned as riotous and degenerate, such as dicing,
quoits, football and tennis. Archery was a generalized skill, shared by
king and countryman. Henry VIII showed off his abilities before the
crowned heads and nobility of Europe at the Field of the Cloth of Gold
in 1520. Seventeen years later an archery contest at Binham (Norfolk)
was used as a convenient cover for plotting an abortive rural rebellion.

Robin's second skill was with the sword. This is the weapon which
he and his men use in personal combat throughout the early tales. It is
more than a weapon; it is a symbol of honour, for it is on Robin's
'bright bronde' that the sheriff swears his oath never to bring harm to
the outlaws. The weapon was a knightly one, but not exclusively so,
and it is not the knightly combat of the lists which the tales describe, but
the art of fencing. Fencing was an entertainment. The minstrels who

attended the great feast of 1306 included 'skirmishers', and it is as an entertainment and in the schools which entertainers and professional champions established that swordsmanship was cherished. In the Robin Hood tales there are three displays of swordsmanship. In the *Gest* (167):

| | |
|---|---|
| *Lytell Johan drew a ful gode sworde,* | Little John drew a full good sword, |
| *The coke toke another in hande;* | The cook took another in hand; |
| *They thought no thynge for to fle,* | They thought not to flee, |
| *But stifly for to stande.* | But stoutly to stand. |

They fight for an hour, at the end of which John pronounces the cook 'one of the best sworde-men that ever yit sawe we'. In *The Potter* Robin takes on the potter with sword and buckler, the latter essentially duellist's equipment. In *Guy of Gisborne* Robin and Guy display the duellist's art to the full in a fight lasting two hours. Guy is 'quicke and nimble with all' and wounds Robin in the left side, but Robin recovers with 'Our Lady's' help (40):

| | |
|---|---|
| *And thus he came with an awkwarde stroke* | And thus he came with an awkward stroke |
| *Good Sir Guy hee has slayne.* | Good Sir Guy he has slain. |

These scenes evoked skills which were best appreciated by those who had watched fencers at work, and fencers, like other entertainers, went where there was sustenance and money. By the end of the thirteenth century they were no longer in demand as professional champions in legal actions, for the judicial duel was by then restricted to appeals for treason. They established schools in London where they were tolerated, despite regulations restraining them. They also found an audience in the great occasions of the royal court. They travelled the roads of England wheresoever their skill might gain reward. The surnames Champion and Scrimshaw (skirmisher) bear witness to a profession or attainment already widespread by 1300. It is their art which the Robin Hood tales evoke. It was an art on display in the market-place as well as in the baronial hall. Captain Cox was 'very cunning in fens'. In London in the middle of the fifteenth century Philip Treher, fishmonger, received payment from the crown for training combatants in appeals of treason. It ran in the family: in 1281 two young men called Treher were bailed by the fishmongers after being charged before the mayor for swaggering in the city with sword and buckler after nightfall.

Hence certain elements in the story had a wide-ranging appeal. But social diffusion does not seem to have dissolved the essential qualities of the legend. Before the end of the fifteenth century men could watch a play of Robin Hood in the market-place or at a fair, or see him participate in the May Games in widely scattered parts of England, but

Robin did not originate in a municipal context. He never fully emulated William of Cloudesley, who escaped from Carlisle over a trail of dead and wounded including the mayor and all the bailiffs, but there can be no doubt that he was an enemy of the people of Nottingham. He goes there secretly and in disguise; they flee 'both yemen and knaves and olde wyves that myght evyll goo' at the approach of Robin and the king all clad in Lincoln green. Likewise, tales of Robin may have been told in monasteries or collegiate churches, for ecclesiastical denunciations of the story were not based on ignorance; but the tale cannot have originated in such a context, for the *Gest* and *Robin Hood and the Monk* are unremitting in their scorn for the monastic order. Finally, ploughmen may have sung of Robin, but their rustic background makes no impression on the earliest surviving versions of the legend. It is difficult to imagine that they would readily accept 'churlish' as a term of abuse synonymous with 'boorish', and it is the term 'churl' that Little John uses to upbraid the monk. That the ploughmen of *How the Plowman Learned His Pater Noster* sang a gest is in any case incongruous. What a ploughman really might have sung of Robin will never be known.

At many social levels the tale provoked an overwhelmingly critical and hostile reaction. In *Piers Plowman* it is Sloth, the personification of one of the seven deadly sins, who knows his rhymes of Robin Hood. The clergy who were the first to mention the tales regarded them as ribaldry, as fables, 'jests' and 'trifles' which distracted good men from their devotions, and appealed to the stupid populace, the *stolidum vulgus*, to use Bower's phrase. This almost universal hostility was not simply an expression of clerical stuffiness. Caxton found no room for the tales in his *Book of Curtesye*: instead he recommended a literary diet of Gower, Chaucer, Occleve and Lydgate. To laymen, too, Robin was a symbol of unrest. The tenants of Tutbury who, in their petition to parliament of 1439, likened Piers Venables and his gang to Robin Hood and his *meinie*, were in no doubt that the outlaw hero was a criminal. Occasionally, amidst this almost universal disapprobation, other voices were heard. The clerk of the sheriff of Wiltshire included in his acrostic of 1432 'Good man was hee', and in time Robin became so diversified a personality that he provoked varied responses. But the tone of disapproval still sounded in the sixteenth and seventeenth centuries. Puritan divines were as hostile as Catholic monks, and Elizabethan statesmen, like fifteenth-century juries, still used Robin as an exemplar of criminal disorder.

This tone of sharp disapproval is not to be dismissed as a reaction by the establishment to a sub-culture of which it knew little and comprehended less. Nor did it simply express hostility in members of a ruling class to a manifestation of social discontent by the lower orders. That such interpretations, dependent as they are on modern jargon, will not work is demonstrated by one single example, the action initiated against Roger Marshall of Wednesbury, alias Robin Hood, in the Court of the Star Chamber in the summer of 1498. In this, those who complained of the conduct of a 'Robin Hood' were of the same class and background as those against whom they laid complaints. The burden of these complaints was not that those charged wanted to change the established social order, but that they had made riotous assembly and threatened personal violence; and the quarrel originated in a dispute over local jurisdiction:

To the King our Sovereign Lord

Humbly sheweth unto your highness, your faithful subject and true liegeman Roger Dyngley, Mayor of Walsall, and Thomas Rice, of the same town, with all the inhabitants and tenants of your said town of Walsall, that whereas your said orators [petitioners] on Wednesday next before Trinity Sunday, the 13th year of your reign, were in God's peace and yours, in your said town of Walsall, thither came one John Cradeley, of Wednesbury, and Thomas Morres, of Dudley, in your said county, and then and there made affray upon the said Thomas Rice, 'and hym soore wounded and bett', so that he was in peril of his life. Whereupon the said Mayor with other inhabitants did arrest the said John Cradeley and Thomas Morres, and there put them in prison, according to your laws, there to remain till it were known wether the said Thomas Rice should live or die. And incontinent [immediately] thereupon one John Beamonde, Squyer, Walter Leveson, of Wolverhampton, Richard Foxe, priest, of the same town, and one Roger Marshall, of Wednesbury, 'arreysed' [raised] and riotously assembled themselves at Wednesbury with other riotous persons to the number of 200 men, arrayed in manner of war, that is to say, with bows, arrows, bills, and glaives, with other unlawful weapons there gathered and assembled, to the intent to have come to have destroyed your said town of Walsall, saying openly that they would fetch out of prison the said John Cradeley and Thomas Morres, and destroy your said town of Walsall. And thereupon William Harper and William Wilkes, Justices of the Peace, charged the said riotous persons to keep the peace upon a great pain to be forfeited to your grace. By reason whereof the said rioters for that time ceased from further riot. And whereas the said Justices of Peace, knowing that the said rioters intended to make more riot, and to execute their malice in doing some mischief or hurt to the said town or to the inhabitants thereof, for eschewing any riot or breach of the peace, commanded the inhabitants of Walsall, Wednesbury, and of divers other towns, their adherents, that they should not assemble together out of their said town, and should not come to a fair that should be holden at Willenhall on Trinity Sunday then next following. And the inhabitants of Walsall the same day kept themselves at home. Notwithstanding, came one from Wolverhampton, whose name is William Milner, calling himself the abbot of Marram, and one Walter Leveson with him, with the inhabitants of Wolverhampton to the number of four score persons in harness, after the manner of war, to Willenhall to the said fair. And also one Robert Marshall of Wednesbury, calling himself Robyn Hood, and Sir Richard Foxe, priest, with divers other persons to the number of 100 men and above, in harness, came in likewise, and met with the said other rioters at the said town of Willenhall, and then and there riotously assembled themselves, commanding openly that if any of the town of Walsall came therefrom, to strike them down, and in the said town continued their said riotous assembly all the same day, and if any man of Walsall at that day had been seen at that fair, they should have been in jeopardy of their lives.

This complaint leaves no doubt as to what sort of behaviour the mayor and folk of Walsall expected from a Robin Hood. But that is only one side of the story. Roger Marshall's answer tells another:

The bill is only feigned against him of pure malice for his great trouble and vexation, and loss of his goods. He did not riotously assemble with any persons in arms, nor is he guilty of any riot. As for the coming to the said fair of Willenhall 'hit hath byn of olde tymes used and accustumed on the said fere day that wyth the inhabitantes of the sede townes of Wolverhampton, Wednesbury and Walsall have comyne to the said fere with the capitanns called the Abot of Marham or Robyn Hodys to the intent to gether money with ther disportes to the profight of the chirches of the seid lorshipes,' whereby great profit hath grown to the said churches in times past. Whereupon the said Roger Marshall with his company at the special desire of the inhabitants of Wednesbury, came in peaceable manner to the said fair, according to the said old custom, and there met with one John Walker, of Walsall, and divers others of the said town, and then and there 'they made as gud chere unto them as they shuld do to ther lovying neyburs', and he denies that they came riotously.[20]

Precise details of what happened at the fair of Willenhall on Trinity Sunday 1498 must remain in doubt. But it seems probable that Roger Marshall brought a party, dressed up as Robin Hood and his men, contrary to the prohibition of the justices of the peace. What to Roger was a charitable exercise and traditional good fun seemed to others like a riotous assembly. The simple heroism of the outlaw hero which inspired the one could look like banditry to others.

This case is complicated by its association with the May Games. Robin is mentioned alongside the abbot of Marham, one of the traditional Lords of Misrule in the west Midlands. And it seems plain that the local justices, after quelling the first riot occasioned by the arrest of the Wednesbury man in Walsall, feared that the summer games at Willenhall might be used as cover for another. However, it would be a mistake to think that Robin was associated with riot simply because he appeared in the May celebrations alongside a Lord of Misrule. The earliest known disapprobation expressed by laymen was free of any such association. The complaint which the tenants of Tutbury made to parliament in 1439 placed Robin firmly in the context of straightforward banditry, unadorned by any play-acting or possible charitable purpose:

To the right nobles, wise and discrete communes of this present parlement; besechen mekly William atte Loue, and other tenaunts of oure lorde the kynge, as of his castell and honure of Tutbury, parcell of his duchie of Lancastre, dwellinge atte Scropton in the countee of Derby. That where as one John Forman, of the towne of Snellestone in the seide countee of Derby, for diverse grete and notable causes and offenses done by the same John, withinne the fraunchise and jurisdiction of the saide castell and honoure, was lawefully arrested atte Barton Bakepuz withinne the same fraunchise, by Sir Thomas Blount Knyght, depute unto the worshipfulle lorde the erle of Stafford, steward of the saide castell and honure, and othere officers there, and there uppon committed unto the saide William Supliaunt, and othere tenaunts forseide, saufly to kepe and bringge hym unto the saide castell of Tuttebury; and as they were goynge to bringe hym there, on Sonday after Cristemasse day laste passed, atte Sudbury withinne the saide fraunchise, cometh one Piers Venables of the towne of Aston gentilman withinne the saide countee of Derby, with many othere unknowen, in manere of werre, riote, route and insurrection arraied with force and armes, and made a rescours [rescue], and toke awey the saide John Forman fro theyme, and in the saide William and othere tenaunts made an assaute, and thaym bedde, wounded and evil tretid there. And after that tyme, the same Piers Venables, havynge no liflode ne sufficeante of goodes, gadered and assembled unto him many misdoers beynge of his clothinge; that is to wete, Thomas Sayne of Aston in the saide countee of Derby yoman, Herry Hele of Dowbrigge (Doveridge) in the saide countee yoman, Robard Bochere of the said towne yoman, Nicholas Normanton of the saide towne yoman, Thomas Tailour of the saide towne yoman, Thomas Hobbessone of the saide towne yoman, John Flecchere of the saide towne yoman, John Savage of the saide towne yoman, Nicholas Smyth of West Broughton in the saide counte yoman, John Smyth of the said towne yoman. Thomas Smyth of the saide towne yoman, Thomas Warde of Sudbury in the saide counte yoman, Robert Forman of Eveston Aroungomery (Marston Montgomery) in the saide counte yoman, Rogere Laude of the saide towne yoman, Thomas Bene of Snellestone in the saide counte yoman, with many other unknowyn; and, in manere of insurrection, wente into the wodes in that contre, like as it hadde be Robyn hode and his meyne [meinie, retinue]; and so after that tyme they come diverse tymes withinne the fraunchise atte Scropton forsaide, called Scropton home, and othere places withinne the saide fraunchise, and the saide William and alle othere tenaunts there duellinge, fought and manassinge to fcle [slay], so that the saide tenaunts dare nat abide in thaire tenures and places, ne no laboure there do, neither bailifs, clerkes, ne other officers there, dare nat come there to holde the courtes, withoute grete power and strengthe, and so they kepyn the wodes and strange contrays: and atte fome tyme they gone in to Chestreschire, that they can nat be take to be justefied by the lawe, but ryde and gone as outelawes, waitynge a tyme to murdre, sclee, and other grete harmes in that contray to do, but yf it be remedied, in contempt of oure lorde the kyng, and ayene alle his lawes and statutes in this partie made.[21]

No defence is recorded. What Piers Venables might have said could well alter the rights and wrongs of the case. But it could not change the fact that the petitioners thought that the behaviour of men who were 'in manere of werre, riote, route and insurrection arraied' and who 'in manere of insurrection wente into the wodes in that contre' was 'like as it hadde be Robyn hode and his meyne'. And in this case and that of Roger Marshall sixty years later there was a common element: action began with armed intervention to rescue a prisoner arrested by lawful authority. What was more likely to provoke thoughts of Robin?

In this the analogy with Robin is quite precise. Piers Venables and his supporters had taken to the woods and resorted to all that that implied in lawless conduct. The petitioners may also have been conscious of social parallels. Piers had 'no liflode ne sufficeate of goodes', but he was 'of the towne of Aston gentilman'. Every man jack of his company is identified as a yeoman. In this there can have been no mistake. The petitioners came from Scropton, little more than a mile to the west of Tutbury on the north side of the Dove. Aston, the home of the chief offender, is less than two miles further west. Sudbury, where Forman was freed, lies half a mile beyond that. Venables' gang of yeomen all came from villages in the immediate neighbourhood. The appellants must have known all those whom they accused. They were neighbours. And what inspired them to think of Robin Hood was not yeomen fearlessly asserting the sturdy independence of their class, still less peasants rebelling against the burdens of the manorial regime, but a band of marauders who had released a prisoner lawfully arrested, who imposed themselves on the local community of Scropton and made it their home, and there and elsewhere 'fought and manassinge to fcle [slay], so that the saide tenaunts dare nat abide in thaire tenures and places, ne no laboure there do, neither bailiffs, clerkes, ne other officers there, dare nat come there to holde the courtes, withoute grete power and strengthe'.

Such impressions survived long. Nearly a hundred and seventy years later the tenants of Tutbury had as their successor no less than Robert Cecil, earl of Salisbury, principal secretary to Elizabeth I and James I. They saw Robin in their brigandly neighbours, he in the tawdry gentry who enmeshed themselves in the Gunpowder Plot. On 9 November 1605, four days after the discovery of the plot, he wrote to Sir Charles Cornwallis, English ambassador in Spain:

I do now send you some proclamations, and withall think good to advertize you that those persons named in them, being most of them gentlemen spent in their fortunes, all inward with Percey and fit for all alteration, have gatheered themselves to a head of some fourscore on a hundred Horse, with purpose (as we conceave) to pass over seas. . . . It is also thought fit that some martial men should presently repair down to those countries where the Robin Hoods are assembled to encourage the good and to terrifie the bad. In which service the Earl of Devonshire is used, and commission going forth for him as generall; although I am easily perswaded, that this faggot will be burnt to ashes before hee shall be twenty miles on his way.[22]

Men thought of Robin Hood within a frame of reference made up of riot, resistance to lawful officials, release of lawfully arrested wrong-doers, and the browbeating of the local community by force and the threat of force, all of which was perpetuated by armed gangs too powerful for authority to control. He was an example of the 'lack of governance' which was the perennial complaint in later medieval England. Some such gangs had recognizable political and social objectives: they arose from factional division or injured interest. Some were merely criminal, but found political cover convenient. All were violent and murderous. The operations of some are now well known. The Folville brothers whose activities opened with the murder of Roger Bellars, baron of the Exchequer, in 1326, and the kidnapping and ransoming of Sir Richard Willoughby, justice of the king's bench in 1332, were members of a knightly family in Leicestershire. Some of them continued in a criminal career for nearly fifteen years. They were associated with the Coterel brothers who operated in the same period in Nottinghamshire and Derbyshire. The Coterel gang murdered Sir William Knyveton and John Matkynson at Bradley (Derbyshire) in 1330. In the words of a Bakewell jury which indicted them, they 'rode armed, publicly and secretly, in manner of war, by day and night'. Their chief tactic was to demand money with menaces. In 1332 they joined the Folvilles in the kidnapping of Justice Willoughby and took a small share of the profits. Some ten years later John Lord Fitzwalter directed a ruffianly band which took the law into its own hands in the county of Essex and levied blackmail on the citizens of Colchester. At about the same time Sir John Molyns was terrorizing Buckingham-shire, taking to kidnapping and organizing murder in revenge for his dismissal from royal service. Between 1387 and 1392 William Beckwith organized a band based on Knaresborough Forest in Yorkshire which continued still active in the area two years after Beckwith was killed in 1392.

Such criminal bands were not a new phenomenon in the fourteenth century. In the winter of 1231–2 there were risings and demonstrations against foreign clergy who enjoyed benefices in England by papal provision. Papal messengers were attacked, one was killed. Some Roman clergy went into hiding; others were captured and ransomed. Armed bands attacked and pillaged the foreigners' estates and disposed of the corn. The leader who took the name William Wither was a knight, Robert of Thwing, who claimed that he had been deprived of the advowson of one of his livings unjustly as a result of papal letters of provision. These were violent men with a cause. The men who robbed Brabantine merchants in the 'pass of Alton', Hampshire, in 1248 seem to have been less principled. They were simply a gang organized by two local men of knightly family, John de Bendinges and John Barkham, who pulled off an adventurous robbery with a haul of 200 marks.

The historical research of the last twenty years or so, which has pieced together much of the activity of these bands, has concentrated on the upper crust of criminals. They made a splash; they were dealt with in the royal courts; they might provoke action by the king. All this has brought them to the historian's attention. Lower down the social scale and in the local courts the picture is perhaps less complete but is otherwise identical. In 1329–30 the court of the manor of Wakefield received the following report:

It is found by inquisition of the twelve jurors appointed by the Steward that Thomas Drabyl used strangers to lie in wait for Edmund Barndside, Thomas son of Simon, Richard son of Simon and Thomas of Billeclif, so that the aforsaid Edmund, Thomas, Richard and Thomas, tenants of the lord, dared not leave the lord's liberty. He is therefore in mercy for contempt of the lord. Likewise it is found by the same jurors that the same Thomas broke the peace twice against John son of Thomas son of Simon and the same John broke the peace the same number of times against the aforesaid Thomas. Therefore it is ordered that the same Thomas and John are to be attached to answer the lord for the same trespass. Likewise it is found by the jurors that with the participation of various strangers the same Thomas Drabyl, by extorsion and threats compelled and ransomed Adam son of John of Hepworth for half a mark, for which sum the same Thomas received 2s. 4d., from the aforsaid Adam. Therefore it is adjudged that the said Thomas be attached to answer the lord for the same trespass. Afterwards at the suit of Edmund Barndside, Thomas son of Simon, Richard son of Simon and Thomas of Billecliff, it is found by inquisition of the twelve jurors, on which the same Edmund, Thomas, Richard and Thomas Drabyl put themselves, that by the threats of the gang of the same Thomas the aforesaid Thomas, Edmund, Richard and Thomas lost their own merchandise. Damages half a mark. Therefore it is adjudged that the aforesaid Edmund, Thomas, Richard and Thomas should recover half a mark from the aforesaid Thomas Drabil and that the same Thomas is in mercy for the offence.[23]

At this lower social level, too, criminals had their aiders and abettors, willing and unwilling, among the local population. The Wakefield court roll of 1318 runs:

Richard of Windhill, taken as a suspected thief, because he came with a message from several thieves to the wife of the late William of Stodlay seeking victuals for the said thieves, and because he threatened the woman to burn her unless she sent food and money by him for this, and shot at the said foresters with arrows; being asked what he says denies the charges and places himself on the court. An inquisition is taken on oaths of . . . by whom he is found not guilty of frequenting the company of thieves etc.[24]

Such criminals were unaffected by the plight of their victims. Among the known criminal bands only William Wither and his gang were reputed charitable. They sold the grain they seized at low prices 'for the benefit of the many' and even gave it away to the poor. At the lowest social level, among the poor and unprotected, guilt and innocence are beyond true assessment. The history of the hermit Robert of Knaresborough, who died in 1218, sums it up. His hermitage at Rudfarlington was ransacked and rendered uninhabitable by bandits. It was rebuilt for him but was then destroyed by William de Stuteville, lord of Knaresborough, for Robert's harbouring of thieves and outlaws. The vulnerable could not win.

At all these different social levels there was much in real-life crime which tallied with the tale of Robin Hood. The weapons, naturally enough, are the sword, the bow and arrow. The tactic of a robbery or kidnapping was almost always the ambush. The occasion for a riotous assembly and assault is not infrequently the delivery of a prisoner. The criminals were almost as invulnerable as Robin. The outlawry pronounced against them was often no more than a formal step in a lax procedure. Like Robin, most of them, including the murderers, were pardoned. In 1340-1 Richard de Folville, one of the brothers who was a priest, was chased into the tower of his church at Teigh, Rutland. He shot and killed one of his pursuers with an arrow and wounded others. He was then dragged outside and summarily beheaded. But Eustace de Folville, the leader of the gang, against whom there were five charges of murder, was pardoned in 1333 on condition that he made himself available for royal service when required; he ended his days in peaceful enjoyment of his estates. Of the Coterels, James, John and Nicholas never apparently paid for their crimes. Nicholas later became Queen Philippa's bailiff of the High Peak and, like Falstaff, stole his soldiers' wages. Some of the lesser fry involved in the Alton robbery of 1248 were hanged but the leaders were pardoned. Lord fitz Walter had to pay a heavy penalty for his activities, but he remained at large. Sir John Molyns was pardoned.

The ineffectiveness of the procedures for arrest, the failure of prosecution at trial and the frequency of pardon all reflected the local support and powerful patronage which criminals enjoyed. The Folvilles were members of the household of Sir Robert Tuchet of Markeston and wore his livery. The Coterels gained support from Sir Robert Ingram and backing and employment from the dean and chapter of Lichfield. The Alston robbers were pardoned through the intercession of members of the royal family and the king of Scotland. And around the higher placed friends were more lowly hangers-on, hired men and assistants who carried news and messages, or brought food, horses and weapons, or provided hiding when the gang was hard-pressed. Each band, in short, was surrounded by its profiteers, its receivers, its patrons who could benefit now and then from an ability to call up illicit force, and its meaner handy men looking simply for pay.

This makes it easier to understand how a legendary criminal hero could be idolized. The criminal public with an interest in the matter was considerable, in numbers, social status and influence. Its bounds were widened and its moral stature increased by the difficulty of defining crime, especially by the haziness of the borderline between crime and politics, and by the violence of political life. William Wither took to the road against the papal intrusion of Italian clerks into English benefices. It was said at the time that the Folvilles' original crime, the murder of Roger Belers, was in revenge for the injuries he had done them. Their later kidnapping of Justice Willoughby was a criminal act, but they chose their victim well for he was later charged 'by clamour of the people' with 'selling the laws like cows', and he had to fine with the king for £1,000. William Beckwith began his criminal career in Knaresborough forest after he had been refused a forestership; he directed his activities specifically against the forest officials. Crime, local rivalries, the control of local government, the bringing to bear of the authority of the crown, all intermingled. This made it easier to imagine that the criminal had some right on his side. He gained social approval. The Folvilles provided the exemplar. Rough and ready justice, the violent redress of wrong, came to be known as Folville's Law, and when in *Piers Plowman* Langland recounted the qualities with which Grace endowed men to repel the attacks of Antichrist, he included:

| | |
|---|---|
| *And some to ryde and to recovere that unrightfully was wonne:* *He wissed hem wynne it agein thorugh wightnesse of handes* *And fecchen it from false men with Folvyles lawes.*[25] | And some to ride and recover what was wrongfully taken He showed them how to regain it through the might of their hands And wrest it from false men by Folville's laws. |

That was both an apotheosis and justification of violent crime.

This was not the only possible conclusion. To the crown the yeoman archer, of whom Robin was the paragon, could seem a menace to law and order. The Statute of Livery and Maintenance of 1390 gave them a specific mention:

No such noble shall give such a livery to any *valet* called a yeoman archer nor to any other person of lower estate than esquire unless he is a family servant living in the household.[26]

Local communities were equally wary of foresters. After the execution of Thomas earl of Lancaster in 1322, the men of the neighbourhood of Pickering brought the following petition to the attention of Edward II:

After the decease of Earl Edmund he was succeeded by Thomas, late Earl of Lancaster, in whose time many strange things were done by the bailiffs, foresters and verderers in prejudice of the rights of the Crown, such as purprestures and enclosures contrary to the assizes of the forest, to the great destruction of the game, and to the injury of the King and those of his subjects who are commoners there. Moreover, the bailiffs, foresters and verderers have committed offences whenever they could against the King, often rebelling against him and making others who are the King's tenants rebel, to wit, first when they besieged Scarborough castle with three hundred men clad in green jackets, who were arrayed and led by John Dalton, then bailiff of Pickering, and kept up the siege until the then Earl of Cornwall,[27] who was there by the King's order, surrendered himself into the hands of the great men who were there. Afterwards, by their violence and imprisonment, they made the King's liege subjects go, at their own cost, with the Earl of Lancaster's men into the West Country to take Sir Adam de Banastre[28] and his force and put them to death. Afterwards they have many times been arrayed by the bailiffs, foresters and verderers to go with force of arms against their liege Lord at York at the time of several parliaments, at Pontefract when the King was opposed on his own land, at Newcastle-on-Tyne when the Earl of Lancaster rode against the King and at the siege of the castle of Tickhill, but against the enemies from Scotland they would not array or allow to be arrayed, one man.

Moreover, those that claim to be foresters have felled oaks without number in the time of the Earl of Lancaster, made arrays and indicted and ruined the people of the country by their power, so that the latter are beggared while the former are rich in lands, tenements and fine manors, though, when they came into the country, they had nothing but their bows and arrows and the clothes they walked in.[29]

The circumstances to which men could relate the tales of Robin Hood varied widely. The imagery which crime and violence evoked was just as diverse. In the fourteenth century rogues and thieves were sometimes colloquially described as 'Robert's men'. In 1331 the phrase was included in an Act of parliament which referred to the 'robberies, homicides and felonies done in these times by people called Roberdesmen, Wastours and *Drahlacche* [Drawlatch]'. It was repeated when this statute was confirmed in 1385. Robert's knaves appear as robbers in *Piers Plowman* and so too does Robert the Robber himself who has 'leyen by *Latro*, luciferis Aunte'.[30] He reappears in a famous letter which the priest John Ball addressed to the peasant rebels of 1381:

Iohon Schep . . . greteth wel Iohan Nameless, and Iohan the Mullere, and Iohon Cartere, and biddeth hem that thei bee war of gyle [they should beware of guile] in borugh, and stondeth togidre [together] in Godes name, and biddeth Peres Plouyman go to his werk, and chastise wel Hobbe the Robbere, and taketh with yow Iohan Trewman and alle hiis felawes.[31]

In a companion letter of Jakke Carter the instruction is:

Lokke that Hobbe robbyoure be wele chastysed for lesyng [losing] of youre grace, for ye have gret nede to take God with you in all your dedes.[32]

Hobbe the Robber has been identified as the treasurer, Robert Hales, whom the peasants executed on Tower Hill, but there is no compelling reason for accepting this. If a real person was intended it could equally well have been Sir Robert Belknap, chief justice of the king's bench, who was carrying out a commission of trailbaston in Essex when the peasants caught him. It may simply be that Hobbe the Robber was simply another folk version of Robert the Robber as the archetypal criminal. Whatever lay behind this mysterious allusion there can be no doubt that both Hobbe the Robber and Robert the Robber were objects of censure. It remained for Sir Edward Coke, chief justice of the king's bench of James I, to conclude that Robert the Robber and Robin Hood were one and the same. That was a false identification imposed by the anachronistic logic of a lawyer on the heterogeneous responses of medieval people to the crime in their midst. Langland provides a better guide. At one and the same time he could approve of Folville's Law and call Robert the Robber to repentance. He was also the first poet to mention Robin Hood.

The evidence leaves two final related impressions which are not easy to delineate. First, it seems that the tales were aimed at *les jeunes*, young men without responsibility. This may explain why the outlaws lack both wives and property. Quite apart from that, yeomen in service were largely drawn from younger sons, from those seeking to make their way. So also were criminal gangs like the Folvilles; Eustace, the leader, had an elder brother, John, who remained in possession of the family patrimony and had little if any connection with his notorious brothers. Secondly, Langland must have picked up much of what he knew of Robin Hood, Robert the Robber and Folville's Law in the taverns of London. That is of a piece with *Pierce the Plowman's Crede*, of the late fourteenth century, in which the 'Robertes Men':

| | |
|---|---|
| . . . *raken aboute* | . . . roam about |
| *At feires and at ful ales and fyllen the cuppe.*[33] | At fairs and full-ales and fill the cup. |

It was at the fair of Willenhall that Roger Marshall appeared as Robin and so provoked the good men of Walsall to take their case to the Star Chamber. It was as Ale-conner of Coventry that Captain Cox topped off his many literary and practical accomplishments. The audience of Robin Hood must have included criminals. It is probable that it also included many more who talked of crime, hangers-on, young men who followed the real outlaws with admiring eyes, habitués of the local tavern who, in their cups or in their dreams, always killed the sheriff stone dead, but never dared to let an arrow fly in anger.

So men imagined and played out roles, often perhaps as a substitute for crime. Roger Marshall mentioned Robin in the same breath as the Abbot of Marham, the lord of misrule who turned the world upside down at Christmas tide. And play-acting is also suggested by an earlier incident from 1357. In that year, following his victory at Poitiers, the Black Prince brought King John of France and other captives home to England. Crowds gathered to meet them as they rode towards London and:

> one day, as they neared a forest, up to 500 men lay in ambush clad in tunics and cloaks of green, and as the King of France passed by they sprang out on him as if they were a band of robbers and evil-doers, with bows and arrows, swords and bucklers. The King was astonished and asked what manner of men they were; and the Prince replied that they were Englishmen, living rough in the forest by choice, and that it was their habit to array themselves so every day.

It would seem that already men liked to dress up as Robin Hood and his merry men. In 1357 such role-play passed easily into real crime and violence. The incident was recorded up to forty years later in, of all places, the Anonimalle Chronicle of St Mary's Abbey, York, Robin Hood's notorious victim.

The atmosphere of the tales comes close, as the audience must have done sometimes, to Falstaff and his cronies. Shakespeare pulled all the threads together, for he took the criminal gang-leader, stereotyped in Robin Hood, and turned him into a preposterous, gargantuan comic figure, full of rhetoric, boastful bravado and moving pathos. But some of the older tradition came through this transformation. Shakespeare knew that Gadshill, like Alton and Barnsdale, was a famous haunt of robbers. He saw no improbability in having Sir John declare – 'What, ye knaves, young men must live' – and no incongruity in having him declaim – 'There lives not three good men unhanged in England and one of them is fat and grows old'. And he hit the nail on the head when he had Justice Silence sing of Robin Hood, Scarlett and Little John after his drunken feast with the fat knight. In Shakespeare's England the old style of criminal gang had indeed 'grown old'. He might have written **differently if he had known the borders rather than the forest of Arden**. As it was he dismissed the past – 'I know thee not old man: fall to thy prayers'.

But men still knew Robin Hood. That was because Robin himself had been changed.

# VII
# The Later Tradition

In the course of the fifteenth century Robin Hood was adopted into the May Games. There he mingled with other characters and his tale absorbed extraneous traditions. Within a few years of the end of the century parts of the legend were in print, and within the next two centuries the stories were repeated over and over again in cheaper and cheaper formats. These changes altered the lines along which the tales were handed down. They broadened and further diversified both the means of communication and the audience. This in turn affected the content of the legend. Minor elements in the old stories were now developed into major themes. New tales were concocted. Socially, Robin became all things to all men. At one end of the range he acquired breeding, even became the outlawed earl of Huntington, while at the other he engaged in rustic combat with butchers, tinkers and beggars. In its earliest written versions the legend was already contaminated. Now it was to be adulterated.

Seasonal festivals such as the May Games were far older than the tale of Robin Hood. May Games and mell suppers, the Feast of Fools and the play of the King and the Queen had been condemned by reforming bishops, Robert Grosseteste of Lincoln and Walter Cantilupe of Worcester, in the 1230s and 1240s. Puritan divines still thundered against such sprees in the sixteenth century. Robin seems to have moved into them in the course of the fifteenth century by way of the plays. The dialogue, the duelling, the disguises and much else in the action were easily translated from poetic recital into some dramatic form. The earliest known dramatic fragment of *c.*1475, which matches *Guy of Gisborne*, has no obvious specific connection with the May Games, but two other plays, of the later sixteenth century, based respectively on *Robin Hood and the Curtal Friar* and *Robin Hood and the Potter*, were plainly written for them. Moreover, the servant who played Robin Hood and the sheriff of Nottingham in John Paston's household in the early 1470s also gave a rendering of St George, and the saint, like Robin, was a figure in the May Games. By the end of the fifteenth century it was probably through the games that Robin was most widely known. He was apparently a traditional participant in the summer games at Willenhall in 1498 when this function provided cover for Roger Marshall's alleged riot. He appears at Croscombe, Somerset, in 1476, at Wells in 1498, at Reading in 1498–9 and Kingston-on-Thames in 1507. In Scotland he turns up at Edinburgh in 1492, and Aberdeen in 1508. In the course of the sixteenth century he became one of the most universally represented figures in the springtide festivals.

This introduced new characters into the tale. The queen of May and the friar were traditional participants in the morris dance. In origin they were quite independent of Robin's legend and they were still represented separately in their role in the morris dance, entirely without Robin or anything to link them with his tale, in Tollet's window executed for Betley Hall, Staffordshire, *c.*1621. Whether the friar of the morris dance was in origin one and the same as Friar Tuck is problematical. It has already been suggested that Friar Tuck originated in Sussex in 1417,[1] but this does not preclude some link with a friar of the springtide games. The association of Robin and Maid Marian drew ultimately through the spring and summer festivals, on a literary source, the French pastoral play *Robin et Marion*, composed *c.*1283 by Adam de la Halle, in which the shepherdess Marion, loyal to her lover Robin, successfully resists the advances of a knight. The story contributed to the May Games in France, and it was taken over by an English poet, John Gower. In his *Mirour de l'omme* or *Speculum Meditantis* of 1376–9, a long poem on vices and virtues, written in French, he had Robin and Marion participating in rustic festivals and condemned the revels of monks with the comment that they obeyed the rule of Robin rather than that of St Augustine. Hence Robin, Marion or Marian and popular festivals were already associated at a remarkably early date, within a year or two at most of Langland's first reference to Robin Hood. In view of this it is striking that the earliest stories of Robin make no mention of Marian and betray no hint of any debt to the French *pastourelle*. The evidence does not allow any other conclusion but that the two traditions developed side by side and independently one of the other in the course of the fifteenth century. The poet Alexander Barclay, writing shortly after 1500, is the first person known to juxtapose Robin Hood and Marian but he implies that their tales were still distinct–'some merry fytte of Maid Marian or else of Robin Hood'. But by then or shortly afterwards, they had come together through Robin Hood and the Robin of the games being made one and the same. Marian was queen of May. Robin became her King. Together they presided over the May Games in the sixteenth century.

For some this change in context had little effect on Robin's unruly reputation. In 1555 the Scottish parliament prohibited any further annual celebrations in which there were impersonations of Robin Hood, Little John, the abbot of Unreason and the queen of May. Those who participated in choosing such within royal burghs were made liable to five years' imprisonment; those chosen were to be banished from the realm; similar actions in the countryside were to be punished less severely. But, although Robin might figure in the games as the leader in an annual ritual of disorder, in which for a day authority was overturned, he became stylized by that very role. Moreover, this was not the only role he played as a result of his association with the games. In some contexts he retained his courtesy and became a genial host, exemplifying an idealized existence in the greenwood. It was thus that he figured in 1515 in the Maying of Henry VIII's court:

The King and Queen accompanied with many lords and ladies rode to the high ground of Shooters Hill to take the open air; and as they passed by the way, they espied a company of tall yeomen, clothed all in green with green hoods and bows and arrows, to the number of two hundred. Then one of them, which called himself Robyn hood, came to the King, desiring him to see his men shoot, and the King was content. Then he whistled, and all the two hundred archers shot and loosed at once, and then he whistled again, and they likewise shot again; their arrows whistled by craft of the head, so that the noise was strange and great, and much pleased the King and Queen and all the company. All these archers were of the King's guard and had thus apparelled themselves to make solace to the King. Then Robyn hood desired the King and the Queen to come into the green wood, and to see how the outlaws live. The King demanded of the Queen and her ladies, if they durst adventure to go into the wood with so many outlaws. Then the Queen said, that if it pleased him, she was content. Then the horns blew till they came to the wood under Shooters Hill, and there was an arbour made of boughs, with a hall and a great chamber and an inner chamber very well made and covered with flowers and sweet herbs, which the King much praised. Then said Robyn hood, Sir, outlaws' breakfast is venison, and therefore you must be content with such fare as we use. Then the King and Queen sat down, and were served with venison and wine by Robyn hood and his men, to their great contentation.[2]

This remained an important feature of the tradition. Shakespeare alluded to Robin in a bawdy, drunken context in *Henry IV*. But he also used the Robin of the idyllic greenwood in *As You Like It*, where the duke's exiled court provides a theatrical example:

They say he is already in the forest of Arden, and a many merry men with him; and there they live like the old Robin Hood of England: they say many young gentlemen flock to him every day and fleet the time carelessly, as they did in the golden world.[3]

Robin's participation in the games not only diversified the tradition. It also prepared the ground for its theatrical development. The most important surviving examples of the plays on Robin are Anthony Munday's *The Downfall of Robert Earl of Huntington* and *The Death of Robert Earl of Huntington*, written in 1598. In these, Munday divested Robin of his association with the Mayings:

> *Me thinks I see no ieasts of Robin Hoode,*
> *No merry morices of Frier Tuck,*
> *No pleasant skippings up and downe the wodde,*
> *No hunting songs, no coursing of the Bucke.*
> *Pray God this play of ours may have good lucke,*
> *And the King's Maiestie mislike it not.*[4]

He then took up the tradition, expressed by Leland and Grafton, which claimed Robin to be noble, and firmly identified him as Robin earl of Huntington. Apparently relying on Major's dates, he set his fictitious earl in the reign of Richard I. That done, he stirred in ingredients from other legends. Maid Marian became Matilda, daughter of Robert fitz Walter, who, in tradition since the early fourteenth century, had been the object of King John's lecherous attentions. In the second play Robin is dispatched by poison in scene 5 and the tale of Matilda and King John takes up the remainder of the plot. How much of this Munday himself invented it is impossible to say; the main components of the play were borrowed; much of the material on John was derived from the anonymous play *The Troublesome Reign of King John*. But he is the first-known dramatist to express the tradition of a noble Robin firmly set in a context which associated him with Richard I and John, and he is the first-known writer of any kind to give him the title of earl of Huntington. It cannot be proved that Robin's ennoblement originated in the theatre; the first hints of it in Leland antedate the first surviving plays to include it by sixty years; but dramatists' views of the tastes of the theatrical audience, especially at court, certainly encouraged and shaped it. Theatrical production imposed its own requirements. Patrons and audiences paid for what they wanted. The result was a Robin cast in a gentle, aristocratic mould. Munday not only traduced the yeoman hero but also translated his story into a tale of court intrigue. His work was influential; it infected the antiquarian investigation of Robin's origins and hence continued to contaminate the tradition down to the movies and the television dramas of the twentieth century.

The general literary development of the tale was much more varied. Increasingly in the sixteenth and seventeenth centuries printers exploited the possibilities of a 'mass' market. Tales were printed in cheaper and cheaper versions: as broadsides, that is single sheets printed on one side only, as 'garlands' or anthologies, or as chapbooks in small octavo or duodecimo format specifically designed as chapmen's wares for sale in markets or from packhorses at 2*d*. or 1*d*. a copy. They were part of an extraordinary expansion of the market which, in addition to the ballads and 'merriments' embraced 'small godly books' or 'Godlinesses', 'histories' and almanacs. They accompanied a marked improvement in the level of literacy both among the gentry and the rural yeoman class between the late sixteenth and the mid-seventeenth century. On the evidence of signatures, and subject to considerable geographic and terminological variation, roughly half of those classed as yeomen were illiterate in the 1560s. By the 1660s the proportion had fallen to a quarter. At least three-quarters of those classed as tradesmen and craftsmen were illiterate in the 1560s. By the early seventeenth century this was true of less than half, a century later of only a third. The new formats were designed to educate and entertain this widening reading public.

In addition to the earliest surviving versions, Child's great collection of ballads includes thirty-three of these later tales of Robin Hood, some with variants which are separate compositions, in style if not in subject-matter. Some are derived from the Percy Folio,[5] some from broadsides. Most come from garland collections of 1663 and 1670 and from the collections of chapbooks of the diarist Samuel Pepys, and of others who were interested in the new literary vogue. A few are preserved only in late versions of the eighteenth century; Child included these where the titles had been mentioned earlier or where there were other grounds for thinking them traditional. He excluded some ditties as not constituting genuine ballads. Some titles he could not trace. One story of some interest he apparently overlooked.[6] But the collection he made has never been superseded. It is comprehensive enough to present a much more complete picture of the development of the legend between the sixteenth and the eighteenth centuries than the earliest surviving versions can possibly provide for its origins. Nevertheless, there is scarcely anything to suggest that it preserves older traditions ignored or bypassed in the earliest stories. On the whole, these later ballads are derivative, secondary and second-rate.

Of the thirty-three later tales preserved by Child twelve do little more than rehash parts of the legend preserved in the earliest versions. Three of these, *Robin Hood and the Bishop*, *Robin Hood's Golden Prize* and *Robin Hood and the Bishop of Hereford*, take up the theme of the outlaw's enmity for the clergy. In all three, priests or bishops are bamboozled, ransomed or robbed. Two stories, *Robin Hood Rescuing Three Squires* and *Robin Hood Rescuing Will Stutly* are blood-and-thunder adventures in which men condemned to death at Nottingham are rescued. The sheriff of Nottingham figures as the villain; in the former tale he is hanged on his own gallows after the squires have been rescued. *Robin*

*Hood and Queen Katherine*, *Robin Hood's Progress to Nottingham* and *The Golden Arrow* all have archery contest as their centre-piece. *Robin Hood's Chase* is a sequel to *Queen Katherine* in which King Henry pursues Robin through the northern counties only to return empty handed to London. *The King's Disguise and Friendship with Robin Hood* is a much more direct derivation of the encounter between Robin and the king first recounted in fyttes seven and eight of the *Gest*.

In most of these tales the *Gest* or the components of the *Gest* seem to have been the chief source. *Robin Hood and the Potter* also played a part in providing the prototype of Robin in disguise. In *Robin Hood and the Bishop*, he takes the guise of an old woman, and in the *Three Squires* of a beggar in one version and of an old man in another. *Robin Hood and the Monk* may well have contributed to the hostility to the clergy expressed in *The Bishop*, *The Bishop of Hereford*, and the *Golden Prize*, and also to the murderous antipathy between Robin and the sheriff. *Guy of Gisborne* may have been a distant source for the plot of *Robin Hood and the Valiant Knight* in which Robin is brought to battle by 'a trusty and worthy knight' of the uninformative name of Sir Willliam. The battle is a draw; Sir William is killed; Robin falls ill and he too dies at the hands of a monk who lets his blood. By the eighteenth century, from which this story first survives, the traditions were well confused.

It was easy to embody new material in the medieval tradition as it was reworked and adapted. Attempts were made to link the legend with other tales. In one version of *Queen Katherine* King Henry announces to Sir Richard Lee (A,22):

> *Well it is knowen ffrom thy pedygree*
> *Thou came from Gawiins blood.*

But he was optimistic, for the reference to Gawain was not understood and in other variants he was transmuted into Gower. Gamelyn was a more suitable candidate for embodiment in the legend. In *Robin Hood Newly Reviv'd*, he appears as the yeoman Gamwell whom Robin first fights and then enrols in his band, the recruitment being eased by Gamwell's firm assertion that he is Robin's nephew. Another eighteenth-century version of the tale, *The Bold Pedlar and Robin Hood*, tells a similar story of a pedlar named Gamble Gold who announces himself as Robin's cousin. *Robin Hood and the Prince of Aragon*, of the late seventeenth century, identifies Gamwell with Will Scadlock, the lost son of an entirely fictitious earl of Maxfield. Another story coming from the seventeenth century, *Robin Hood's Birth, Breeding, Valor and Marriage*, is more complicated. It begins with the statement that Robin was born (2):

*In Locksly town, in Nottinghamshire,*
*In merry sweet Locksly town.*

It then drags in all and sundry. Robin's father was a forester who could
shoot (2, 3):

> *Two north country miles and an inch at a shot,*
> *As the Pinder of Wakefield does know.*
>
> *For he brought Adam Bell, and Clim of the Clugh,*
> *And William a Clowdesle*
> *To shoot with our forrester for forty mark,*
> *And the forrester beat them all three.*

Robin's mother, the forester's wife, is the niece of Guy of Warwick, and
her brother (Robin's uncle) is Gamwell of Great Gamwell Hall, whose
knave is Little John. This was probably nothing more than an attempt
to link the doings of Robin with other well-known items in the story-
teller's or singer's repertoire.

In some of these tales imagination roamed fancy free. *Robin Hood's
Birth, Breeding, Valor and Marriage* has Robin marry Clorinda, queen of
the shepherds, but Clorinda showed no staying power against the
pervasive claims of Maid Marian. *Robin Hood and the Prince of Aragon* is
in the style of a romance and presents Robin, Scadlock and Little John as
champions who free the city of London by slaying the prince of
Aragon, an infidel Turk, and his two pet giants, who are beleaguering
it. *The Noble Fisherman* takes Robin to sea at Scarborough under the
pseudonym of Simon. He proves an incompetent fisherman and soon
wishes he was back in Plumpton Park, but through his prowess with
the bow, which by good fortune he has brought with him, he is able to
defeat and capture a French raider loaded with treasure.

Such trivial romances were passing fancies which had very little
permanent effect upon the legend. *Robin Hood and Allen a' Dale*, first
surviving in a seventeenth-century broadside, took firmer root and
introduced a new character. It is a light story in which Robin intervenes
to prevent the marriage of Allen's intended bride to a rich old knight
and restore her to her lover. Little John, attired as a bishop, reads the
bans and conducts the wedding ceremony. The tale was first told in the
prose life in the Sloane MS where the forlorn lover is not Allen, but
Scarlock. Unlike most of the other frills fashioned around the legend
this became part of the generally accepted canon in the nineteenth
century. A prim romance, it was a fitter tale for children's eyes than the
rustic celebration of the wedding of Robin and Clorinda in *Robin Hood's
Birth, Breeding, Valor and Marriage* (52, 53):

*Then a garland they brought her, by two and by two,*
*And plac'd them upon the bride's head;*
*The music struck up, and we all fell to dance,*
*Till the bride and the groom were a-bed.*

*And what they did there must be counsel to me,*
*Because they lay long the next day,*
*And I had haste home, but I got a good piece*
*Of the bride-cake, and so came away.*

In one direction there was a more consistent, sustained development. This lay in those variants of the legend in which Robin meets his match in some chance encounter with local official, tradesman or rustic. In these tales Robin ceases to be invulnerable. The outlaw hero who in the *Gest* is knocked down solely by the king now succumbs to beggars, shepherds and pedlars. In some of these stories Robin also seems more plebeian, but this is less striking than the repetitive simplicity of the plots. Usually Robin encounters a stranger. He challenges him. He may ask him to perform a service or make a payment, or he may demand to examine his wares. A fight ensues. The opponent proves a worthy foe, and the fight usually ends in compromise or with an invitation to join the band, which is usually accepted. In some instances the opponent proves decisively the better; Robin is defeated and may even be chastised. If the growing interest in these stories lay among newly literate country yeomen and tradesfolk in the towns, this is what ballad-mongers and printers considered that they wanted to hear and read; and to judge from the number of titles, they were right; this was the chief growth-point in the expanding commerce in the tales.

Of the thirty-three titles in Childs's collection eighteen embody this theme in one form or another. Some of them became integral parts of the legend as it was retold to youngsters in the nineteenth century. It is in this fashion that Robin recruits the friar in *Robin Hood and the Curtal Friar*, Little John in *Robin Hood and Little John* and, less convincingly, Maid Marian in a tale first surviving from the eighteenth century, in which Marian, disguised as a page, fights with her lover for an hour before mutual recognition dawns. In some of these stories the contestant had an independent fictional reputation and the fight is used to concoct a link with Robin's legend. In *Robin Hood Newly Reviv'd* the opponent is Gamwell; in *Robin Hood and the Pinder of Wakefield* it is the pinder, who had a separate literary existence in ballad and play, both under that name and as George a' Green, which can be traced back to the sixteenth century. In some of these tales the choice of opponent lies within Robin's traditional environment and perhaps serves to link the antipathy to the royal forest expressed in the medieval legend with the continuing instincts of, and sympathy for, the poacher. In *Robin Hood's*

*Delight*, Robin, Scarlock and John are challenged in Sherwood by three of King Henry's foresters. The outlaws have the worst of it and eventually settle for a drinking bout in Nottingham (21–2):

> *'We will fight no more', sayes bold Robin,*
> *'You be men of valour stout;*
> *Come and go with me to Nottingham,*
> *And there we will fight it out.*
>
> *'With a but of sack we will bang it out,*
> *To see who wins the day;*
> *And for the cost, make you no doubt*
> *I have gold and money to pay.'*

In *Robin Hood and the Ranger* the combat is restricted to Robin and a single forester. He too proves the better and Robin promptly invites him to join the band. Some variants, like one of the tales of the beggar, which was printed in Aberdeen and Glasgow, and *Robin Hood and the Scotchman* were adaptations for a local market. *Robin Hood's Birth, Breeding, Valor and Marriage* was composed for the annual bull-running at Tutbury; the publisher announced hopefully that 'it was calculated for the meridian of Staffordshire, but may serve for Derbyshire and Kent'. However, in most of these publications there is little distinct purpose other than that of ballad-mongers and printers ringing the changes, with little artistic or didactic intent, simply in order to enliven the market for their wares. In this self-sustaining exercise in 'educating' popular taste Robin was made to fight a butcher, a tanner, a shepherd, a beggar (in two distinct versions), a 'bold pedlar' and lastly three pedlars, in company with Scarlet and Little John. In some tales Little John is defeated by the combatant before Robin tries his arm. In some he offers to take up the challenge after Robin's defeat. In *Little John a'Begging* he stands alone, but this tale is of different stock for here John defeats the beggars and makes off with their gold in a triumphant return to Sherwood.

In these combats Robin is soundly beaten by the ranger, the shepherd, the three foresters, the tinker and, in one version, by the beggar. The rest end in a draw, although it is almost always Robin who cries quit. Where Little John enters the fray he too suffers the same fate; only the friar gives him best for his skill as an archer. Most combatants accept the invitation to join the band: the stranger, who becomes Little John, the pinder, the ranger, the tanner, the Scotchman, the tinker, Gamwell in *Robin Hood Newly Reviv'd*, and presumably the curtail friar. The beggar and the pedlars turn the invitation down or go their own way. In two tales, the *Bold Pedlar* and *Robin Hood's Delight*, the bout ends with a friendly drink, and in *The Shepherd* simply with a comment on his prowess. These variations seem quite haphazard. If there was any change of emphasis between the sixteenth and the eighteenth centuries it was that, as time passed, these trivial stories show fewer and fewer traces of the original legend. *Robin Hood and the Pedlars*, which expresses Robin's degradation more completely than any of the others, survives in a version no earlier than the eighteenth century. Here Kit o' Thirsk, the pedlar's leader, knocks the outlaw unconscious and then administers medicine to him as he lies on the ground (25–9):

> *'In my packe, God wot, I a balsame have got*
> *That soone his hurts will heale';*
> *And into Robin Hoods gaping mouth*
> *He presentlie powrde some deale.*
>
> *'Now fare ye well, tis best not to tell*
> *How ye three peddlers met;*
> *Of if ye doe, prithee tell alsoe*
> *How they made ye swinke and swett.'*
>
> *Poore Robin in sound they left on the ground,*
> *And hied them to Nottingham,*
> *While Scarlett and John Robin tended on,*
> *Till at length his senses came.*
>
> *Noe sooner, in haste, did Robin Hood taste*
> *The balsame he had tane,*
> *Than he gan to spewe, an up he threwe*
> *The Balsame all againe.*
>
> *And Scarlett and John who were looking on*
> *Their maister as he did lie,*
> *Had their faces besmeard, both eies and beard,*
> *Therewith most piteously.*

The moral is clear enough. The rustic, tradesman or beggar is as doughty as the outlaw. This does not depend simply on Robin's discomfiture. In its earliest expression in *Robin Hood and the Potter* the potter is allowed to deliver some sound advice after smiting Robin to the ground (22–3):

| | |
|---|---|
| *'Het ys fol leytell cortesey', seyde the potter,* | 'It is very little courtesy', said the potter, |
| *'As y haffe harde weyse men saye,* | 'As I have heard wise men say, |
| *Yeffe a pore yeman com drywyng on the wey,* | If a poor yeoman comes driving on the way, |
| *To let hem of hes gorney.'* | To hinder him on his journey.' |
| *'Be mey trowet, thow seys soyt', seyde Roben,* | 'By my troth, you speak truth', said Robin, |
| *'Thow seys god yemenrey;* | 'You speak good yeomanry; |
| *And thow dreyffe fforthe yevery day,* | If you drive forth every day, |
| *Thow schalt never be let ffor me.'* | You shall never be hindered by me.' |

A fight with staff. Robin Hood and the Tanner after an
engraving by Thomas Bewick, *c*.1795, from Ritson's *Robin Hood*.

The tanner, Arthur a'Bland, takes a coarser line (9–11):

*'For thy sword and thy bow I*
　*care not a straw,*
*Nor all thine arrows to boot;*
*If I get a knop upon thy bare scop,*
*Thou canst as well shite as shoote'.*

*'Speak cleanly, good fellow', said*
　*jolly Robin,*
*'And give better terms to me;*
*Else I'le thee correct for thy neglect,*
*And make thee more mannerly.'*

*'Marry gep with a wenion!'*
　*quoth Arthur a Bland,*
*'Art thou such a goodly man?*
*I care not a fig for thy looking so*
　*big;*
*Mend thyself where thou can.'*

'For your sword and your bow I
　care not a straw,
Nor all your arrows to boot;
If I fetch a crack on your bare scalp,
You can as well shit as shoot.'

'Speak cleanly, good fellow', said
　jolly Robin,
'And give better terms to me;
Else I'll you correct for your neglect,
And make you more mannerly.'

'Marry, get along with a plague
　on you,' quoth Arthur a Bland,
'Are you such a goodly man?
I care not a fig for you looking so
　bold;
Mend yourself where you can.'

*Robin Hood and the Pedlars* is perhaps the most direct of all (24, 30):

> *'But lett him learne to be wise in turne,*
> *And not with pore peddlers mell.'*

and

> *Thus ended that fray; soe beware alwaye*
> *How ye doe challenge foes;*
> *Looke well aboute they are not to stoute,*
> *Or you may have worst of the blowes.*

In these tales, in varying proportions, Robin is at once hero and butt. It is as both that he survived in popular imagination in the seventeenth century.

It is tempting to suppose that these tales embody ancient tradition, stemming from the very source of the legend, in which Robin, if not always the hero, was at least the property of the folk. For this, there is a little, but only a little, to be said. Certainly by the seventeenth century Robin had become a household name. Robin Hood proverbs, like Robin Hood place names, abounded, Men bought or sold bargains as Robin Hood's pennyworths, or went the long way round by Robin Hood's barn or mile, or overshot Robin when they boasted. On occasion this popular appreciation was by no means casual; it could acquire a socially critical edge. Sir Robert Cecil might sneer at the Gunpowder plotters as 'Robin Hoods' but he himself was the target when his tenants rhymed:

> *Not Robin Goodfellow, nor Robin Hood,*
> *but Robin the encloser of Hatfield Wood.*[7]

Moreover, fanciful though the later tales may often be, they use settings familiar to the audience. Robin or his men are now made to participate in crude slogging matches with the quarter-staff, and the staff was immediately recognizable as the most readily available weapon for rustic combat. In the 103 cases of murder and manslaughter presented to the coroners of Nottinghamshire between 1485 and 1558 the staff figured in 53, usually as the sole fatal weapon. The sword, in contrast, accounted for only nine victims and one accidental death. The realities of the record provided gruesome comparison with the carefree cudgelling of the ballads:

On 4 September (1527) John Strynger late of Babworth, labourer, assaulted Henry Pereson of Babworth with a staff worth 1*d*. which he held in both hands, striking him on the top of the head so that his brains flowed out and giving him a wound 1 inch deep, 2 inches wide and 3 inches long of which he immediately died. Thus John feloniously murdered him, and immediately afterwards he fled about 9 a.m. and escaped. Robert Bramley, a man of good reputation and standing, first found Henry dead.[8]

Yet there is nothing in these versions of the legend which cannot reasonably be put down to 'popular' debasement of themes already expressed in the earliest surviving tales. These contain two possible prototypes for the ballads of combat: the fight between Little John and the cook in the *Gest* and that between Robin and the potter in *Robin Hood and the Potter*. In the former, Little John, like Robin in many of the later ballads, recruits his opponent. In the latter Robin is defeated, offers the potter 'fellowship', and adopts his clothing and takes his wares as a disguise. That was followed exactly in *Robin Hood and the Butcher* and, less precisely, in one version of *Robin Hood and the Beggar*.

The claim that this theme stems from an original folk tradition of Robin therefore has to depend on a more complex argument that the earliest surviving written versions, precisely because they *are* written, are themselves no more than side-shoots from the main stem of the legend which, being oral, cannot from its very nature be defined until it is revealed in the ballads of the sixteenth and seventeeth centuries composed and printed for the popular market. This cannot be either proved or disproved because in the last resort it depends on assertion and invention. The existence of such a folk tradition is easier to imagine than refute; but imagination is no substitute for evidence, and, on the whole, such evidence as there is tells against this hypothesis.

It is apparent, first, that Robin and his men suffered progressive social decline. In the *Gest* Little John and the cook fight with the sword, and this form of duel recurs in *The Curtal Friar*, *The Pinder of Wakefield*, *Robin Hood's Delight* and in Robin's fight with Gamwell both in *Robin Hood Newly Reviv'd* and *The Bold Pedlar*. Except for the last, all these are derived from the Percy Folio, or the garland of 1663, or some earlier broadside version. In *The Potter* Robin contends with the sword against the potter's staff. This form of combat recurs in *The Butcher*, *The Beggar*, *The Shepherd* (where the staff is replaced by the shepherd's crook), and *The Tinker*. These also, except for the last, are no later than the garland of 1663. In *The Ranger* Robin and the ranger fight first with swords, which they break, and then with staves. The staff alone is used in *The Tanner*, *Robin Hood and Little John* and *The Pedlars*, but then only after Robin has laid aside his bow, or threatened with his bow before taking up the staff. Of these *The Tanner* comes from the garland, but the other two, like *The Ranger*, are late versions surviving in their present form from the eighteenth century. It seems that Robin's weapons tended to become more rustic as time passed. His use of the staff was not part of the earliest ballads of combat. It came into them late and usually had to be explained or excused as though it was in some way out of character. This most plebeian aspect of his prowess was not part of the original story.

At the same time the general social milieu of the tales was depressed. Some preserve a notion of service ultimately inherited from the medieval retinue. To Little John Robin promises (26–7):

> . . . *if thou wilt be mine*
> *Thou shalt have my livery strait,*
> *And other accoutrements fit for a man,*

and he asks the pinder (B, 4):

> '*But wilt be my Man*' . . .
> *And come and dwell with me?*
> *And twice in a yeere thy clothing be changed*
> *If my man thou wilt bee,*
> *The tone shall be of light Lincolne greene,*
> *And tother of Picklory.*'

But in most of these later tales the retinue has been replaced by the gang: part neighbourhood association, part poaching organization, part criminal enterprise. Robin had once waylaid the potter in order to charge him *pavage*. He now challenges the casual passer-by without either provocation or objective unless it be simple robbery. His function as leader is to take on the victim in personal combat; if he is defeated other members of the gang, as in *The Beggar*, will seek to avenge him. None the less it is through such combats that the gang recruits; indeed, holding one's own with the staff or sword against the outlaws is the sole route to entry. It is facilitated if the combatant can claim kinship with Robin or another of the outlaws. That the combats might be seen in this light is put beyond serious doubt by Alexander Smith's *History of Highwaymen* in 1714:

he was a stout fellow, and would never entertain any of his fraternity before he had made sufficient trial of their courage and dexterity in using their weapons.[9]

Secondly, almost all these later ballads were sung. The tunes still survive. Some share the same tune. Ten of them were sung to the tune of Arthur a' Bland, the name of the tanner of *Robin Hood and the Tanner*. The tune was sometimes described as 'Hey down a down a down', which occurred as a second-line refrain in all these ballads. Their common dependence on it probably explains their more or less consistent use of a middle rhyme in the third line of each stanza. The result was trivial versification. *The Tanner* opens thus:

> *In Nottingham there lives a jolly tanner,*
> *With a hey down down a down down*
> *His name is Arthur a Bland;*
> *There is nere a squire in Nottinghamshire*
> *Did bid bold Arthur stand.*

The origins of this simple form are complicated. Ballads were sung in Chaucer's day, but these were sophisticated lyrics very different in form and content from the broadside ballads of the sixteenth century. The term 'ballad' came to be applied to stories of diverse origins and various forms. This mirrored the repertoire of the local performer who paid scant attention to literary distinctions. Izaak Walton's milkmaid regaled the anglers with the Milkmaid's song, but she knew more than pleasant rustic ditties as her mother revealed:

What song was it, I pray? Was it 'Come Shepherds, deck your herds'? or 'As at noon Dulcina rests'? or 'Phillida flouts me'? or 'Chevy Chace'? or 'Johnny Armstrong'? or 'Troy Town'?[10]

The change in the sense of the word 'ballad' camouflages the transformation of the minstrel's lay into the ballad-monger's song. The Robin Hood ballads themselves provide the best and earliest evidence of this change, and one of them, *Robin Hood and the Butcher*, reveals in some detail how the sung ballad of the sixteenth century was evolved from the minstrelsy of the fifteenth century. There are two versions of this tale. One was the work of a ballad-writer 'T.R.' who, before 1655, composed a version which was certainly intended to be sung, and probably to the tune of Arthur a' Bland for it has the characteristic rhyme in the third line (1):

> *Come all you brave gallants, and listen a while,*
> *With a hey down, down, an a down*
> *That are in the bowers within;*
> *For of Robin Hood, that archer good,*
> *A song I intend to sing.*

The other is derived from the Percy Folio and plainly occupies an intermediate position between T.R.'s version and *Robin Hood and the Potter*, from which both were ultimately derived. It lacks the third-line rhyme; it has no second-line refrain; and it comes closer in its detail to the original tale of the potter. This is symptomatic of a more general trend. The more the tales acquired the form of the popular ballad the less accurately did they tend to preserve the original legend.

Play-acting also contributed to the new form, either within or separately from the May Games. The challenge, the combat, the recruitment to the band were almost a ritual, easy to present theatrically. *Robin Hood and Little John* ends:

> *Then musick and dancing did finish the day;*
> *At length, when the sun waxed low,*
> *Then all the whole train the grove did refrain,*
> *And unto their caves they did go.*

In *Robin Hood and the Tanner* Arthur a' Bland joins the band and identifies himself as Little John's kinsman and:

> *Then Robin Hood took them both by the hand,*
> *And danc'd round about the oke tree;*
> *'For three merry men, and three merry men,*
> *And three merry men we be.'*

There is a similar scene in *Little John a'Begging*, whilst in *The Bishop of Hereford* Robin partners the bishop in a dance. *Robin Hood's Birth, Breeding, Valor and Marriage* suggests a veritable pageant (44–8):

*This battle was fought near to Titbury town,*
*When the bagpipes bated the bull;*
*I am king of the fidlers, and sware 'tis a truth,*
*And I call him that doubts it a gull.*

*For I saw them fighting, and fidld the while,*
*And Clorinda sung, Hey derry down!*
*The bumpkins are beaten, put up thy sword, Bob,*
*And now let's dance into the town.*

*Before we came to it, we heard a strange shouting,*
*And all that were in it lookd madly;*
*For some were a bull-back, some dancing a morris,*
*And some singing Arthur-a-Bradly.*

*And there we see Thomas, our justices clerk,*
*And Mary, to whom he was kind;*
*For Tom rode before her, and calld Mary, Madam,*
*And kist her full sweetly behind.*

*And so may your worships. But we went to dinner,*
*With Thomas and Mary and Nan;*
*They all drank a health to Clorinda, and told her*
*Bold Robin was a fine man.*

It is easy to imagine that that aroused visual memories in the audience.

By 1700 the accession of secondary material to the legend was largely at an end. Repetition had overtaken invention. The printed versions of the ballads established a kind of canon. The tales were also issued in prose versions, as simple escapist literature which satisfied the taste for adventure and the antiquarian interests of the semi-educated. The new tales add nothing of any consequence to the historical content of the legend. Frills were borrowed from romance, and in the ballads of combat minor features of the original legend were developed and diversified to play a predominant part in the new vogue. The tale was still vigorously alive. But this was at the cost of becoming totally fictional. Whatever the historical reality, of political detail or social immediacy, that lay behind the original tale, it was lost amidst the jumble of new names, relationships and circumstances required by artistic or commercial convenience. 'Edward our comely king' now appears as 'Richard Lion-heart' or alternatively as Henry VIII. The friar, incongruously, comes from Fountains abbey. In *Queen Katherine* Robin is identified as 'Loxly'. This was derived from the prose life in the Sloane MS. In other ballads Locksley is either Robin's birthplace and hence his surname, or an alias, or the name of someone else. Little John is so called because of his size or because his surname is Little. He is sometimes also the Miller's son, thereby denying Much any separate identity. Sir Richard at the Lee, essential in the *Gest*, is now a mere

# A True Tale of ROBIN HOOD.

Or, A Brief Touch of the Life and Death of that renowned Outlaw *Robert* Earl of *Huntington*, vulgar-
ly called *Robin Hood*, who lived and dyed in A.D.
1198. being the 9th. year of the Reign of King
*Richard* the First, commonly called *Richard Cœur
de Lyon.*

Carefully collected out of the truest Writers of our
English Chronicles : And published for the satisfaction of those who desire truth from falshood.

By *Martin Parker.*

Printed for *J. Clark*, *W. Thackeray*, and
near *West-Smithfield*, 1687.

A frontispiece of 1687 borrowed from the *Tale of Adam Bell*. See
above, p. 67. W. Thackeray appears as publisher of both.

adjunct, if indeed he is mentioned at all. Robin's clerical victims are no longer necessarily monastic. He now preys on friars and bishops as well.

Martin Parker's *True Tale of Robin Hood* of 1632 is perhaps the best illustration of how far the legend had moved from its original sources. Parker claimed that his tale was 'carefully collected out of the truest writers of our English chronicles. And published for the satisfaction of those who desire to see truth purged from falsehood'. But he made Richard the Lionheart his king and turned Robin into Robert earl of Huntington. In this he followed Munday and the tradition going back to Major, but he also knew the *Gest*, and the contamination of the old legend with the new tradition produced a uniquely flavoured concoction. Parker is unusual among seventeenth-century writers in retaining the abbot of St Mary's as Robin's great enemy. He drew this from the *Gest*, but he then leaves the *Gest* far behind and recounts a series of incidents in which the abbot's and the outlaw's forces clash in arms. He also mixes in the tradition of William Longchamps, bishop of Ely, Richard's chancellor, who was hated for his misgovernment during Richard's absence in the Holy Land, and for good measure, in order to explain the king's pursuit of Robin on his return from the crusade, he has Robin rob a royal treasure train. In the dénouement Robin is abandoned by his men who flee to join the king of Scotland as Richard descends on Nottingham. The king is ready to pardon him, but Robin suffers a fever brought on by the desertion. He is bled to death by a treacherous friar from whom he has sought treatment and is subsequently buried by the prioress of the house under a suitable gravestone. The banality of it all is brought home in the single stanza (96):

> *A treacherous leech this fryer was,*
> *To let him bleed to death;*
> *And Robin was, me thinkes, an asse,*
> *To trust him with his breath.*

Robin Hood was not confined to song, theatre or the written word. There was profit to be made in the claim that he sat, shot, drank, slept or stabled his horse wherever legend and commercial enterprise could be happily joined. At Loxley, three miles north-west of Sheffield, Joseph Hunter recorded in 1819 that 'the remains of a house in which it was pretended he was born were formerly pointed out'. A few miles to the west, at Hathersage, Little John's Grave attracted visitors, along with a cottage where it was claimed he had died; these were traditional associations which certainly went back to the seventeenth century. Meanwhile Robin Hood's Well on the Great North Road, first recorded by Roger Dodsworth, was the centre of a brisk trade. The York printer

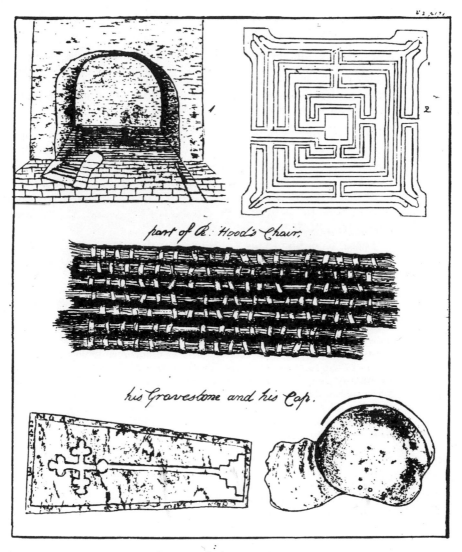

part of R: Hood's Chair.

his Gravestone and his Cap.

Robin Hood obiit xxiv kal Decembris mccxxxxvii

The Robin Hood relics at St Anne's Well, Nottingham,
after drawings by John Throsby, c.1797.

and antiquary, Thomas Gent, attached to his account of Kirklees nunnery which he included in his *History of York* in 1730:

Over a spring, call'd Robin Hoods Well, (3 or 4 miles this side of Doncaster, and but a quarter of a mile only from 2 towns call'd Skelbrough and Bourwallis) is a very handsome stone-arch, erected by the Lord Carlisle, where passengers from the coach frequently drink of the fair water, and give their charity to two people who attend there'.[11]

The well was one of the best known halting places on the road and up to the nineteenth century supported two inns. Except for the domed shelter which Vanbrugh designed for the earl of Carlisle none of this now survives. The plain fact was that in such ventures Nottingham was bound to win. Already in the sixteenth century St Anne's Well, to the north of the town, within the bounds of Sherwood, was famous as Robin Hood's Well.

There, according to his *Travels over England, Scotland and Wales*, first published in 1694, the Kentish person James Brome was shown Robin Hood's Chair. More followed:

Being placed in that chair, we had a cap, which, they say, was his, very formally put upon our heads, and having performed the usual ceremonies befitting so great a solemnity, we receiv'd the Freedom of the Chair, and were incorporated into the Society of that renowned Brotherhood; but that we may not receive such privileges without an honourable mentioning of the persons that left them to posterity; know we must, that the Patent was bequeathed to the inferior Rangers of this forest, by Robin Hood and Little John, honourable personages indeed, being the chief lords of some most renowned robbers in the reign of King Richard the First. . . . Having for some time pleased our selves with our new Brothers that very curteously entertained us, we went from hence into Yorkshire.[12]

In 1797 the local antiquary, John Throsby, noted some decline in trade:

The house which is resorted to in summer time, stands near the well, both which are shaded by firs and other trees. Here is a large bowling-green, and a little neglected pleasure ground. . . . The Well is under an arched stone roof, of rude workmanship, the water is very old, it will kill a toad. . . . It is used by those who are afflicted with rheumatic pains; and indeed, like many other popular springs, for a variety of disorders. At the house were formerly shewn several things said to have belonged to Robin Hood; but they are frittered down to what are now called his cap or helmet and a part of his chair. As these have passed current for many years, and perhaps ages, as things once belonging to that renowned robber, I sketched them.[13]

By this time interest was shifting to Sherwood and its surroundings where, by the next century, Robin had been endowed with a larder, two caves, a stable, yet another well and yet another grave, not to mention a meadow, a farm and sundry hills. It was now claimed that he

Robin Hood slays the foresters in *Robin Hood's Progress to Nottingham*, after an engraving by Thomas Bewick, *c*.1795, from Ritson's *Robin Hood*.

had been married in Edwinstowe church, whilst Papplewick was left with the ceremony which united Allen a'Dale and his bride. Meanwhile, Friar Tuck acquired a well, and Fountain Dale in Sherwood was so named to overcome the difficulty that the curtail friar had been attached in the ballad to Fountains abbey. Nottingham and Sherwood have remained centres of the cult. Nevertheless, with the exception of St Anne's Well and Robin Hood's Hills near Mansfield, first recorded in 1775, none of these associations can be traced earlier than the nineteenth century.

This later preponderance of Nottingham over Barnsdale was inevitable. Nottingham was a county town. Wentbridge was a hamlet; Barnsdale Bar and Robin Hood's Well were wayside halts. Quite apart from its commercial advantages, Nottingham was far more widely known. The result is plainly imprinted in the later ballads. Of Child's thirty-three titles Barnsdale appears in only three: in one version of *The Beggar*, one version of *The Bishop of Hereford*, and in *The King's Disguise*, which also brings in Nottingham. Nottingham or Sherwood, or both, in contrast, appear in seventeen of the tales. In *Robin Hood and Little John* there is even a hint of local pride: 'I'll show you right Nottingham play', is Robin's challenge, and all his bowmen are 'of the Nottingham breed'. Barnsdale could not compete and was almost lost to view. It was a predominantly Nottinghamshire legend which was handed down from the seventeenth century. So it remained until, with Hunter, the tale of the knight in the *Gest* was restored to its proper place.

This leads finally to what the legend did not include or only included to a slight degree. The new stories not only distorted the old; they also jettisoned important parts of it. None of the ballads attempts to refashion the tale of the knight; it is reflected distantly only in Parker's *True Tale*, in which it is Robin, not the knight, who is in debt to the abbot of St Mary's, and in the tales of the capture or robbery of monks or bishops. It seems likely that the nicely balanced story of the monastic mortgage and its repayment was of little interest to the new audience. *Guy of Gisborne* had no obvious successors, unless the tale is vaguely reflected in *The Valiant Knight*, in which the combat is not between individuals but between the knight's retinue and Robin's band. *Guy of Gisborne* was never apparently printed before Percy included it in his *Reliques* in 1765. It survives solely in the Percy Folio and through the accident that it was in the surviving portion of the manuscript which Percy managed to rescue. It may be that it was too localized to get into general circulation.

One other story, unique in atmosphere, has survived in a single manuscript, but this, unlike *Guy of Gisborne*, was never included in the anthologies of Percy, Ritson or Child. It was preserved under the title *Robin Whood Turned Hermit* in a collection of ballads dated 1735, made by the Stamford antiquary, Francis Peck. It is an edifying story based in part on Parker's *True Tale* or on a common source. Peck summarizes the tale in the following argument:

This song is altogether founded upon Fact. Wherein the Author (first touching the former Circumstances of Robin Whood's turning Fisherman, building an Hospital at Scarborough, the Flight of one hundred of his Men, and the staying of the other forty) brings Robin back to his remaining Friends, whom he thanks for their fidelity, then leads them from Sherwood for fear of Danger – from a greater Force coming upon them, and with them sculks about in other Places. At last coming to Lyndric a famous hill near Dale Abbey in Lancashire (*sic*) Robin Whood falls asleep and hath a strange Dream there. Which at his awaking, he relates to his Companions, and then tells them, that he is resolved forthwith to retire, and to turn Hermit. At his taking leave of them, he advises them all to repent and to betake themselves to better course; (especially Little John whom he also exhorts to have a great care how he sets his feet upon St. Michael's ground for that will be very fatal to him whenere he does so). His last Message to his Lady Matilda. His Men depart, everyone to their Homes and Friends. Robin retires to Depe Dale, chuses the penitent Thief for his Patron, and spends the Remainder of his Time in great Penance and Devotion. He falls sick of a fever, Repairs to Kirklees to be let Blood. A revengeful Friar cuts an artery instead of a vein; whereby he quickly bleeds to Death. The Lady Prioress and Nuns bury and lay a grave-stone over him. [14]

Although some if its material is plainly derived from other later ballads, its flavour is far removed from the common taste (23, 4):

*To Depe-Dale come, most wisely Robin Whood,*
*Surveys each Nook and Corner of the Wood*
*At length he finds a lonely rocky cell,*
*And in Devotion there resolves to dwell.*
*There he grows wise and for his Patron taks*
*The Thief repentant, and him thus bespaks*
*Happy Robin Whood! Happy Robin Whood!*

*O thou, who didst upon the Cross repent*
*Teach me, as thou didst, strongly to repent*
*If e'er again I should my Crimes forget,*
*Help me, bless'd Saint, that Falling to regret,*
*Could I, as thou did'st, hear my Savior's Voice,*
*This day shalt thou be with me in Paradise.*
*Happy Robin Whood! Happy Robin Whood!*

Peck commented sententiously: 'This song is, I think, designed in a true Manner. *Docet; delectat; flectit.* It instructs; it pleases; it moves and affects the Reader.' The tale was in fact no more than a concoction blending some of the stories about Robin with the deeds of an anonymous outlaw which were first recorded in a chronicle of the foundation of Dale abbey written by Thomas of Muskham in the thirteenth century. Muskham places the anonymous outlaw in the reign of Henry II (1154–89) when the whole of the area between the rivers Erewash and Derwent was royal forest. He is the unmistakable model for Peck's ballad for he too dreamed of the Cross on Lyndric hill and promptly repented, dismissing his followers and taking to a hermit's life in Deepdale. Peck edited and published Muskham's chronicle in 1732–5. In both his summary of the ballad and his edition of the chronicle he placed Dale in Lancashire – a surprising error for the other place names reveal detailed local knowledge. This simple mistake may well betray his authorship of this peculiar ditty.

The story may have moved Peck, but it had little popular appeal. In a cancelled note he commented: 'The song itself wholly new and never before printed.' It may well be that a repentant Robin seemed incongruous in a world accustomed to his trading blows with friars, beggars, tinkers and tanners. In other tales he remained violent – a 'bold' or 'merry' outlaw.

By the late sixteenth century such terms could be set in a new context of criminology. John Awdeley's *Fraternity of Vagabonds* of 1561 and Thomas Harman's *Caveat for Common Cursitors* of 1566 marked a treatment and categorization of crime and criminals quite unlike anything written in the Middle Ages. Yet the background of the rogues and vagabonds they described overlapped that of Robin Hood. One point of coincidence was with the Robin of the original legend. His robberies were justified by his victims' refusal honestly to declare their wealth. In like manner Harman's 'ruffler' justifies the robbery of an elderly victim who has unwittingly concealed his gold:

Good Lord, what a world is this! How may a man believe or trust in the same? See you not, this old knave told me that he had but seven shillings, and here is more by an angel. What an old knave and a false knave have we here![15]

Again in the later tradition of Robin presented in the ballads of combat there is more than a little of Awdeley's 'upright man':

An upright man is one that goeth with the truncheon of a staff, which staff they call a filchman. This man is of so much authority that, meeting with any of his profession, he may call them to account, and command a share or snap unto himself of all that they have gained by their trade in one month.[16]

Some of Robin's opponents bore similar criminal associations. Tinkers, in Harman's words, lived by 'picking and stealing, mingled with a little work for a colour'. Pedlars played the role of receivers and stood 'in great awe of the upright men, for they have often both wares and money of them'. *Robin Hood and the Pedlars* must have made a splendid story for pedlars rebelling in their imagination against the domination of the 'upright men', a story which the pedlars as packmen with ballads in their packs, must in all probability have helped to spread.

When in the 1660s William Winstanley produced *Poor Robin's Almanac* to compete with the officially licensed version of the Stationers' Company, he lightened dull chronology by including a list of villains' days along with the usual festivals. He drew up a 'Fanatick's Chronology', which began with Cain's murder of Abel and ended with the execution of the Regicides, and a 'Roundheads or Fanaticks Kalendar, with the names of their chief Ringleaders, most eminent for Villany'. There Robin, Little John and Friar Tuck figure among the villains along with the Pinder of Wakefield, Guy of Warwick, Jack of Newbury and Tom Thumb, not to mention Jack Cade, Joan of Arc, the Roman emperors Nero and Caligula, Cesare Borgia, Machiavelli, Copernicus and sundry others, real and fictional. Yet another compilation, the *Calendarium Astrologicum*, attributed to Thomas Trigge, which was designed for those visiting country markets, included in its issue for 1665 that Robin 'greatly molested the highways'. There need be no surprise that Smith included Robin in his *History of Highwaymen*. He made no bones about it, beginning the chapter with the heading 'Robin Hood a Highwayman and Murderer'. What followed was a refreshing, down-to-earth revision:

This bold robber, Robin Hood, was, some write, descended of the noble family of the earls of Huntingdon, but that is only fiction, for his birth was but very obscure, his pedigree *ab origine* being no higher than from poor shepherds, who for some time had lived in Nottinghamshire, in which county, at a little village adjacent to the forest of Sherwood, he was born in the reign of King Henry the Second. He was bred a butcher, but being of a very licentious, wicked inclination, he followed not his trade, but in the reign of King Richard the First, associating himself with several robbers and outlaws, he was chosen their captain.[17]

This was only one of several possible reputations. There was also the romantic Robin protecting London against the prince of Aragon. There was Munday's aristocratic Robin. There was the genial host of Henry VIII's maying. There was the Robin of the Tutbury bull-running. He had become multi-purpose. Imagination could roam in splendidly erratic fashion. Peck interpreted a version of *Robin Hood and the Scotchman*, which he included in his collection, as a Cavalier song, sung after the battle of Worcester of 1651, in which Robin Hood stood for Charles II and the Scotchman for the Scottish general, David Leslie. In yet another gloss on the ballad tradition Peck equated Richard I with Charles II, Saladin with Oliver Cromwell, the king's daughter with the realm of England, 'and what if by Robin Whood . . . he meant the Concern which every good man naturally feels stir in him for his distressed Country, when it is in a State of Slavery, as England was, in the Usurpate of Oliver Cromwell?' What indeed!

Whatever strange fantasies Robin's name aroused one was notably absent. So far no one had suggested that he stood for the oppressed Anglo-Saxon, the genuine Englishman struggling against the Norman oppressor. That role was foisted on him by Sir Walter Scott in *Ivanhoe* in 1820 and by Augustin Thierry in his *Histoire de la conquête de l'Angleterre par les normands* of 1825. There was nothing to support it. In placing his Locksley in Richard the Lionheart's reign Scott simply followed the traditional chronology for Robin originating with Major and now enshrined in Ritson's 'Life'. The rest was his own romantic inspiration. His historical premise that 'four generations had not sufficed to blend the hostile blood of the Normans and Anglo-Saxons, or to unite, by common language and mutual interests, two hostile races, one of which still felt the elation of triumph, while the other groaned under all the consequences of defeat' was false. Richard the Lionheart was Angevin by birth and Poitevin by experience. By his time statesmen had ceased to be concerned about the conflict between English and Norman and noted that among freemen the two could no longer be distinguished.

One final trait is noticeable, if not by its absence, then by the very minor part it retained in the composite picture of Robin Hood. That Robin robbed the rich and gave to the poor was now clearly enunciated. This was derived from the original tale of the knight and the abbot and from the social objectives which the author gave his hero in the opening stanzas of the *Gest*.[18] In 1521 Major commented that Robin and Little John took the goods of the rich and killed only those who tried to resist or attack them.

He permitted no harm to women, nor seized the goods of the poor, but helped them generously with what he took from abbots.[19]

The Elizabethan antiquary, John Stow, had much the same story:

Poor men's goods he spared, abundantly relieving them with that which by theft he got from abbeys and houses of rich earls.[20]

Parker embodied it in the poetic tradition in *The True Tale* of 1632 (51–3):

> *Poore men might safely passe by him,*
> *And some that way would chuse,*
> *For well they knew that to helpe them*
> *He evermore did use.*
>
> *But where he knew a miser rich,*
> *That did the poore oppresse,*
> *To feele his coyne his hand did itch;*
> *Hee'de have it, more or lesse.*
>
> *And sometimes, when the high-way fayld,*
> *Then he his courage rouses;*
> *He and his men have oft assayld*
> *Such rich men in their houses.*

None of this had much immediate effect. *The True Tale* was reprinted in 1686 at the height of the great trade in the ballads, but Parker's doctrine failed to spread into the popular tales which became its common jargon. Peck noted that

> *Priests parted with their Gold t'increase their Store,*
> *But never would they rob or wrong the Poor*

but the plain truth was that an outlaw who fought with beggars and tinkers and tried to waylay pedlars was not characterized by a desire to assist those in poverty-stricken distress. Robbing the rich to give to the poor was very much Parker's special slant. It was reinforced by the role which Robin came to play in collecting money at the spring festival, which is discussed in the Postscript. But the weight which it ultimately acquired came largely from one man, Joseph Ritson.

Ritson made an enormous contribution to the study of Robin Hood. His is the first comprehensive collection of the ballads and the earlier tales. He established many of the texts, and proved a cantankerous critic of Percy who had tampered with some of them. But Ritson's own scholarship was not invulnerable. In accepting the traditional identification of Robin Hood he was quite uncritical.[21] And in backing

Parker he surrendered to his own political predilections. These were somewhat volatile. He began as a Jacobite and ended as a Jacobin. He was also one of the first vegetarians. He could scarcely make Robin a vegetarian but he certainly reconstructed him in the image of a radical:

a man who, in a barbarous age, and under a complicated tyranny, displayed a spirit of freedom and independence which has endeared him to the common people, whose cause he maintained (for all opposition to tyranny is the cause of the people), and, in spite of the malicious endeavours of pitiful monks, by whom history was consecrated to the crimes and follies of titled ruffians and sainted idiots, to suppress all record of his patriotic exertions and virtuous acts, will render his name immortal.[22]

This was new. With Parker, Robin's gifts to the poor illustrate Christian charity and penitence for crime rather than any deliberately conceived social policy. Parker was no revolutionary. He became an ardent royalist, best remembered for his *When the King Enjoys His Own Again*. Ritson was different. Politically, in different circumstances a century and a half later, he went the other way, and transformed Robin into a social rebel.

This was imposed on the legend. The popular ballads still current in the eighteenth century, like the terminal growth of a great oak, stemmed from the original root. The work of Ritson and Scott, each fashioned in its own way, clung to it like ivy. Some, like Keats, sensed with poignancy that the tree was now dead.

> *Gone, the merry morris din;*
> *Gone, the song of Gamelyn;*
> *Gone, the tough-belted outlaw*
> *Idling in the 'grene shawe';*
> *All are gone away and past!*
> *And if Robin should be cast*
> *Sudden from his turfed grave,*
> *And if Marian should have*
> *Once again her forest days,*
> *She would weep, and he would craze:*
> *He would swear, for all his oaks,*
> *Fall'n beneath the dockyard strokes,*
> *Have rotted on the briny seas;*
> *She would weep that her wild bees*
> *Sang not to her — strange! that honey*
> *Can't be got without hard money!*[23]

Keats was right about the past but wrong about the future. 'Hard money', among other influences, ensured Robin's continued vigour. Keats composed his poem in 1818. *Ivanhoe* followed in 1820, Thomas Love Peacock's *Maid Marion* in 1822, Thierry's *History* in 1825. Pierce Egan's *Robin Hood and Little John* in 1840 was the first comprehensive story deliberately written for children. Indeed, Peck had already answered Keats:

A man would think that when Robin Whood (or anybody else) is once dead and buried, and a good hard stone laid upon his Belly; nothing would fetch him to life again, but a Miracle. And yet, here you see, Robin Whood is revived? Why, yes: Tom Thumb lived in the days of King Arthur and revived in the days of King Edgar. And why then might not Robin Whood live in the days of King Richard I and revive in the days of King Charles II?

Artistic licence, in short, covered all. And the romantic interest in the medieval past which Ritson foreshadowed and Scott expressed was concerned more with atmosphere than accuracy. Tennyson began *The Foresters* with Sir Richard Lee, like some distressed Victorian gentleman, eating 'his heart for want of money to pay the Abbot', and turned Maid Marian into Sir Richard's daughter. Robin was rendered neo-Gothic. This was the first of many transmutations he has suffered in novel, poem, theatre, movie and television play in the last hundred years.

# VIII

## *Postscript*

The surname 'Robinhood' is the earliest indication there is of the legend. Such a name-formation – of a given name and a surname in a combined surname – is very rare. 'Robinhood' probably provides the best early example. The name invites explanation. The most likely is that a man so called, and those who gave him the name, knew something of Robin Hood. It would follow, therefore, that the legend was in circulation by the time such names were used.

In 1981, when the first edition of this book was written, only a very few such names were known. These occur in London and in Sussex; one such name, coming from Fletching, Sussex, seemed particularly significant because of its early date, 1296, and because Fletching was a manor of Thomas of Lancaster.[1] Since 1981 more thirteenth-century examples of such names have been found: not a lot, but enough. Altogether seven further examples have been collected, all dated between 1261 and 1296. These have come to hand casually. No sane man goes in search of 'Robinhood' or any other unusual surnames through unprinted and unindexed government records. So the names have been collected in the course of other work, and no doubt others will come to light in the course of time.

The collection made so far is none the less of great significance. Two such names come from Huntingdonshire, two from Hampshire, one from each of the counties of Suffolk, Essex and Berkshire; if the example from Fletching, Sussex, is added, it is plain that there is a total concentration in south-eastern England. This distribution is probably insignificant: it simply reflects the fact that far more judicial records survive for south-eastern England than for the north and that they happen to have been studied more intensively during the last few years. But the spread can only mean that 'Robinhood' was widely known and used in counties far away from Robin's home ground of Barnsdale and Sherwood. If the interpretation of the name is correct, the legend must have become a national one by the second half of the thirteenth century.

The new evidence leaves no real doubt that the interpretation is indeed correct, for in a high proportion of these cases the 'Robinhoods' were suspected or outlawed criminals. Of the total of eight names, only three are behaviourly nondescript. Gilbert Robynhod of Fletching was apparently peacefully submitting to his tax assessment in 1296, and the two examples from Huntingdonshire, from 1285 and 1296, were to all appearances law abiding. But, as for the rest: Alexander Robehod was sought for theft in Essex in 1272; Gilbert Robehod was released to pledges by the justices after an unspecified charge in Suffolk in 1286; Robert Robehod was indicted in Hampshire in 1294 on a charge of stealing sheep, a crime somehow inappropriate to the name; John Rabunhod, of rougher metal, was charged with others in 1272 with the murder of John son of Simon after a quarrelsome brawl in a tavern near Fareham, Hampshire; he had promptly fled and was outlawed; finally William Robehod appears in Berkshire in 1261–2 as a member of an outlaw gang suspected of robberies and of harbouring robbers. Now names are found in the context in which they are sought. All these come from the plea rolls; it is therefore no surprise that these 'Robinhoods' were criminals, suspects or outlaws. Still, the names are found on the criminal, not the civil, side of the courts' record, and, whatever the impression of a balanced selection drawn from all classes of record might be, these instances surely suggest that 'Robinhood' had become a criminal nickname. It was not without familiar company: in 1292 a Little John and a Petit Johan were both appealed of robbery.

   Much the most important of these cases is the earliest of all, William Robehod who appears in Berkshire in 1261–2, which was discovered by Dr David Crook. This comes from the King's Remembrancer's Memoranda Roll of Easter 1262 where it is noted that the King had pardoned the penalty of one mark imposed on the prior of Sandleford for seizing without warrant the chattels of William Robehod, fugitive. Presumably the prior had claimed the chattels as the fugitive's lord; he came from Enborne where the priory held land. As matters rest, this is the earliest of all the Robinhood surnames. But that is not all. For, by the luckiest chance of survival, the entry on the Memoranda Roll can be matched with the record of the same case on the roll of the Justices in Eyre in Berkshire in 1261. This is an indictment of a criminal gang, three men and two women, suspected of robberies and the harbouring of robbers, who had fled the jurisdiction of the court and were duly outlawed. They included William son of Robert le Fevere (Fevre = Smith), whose chattels, worth 2s. 6d., had been seized by the prior of Sandleford without warrant. This makes it certain that the William son of Robert le Fevere of the Plea Roll and the William Robehod of the Memoranda Roll were one and the same person. So someone along the administrative chain between the Justices in Eyre and the Remembrancer in the Exchequer, one of the clerks, perhaps even the Remembrancer's clerk, changed the name. And what led him to do so was that William son of Robert had Robert in his name and was a member of an outlaw gang indicted for robbery. So he became William Robehod. It follows that the man who changed the name knew of the legend. The earliest reference to Robin Hood must now therefore be taken to be not 1377 but 1261–2. In all senses that is an enormous advance.

The first consequence of this is to establish 1261–2 as a *terminus ante quem*. Obviously any subsequent Robin Hood may have added to the legend, but he cannot have originated it. So much scholarship concerned to establish the 'original' Robin Hood in south Yorkshire in the 1320s, itself suspect on other grounds, can now be even more firmly jettisoned.[2] The Robert Hod, fugitive, of the York assizes of 1225, now has a clearer field; indeed, the nickname which he was given on the Pipe Roll of 1226, Hobbehod, may well reflect the emergence of the legend.[3] Old, well-known evidence, which has been played down in recent years, suddenly looks refreshed. The Scottish historian, John Major, writing in 1521, believed that Robin Hood and Little John were active in 1193–4. The epitaph left by Thomas Gale in 1702 recorded that Robin died in 1247.[4] If we arrange all these items chronologically we seem to have the shadowy outline of a biography: Robin active in the 1190s, an outlaw in 1225, dead in 1247, an interval exactly matching his twenty-two years in the greenwood in the *Gest*; then a figure of legend by 1262. There is nothing to prove it, but it is not impossible. It would make Robin long lived, but no more so than Fulk fitz Warin, another outlaw hero and the original of the romance named after him, who was active in 1200 and did not die until 1256–7.[5] It would also require a quick generation of the legend, perhaps even beginning in Robin's lifetime. But this too is not impossible. Fulk fitz Warin died in 1256–7. The first surviving MS of *Fouke Le Fitz Waryn* was written 1325–40, but this was not the first version, and his story, as we have it, probably drew directly on in-formation from Fulk himself or from someone who knew him. The Romance of Eustace the Monk was also written very soon after Eustace's death.[6] Finally, we may note that Robert Hod was a tenant of the archbishopric of York and that Thomas Gale, who recorded the epitaph, so wondrously convenient in its arithmetic, was Dean of York; he may therefore have had access to local information. So, in a tendentious fashion, it can all be made to work.

Yet there are good reasons for not relying on such a neat and easy solution. One is that this chronology locates Robin in the disturbances led by Count John during Richard Lionheart's crusade, in the reign of John as King and in the civil war which ended it, and in the minority of Henry III. From John's accession in 1199 the record of the day-to-day workings of government becomes ever more complete; the minority of Henry III encouraged a mass of informal correspondence between the governing magnates. If Robin was important enough to generate a legend he could perhaps be expected to figure somewhere in this mass of material other than in the single Pipe Roll entry of 1225 and subsequent years. In particular, if he was active in Sherwood we might expect some recorded reaction from that frequent visitor to Clipstone, King John. Nothing is apparent.

There is also another much more powerful objection. The real importance of the Berkshire case of 1261–2 is that it reveals how a Robin Hood was created and how his legend might have grown. William son of Robert le Fevere was a member of an outlaw gang indicted for robbery. So, in the mind of the clerk who changed the name, he became William Robehod. That confusion of a real criminal with the legend of a criminal hero takes us to the area of consciousness where fact and fiction mingled and the growing legend struck its roots. For, unless we are to say that the legend is all fiction, which is demonstrably wrong, we must construct some explanation of its factual content. And the Berkshire example suggests one, namely this: that there was not just one 'original' Robin Hood, real or fictional, but many. Each one acknowledged the legend by adopting the surname or by accepting it from others. Each one contributed to it and thereby became difficult to distinguish from the legend itself. Each one was real, committing real crimes, engaged in real adventures; but each one was moulded by the legend he adopted or had imposed upon him with the name, and each one allowed or ensured that his own activities might in turn be embodied in the tale; the whole exchange from fact to legend and legend to fact being decorated all the time with purely fictional embroidery.

Such a process was common enough. In Kent in 1313, for example, among those sought on charges of homicide was 'Johannes dictus Petit Jehan de Shorne' – John of Shorne, called Little John. The alias or nickname was part both of the common equipment of the criminal and of the community's reaction to him. The answer then to the question 'Who was Robin Hood?', must be 'There were more than one.'

That still leaves room for an original, but there can be no certainty as to who it may have been. For the use of the alias casts doubt on every Robin Hood. All the surnames or nicknames must be spurious. The Robert Hod of the Pipe Roll of 1225 is less likely to be so, but even that, with its form Hobbehod in 1226, is not entirely beyond suspicion. The search for Robin Hood, therefore, ends in obscurity created by his own fame. Real people move in the shadows, their crimes revealed before the courts, but by borrowing his reputation they dissolved his identity.

Other matters become a little simpler. It is easier to understand how crime and fiction intermingled. A suspect or outlaw might adopt or acquire the name in random fashion. If so, we no longer need to look for criminal likenesses who bore the name. Roger Godberd now looks even more convincing as a contributor in some way to the tale of Robin and the knight. Roger was the leader of an outlaw gang; he was pursued by a posse; he was protected by a knight whose estates were scattered between the verges of Sherwood and the neighbourhood of Barnsdale; and, if the final charges laid against him are correct, he and other malefactors robbed an abbey of a great sum of money, horses and other goods, and slew a monk; unfortunately it was the abbey of Stanley, Wiltshire, and not St Mary's, York.[7] Likewise, as Dr David Crook has suggested, it may be that the tale of Guy of Gisburn somehow embodies the grim demise in 1225 of Robert of Wetherby whom the sheriff of Yorkshire was instructed to 'seek, take and behead' as an 'outlaw and evildoer of our land', and who was quickly caught and hanged in chains.

There are two further consequences of the early dating which the new evidence has confirmed. Hitherto literary scholars, relying on the passage in Piers Plowman in 1377 as the earliest reference to the legend, have assumed very reasonably that the analogues shared by the tales of Robin, Fulk fitz Warin and Eustace the Monk came from one-way traffic, from the knightly romances to the yeoman ballads. It is now apparent that they were all taking shape at one and the same time. It is easier to understand how they came to share material, but it can no longer be so certain which was the source and which the recipient. It may be that the romances and the Robin Hood tales alike drew on a common fund of fictional situations and adventures which each adapted to its purpose. It is no longer certain, as it seemed in the past, that a legend written in English tapped sources written in French.

There remains the most difficult problem of all. What was the content of the legend in its earliest form or forms? Hitherto the relatively short span of time between the old date of 1377 and the earliest manuscript tales of *c.*1450 has not attracted much attention, perhaps because it has not seemed too wide or too difficult to bridge. But an interval stretching back from 1450 to before 1261–2 is a much more serious gap. We can assume that the clerk who gave the nickname Robehod to William son of Robert le Fevere in 1261–2 knew some sort of tale of Robin Hood. But we do not know whether it was oral or written. And we certainly cannot tell how, if at all, it was related to the diversified tales which survive as written verse from the middle of the fifteenth century. There are only two threads stretching across those two hundred years or more. In 1261–2 as in 1450 the context was crime: Robin Hood was a criminal hero. And at both the earlier and later dates the tale circulated within the civil service.

For the rest, there is very little to go on. A literary investigation cannot proceed without written evidence. We cannot know what the legend was like in 1261–2. We do not know how much of it was lost by 1450. We know very little of what was added during this interval of two hundred years. We do not even know how much of the legend has survived in the written versions which remain.

Yet something can be attempted. First, it is worth recalling the few indications there are of stages in the development of the legend. In reverse chronological order these are:

1. Maid Marion became Robin's partner in the May Games between 1450 and 1500. She was derived from a French pastoral play and was probably carried into English traditions by John Gower.
2. Reynold Greenleaf, an alias of Little John, was part of the legend by 1432 when he appears in the parliamentary return for Wiltshire.
3. Friar Tuck entered the legend after 1417 when the name was adopted, apparently for the first time, by Robert Stafford.
4. The section of the legend which deals with the visit to Sherwood of 'Edward our comely king' tallies exactly with Edward II's journey through the northern counties in 1323 and with no other royal progress. It cannot therefore have been embodied in the tales until after that date. That means that in 1323 fyttes seven and eight of the *Gest* and the components on which they were based cannot yet have been written in their present form. It is only this last instance which reveals anything of the state of the legend well before 1450. It is not a rich haul. But at least it illustrates how and when new material was embodied as time passed.

There is one further possible indication to which Dr Peter Coss has recently drawn attention. In fytte one of the *Gest*, in his first encounter with Robin, the knight is about to depart on a crusade or pilgrimage to the Holy Land (56, 57):

> '*Hastely I wol me buske,*' *sayd the knyght,*
> '*Over the salte see,*
>
> '*And se where Criste was quyke and dede,*
> '*On the mount of Calvere*';

It then appears in fytte two of the *Gest* that that indeed is where he went. Not only does the prior of St Mary's say that he is 'far beyond the sea' (89) but also the knight himself, before entering the abbey, tells his company to put on their 'symple wedes' that they had 'brought from the sea' (97). Now there is nothing intrusive in the knight indicating to Robin that he was resolved upon a pilgrimage. But that he actually went, that he returned to St Mary's 'from the sea' is a different matter. There is nothing else of that in the *Gest*, and it suggests, as Dr Coss rightly points out, that an independent story of a pilgrim or crusading knight returning to redeem lands pledged to St Mary's may underlie this section of the *Gest*. Indeed more could be made of it, for Yorkshire knights marked their departure for the Third Crusade in 1190 by massacring the Jews of York and burning their bonds before the high altar in the Minster. Monasteries traded in Jewish bonds and made their own covert loans to landed debtors. If Dr Coss is right the tale is likely to reflect these conditions before all others. It must have been absorbed into the Robin Hood legend early in its formation when they were still well remembered and worth recalling.

That is all there is to fill the gap. Much of the tradition must have been oral, the more so the further back in time; and an oral tradition by definition leaves nothing in writing. Visual representation is infrequent and of very uncertain identity before the age of the illustrated printed versions. At St Mary's, Beverley, the church of the Beverley gild of minstrels which preserves much minstrel iconography, there is a misericord of *c.* 1450 which probably represents Robin Hood and the King.[8] In Beverley Minster, among the sculptures in the north aisle which celebrate the work of the local minstrels, there is a spandrel bearing a splendid longbowman, all the more remarkable because he is presented, not as usual in action with bow drawn, but hooded and leaning on his bow in casual style. It is as if the sculptor were recalling the ditty 'Robin Hood in Sherwood [Barnsdale] stood'.[9] The date is *c.* 1340. These are the only two possibilities which an optimistic search for illustration has yielded. There are illustrations of archery in plenty, some of which are reproduced in this book, but apparently there are no others which might have been inspired by the tales of Robin Hood, except in so far as all of them celebrate the skills of the archer.

So we come to a dead end. This is not surprising. It may be that the early written versions of the tales mislead us. They provide texts, a literary corpus, the appearance of firm ground. But they were not necessarily the same as the 'rhymes' which Langland knew or the 'Joly Robin' of Chaucer's *Troilus and Crysede*. The impression of the early evidence is of casual survival: scattered literary allusions from widely different contexts; occasional references in records in the Court of Common Pleas, in a parliamentary return, in petitions and legal actions; even the inconsequential entry of a nonsensical ditty in a fragment of a royal household account subsequently used as fly-leaves to a work of St Thomas Aquinas.[10] It all suggests a wide substratum of oral tradition surfacing here and there, sometimes when an allusion was appropriate, sometimes even as mere doodling. That is consistent with transmission by word of mouth, by minstrelsy more or less professional, and by less formal repetition in varied circumstances, to companions, to juveniles, even to oneself. This was the market within which the manuscript versions found a niche and at which the mass production of the printed versions was later aimed. The survival of written versions reflects nothing more than that from the middle of the fourteenth century more and more English was being written.

The relationship between the substratum of tradition and its literary manifestation is well illustrated by Robin's most enduring characteristic: that he robbed the rich and gave to the poor. Such a doctrine is highly convenient to the criminal. It is sound outlaw practice to maintain a clientele. The poor can be bought; they are not worth robbing; they can provide food and shelter, safe hiding for men and loot, and a network of protection and intelligence. Circumstances wed criminal and poor. So it is no surprise that in the late ballad *Robin Hood and the Bishop* Robin is given shelter by an old woman in return for past favours (9):

> For I well remember, one Saturday night
> Thou bought me both shoos and hose;

Yet there is not a lot in the surviving ballads of Robin's alleged social purpose. In the *Gest* the tale of the knight may be so interpreted; Robin's instructions to Little John are aimed against power and wealth in support of the more humble, although the line is curiously drawn; and the closing stanza tells us that he 'did poor men much good'. These passages seem to underlie the later statements of Major and Stow that Robin robbed abbots and was kind to the poor, but they are scarcely a sufficient source of the more fully developed expression of the theme in Martin Parker's *True Tale* of 1632, still less for the deeply embedded tradition which has survived to the present day.[11] The explanation of this may be that the real source lay not in literature but in pageant, in the role which Robin played in the May Games or spring festival.

By the end of the fifteenth century Robin figured in the spring festival in widely scattered centres in southern England.[12] The geographic distribution is not significant. He also appears in Scotland. Quite apart from that, much of the evidence is taken from church wardens' accounts, and from the period up to 1600 these survive in considerable numbers for the southern province but to a much less degree for the province of York. The likelihood is that his participation was much more widespread than the surviving evidence reveals. In 1500 it was probably through the May Games that Robin was most widely known. This prepared the ground for the proliferation of the broadside and chapbook tales from the later sixteenth century.

The celebration of the spring festival is of course very ancient. In medieval England it began with youths and maidens returning from the woods at dawn decked with sprigs, branches and flowers. As they processed they adorned houses and sought contributions for their display. This collection, 'gathering', or *quête* was an essential part of such processions. Now there was nothing more natural than that the most famous of all denizens of the greenwood should accompany the youth of the parish on their return, and there was no more suitable role for the most successful of all robbers than that he should be put to the charitable purpose of conducting the *quête*. For that is plainly what Robin did. Robin Hood's 'gatherings', which appear in local records before the end of the fifteenth century, are not riotous assemblies of men but charitable collections of money.

In some southern townships, especially at Reading and Kingston on Thames, such celebrations were highly organized; they were controlled by the church wardens and are recorded in their accounts. First, the wardens provided for the expenses of the display: at Kingston in 1509, 12s. 10d. for a piece of Kendal cloth for the coats of Robin and Little John, 3s. for three yards of white cloth for the friar's habit, 3s. 4d. for four yards of Kendal for Maid Marion's hooded cloak, 4½d. for gloves for Marion and Robin and 6d. for six broad arrows. There were also payments for meat and drink for Robin and his company, the largest item being 2s. 8d. for two kilderkins of three-halfpenny beer. Secondly, Robin and his companions must have accounted for their collection to the wardens because the wardens noted the receipts from the 'gathering': at Kingston in 1506, 39s. 10d. 'received of Robin Hood's gathering from Whitsunday unto Fair Day at night', and in 1509 as much as 4 marks 20d. 'received at the Kingham and for the gathering of Robin Hood'. Thirdly, the accounts indicate how the 'gathering' was done, namely by the sale of 'liveries' or pins to the contributors. The numbers involved are astonishing. In 1506 the wardens at Kingston recorded the expenditure of 4s. 2d. paid to John Painter for 1,000 liveries, 3s. 8d. paid to William Plott for 1,200 liveries and 40 large ones, and 10d. to the same for 2,500 pins. The arrangements at Reading were much the same: payments for the dress of Robin or Marion or both in 1501, 1503, 1505; receipts from the 'gathering' recorded in 1498, 1503, 1507; payments for liveries and pins in 1501, although not in such large numbers as at Kingston. In each town there is some hint of a professional touch. At Kingston in 1509 Maid Marion was paid 2s. 'for her labour for two years'; at Reading there were visits by Robin Hood and his company from both Henley and Finchampstead. At both centres Robin's pageant was part of more general entertainment involving morris dancers, taborers, lutists and minstrels; at Reading in 1501 6d. was paid to minstrels 'at the choosing of Robin Hood'.

In this Robin Hood intermingled with an old tradition going back at least to the early fourteenth century in which liturgical plays were performed in church or churchyard and the receipts made over to the church. But he gave it his own flavour. Presumably the purchase of a livery or pin identified the purchaser as a member of Robin's company or *meinie*. Presumably also the methods used were vigorous enough to remind the contributor of robbery. At Willenhall in 1498 Robin and his men were accused of riotous assembly. His reply was that as of old he and the Abbot of Marham had come to town 'to gather money with their disports to the profit of the churches'. So Robin 'gathered' from the rich, from those who had money to buy a favour. That he gave to the poor was less obvious. The money went to the wardens, to those who managed the affairs of the local church, and in the varied arrangements for poor relief which existed before the poor rate and the Elizabethan poor law, the church wardens were called upon to assist only from place to place and occasion to occasion. That Robin took from the rich and gave to the poor could have come about by an easy elision of associations. It could equally have been a brain-wave of some long-forgotten anonymous church warden who envisaged harnessing Robin's reputation to this end. For who was to complain if the money went not on the relief of the poor but on the repair of the church fabric? At all events it is likely that Robin's 'gatherings' left this most enduring mark upon his reputation. He had become the chief collector in a Flag Day.

Such are the main developments in the study of Robin Hood since the first edition of this book was written in 1981. In what ways has the problem changed as a result?

First, and most important, the early date placing the origin of the legend and the 'original' Robin no later than the first half of the thirteenth century, is now beyond serious doubt. The only way to stretch this time limit is by arguing that he became a legend in his own lifetime; and that would only stretch it a little, on no sound ground and to no great effect. So the tentative arguments advanced eight years ago, though still valid, are no longer so necessary. The matter is settled by the evidence of the Robinhood surnames.

This confirmation of the early dating is a great advance. Unquestionably it adds strength to the case for regarding that Robert Hod recorded in the Pipe Roll of 1225 as the 'original', but there is no proof and total commitment to him is still guesswork. For the earliest known surname of all, from 1261–2, indicates how a Robin Hood could be invented. It demonstrates what has always been a possibility, that any outlaw Robin Hood may be an alias. But, if this adds to the difficulty of finding the 'original', it also adds to our understanding of how fact and fiction might mingle – the activity of real outlaws with tales of outlaw actions drawn from fact or fiction. Along with Robert Hod, Eustace of Lowdham assumes greater prominence as a possible prototype of the sheriff, and Roger Godberd, who like Eustace, links Nottinghamshire and Yorkshire, looks a likelier contributor.

However, the main effect of the newly confirmed dating is to open up a vast gulf between the origin of the legend in the middle of the thirteenth century and the first manuscript versions of *c.* 1450. Within this period it is still reasonable to conjecture that the story of Robin Hood, the knight and the abbot of St Mary's was perhaps the first to take shape. Its theme is on balance more fitting for a thirteenth-century audience, and its social flavour is more knightly, hinting at a literary milieu where interchange with the romances might take place. It may be underlain by an earlier tale in which the knight participates in the Crusade or visits the Holy Land. But Edward II's northern progress of 1323 still remains as the one factual element in this long prehistory of the legend. The sections of the *Gest* describing the visit to Sherwood of 'Edward our comely king' must have taken shape after that date. There is still no way of telling how and when the Barnsdale and Sherwood elements of the legend came together.

The new suggestions about the May Games provide some explanation of the pervasiveness of the notion that Robin robbed the rich and gave to the poor. They also indicate how the wider market for the cheap printed versions of the sixteenth and seventeenth centuries originated.

But these were relatively late developments.

The aristocratic and knightly household was at first the main agency in sustaining the performers and providing the audience, and hence in spreading and developing the tale. The importance of the combined honours of Lacy and Lancaster in this matter is indicated by links not only between Barnsdale and Sussex, but also between Pontefract and the Lacy and Lancastrian estates north of Clitheroe. Similar links can be suggested to explain the amalgam of Sherwood and Barnsdale and the incorporation of Friar Tuck in the story. There is no direct evidence before John Paston's well-known reference of 1473 that the legend was so rooted, but it is plain that the earliest tales were primarily addressed to yeomen of the household. They reflect the skills, ambitions and the social assumptions of these men and the conventions of service and reward of the world in which they moved. The earliest tales fit no other context.

The legend developed rapidly. By the end of the fifteenth century Robin was known in Scotland and in a wide scatter of towns and villages in northern and southern England in which he appears in the May Games and where his trail was soon to be marked by derivative place names. The tale was carried out from the household to the tavern and the market-place so that it became familiar to clerks, townsfolk and husbandmen. Judges and gentry also knew it. And it diversified with the audience. In the sixteenth century Robin might be a noble, the fictional earl of Huntington, or king of May, or a gang-leader challenging and challenged by rustics and tradesmen. He was a fit topic for court theatre in one direction and of penny broadsheet ballads in another.

The tales are entertainments, adventure stories. But they are set against a realistic background. In their earliest form they call on a number of responses: against monastic wealth, against the royal forest law and against the local sheriff. But they contain no programme of reform. They do not even cock a snook against all forms of authority, for Robin and his men revere the king.

Robin stands outside the law as an honourable criminal, and the audience is asked to take the outlaw's side. But he was also widely recognized as a riotous marauder. To the staid and respectable his tales were ribaldry. The king's deer apart, his challenge is not to the law itself, still less to the social structure which it cemented, but rather to the manner in which both were corrupted and exploited by men of power and wealth. He changes neither law nor society. He simply procures justice within them by guile and violence. His criminal characteristics are never lost. If anything they were appreciated more keenly in the diverse forms of the story of the seventeenth century. But in all its forms the tale is less a social protest than a form of escape. Robin the social rebel is a later invention.

In recent years some historians have sought to illuminate the past by studying single incidents or events which they have examined in all their social and psychological ramifications. The study of Robin Hood is more difficult. It requires a similar method, for a story, like an incident, can only be fully understood when set in its proper context. But, unlike an incident or a set of events, a story is not fixed in time and place. It provides a continually shifting point of focus. As the circumstances which sustain it change – the audience, the means of communication, the social assumptions and conventions, the intellectual milieu – so the story itself changes. And there is a time-lag. Whatever a new generation makes of such a tale, something of the older appreciation of it is likely to survive. So the relationship of the content of a story to its context involves complex chronology. How otherwise could it come about that a children's hero in the twentieth century should owe his triumphs to the bow and arrow?

This book has sought to clear a path through these difficulties. It does not claim to reduce them to simplicity. Many tasks remain. The earliest stories of Robin still call for modern linguistic analysis; that is how a more precise date for the compilation of the *Gest* is most likely to be established. Much also remains to be done on the social terminology of the later Middle Ages. The development of the popular market for literature in the seventeenth century is still not fully explored. Work in these and other areas may, and should, affect the analysis and suggestions put forward in the preceding pages.

Certain principles will stand. Robin Hood's popularity does not justify pretence. There should be no room for pseudo-history expressing local patriotism or commercial interest. And if Robin is taken over as an expression of present-day social malaise or discontent, so be it. But that is no excuse for advancing modern fiction as an explanation of medieval fact.

But legend is fact of a very peculiar kind. At one and the same time it illuminates and distorts. Of the tale of Robin Hood this is doubly true. It does not, like one of Robin's arrows, cleave direct to the heart of its stock. It is more like a fragmentary section, erratically cut, which records only part of the timber's grain. What the original story was really like, how the plant took root and grew and in what sort of soil, are matters for patient reconstruction. But when that work is done a further task remains. The fancy present in all legends falsifies, and fancy saturates the tale of Robin Hood. It made heroes of outlaws. It confused violence and crime with justice and charity. In bridging the gap between the real and ideal world it presented some of the social problems of the Middle Ages as sharply cut issues of right and wrong. In this it achieved an enduring confidence trick. Playwrights may surrender to it. Sociologists may compound it. We can all enjoy it. But it is also useful to uncover it and understand what made it possible.

# Notes

## I Prologue

**1** *Journal of American Folklore*, lxxix (1966), p. 350.
**2** R. Graves, *The English Ballad* (London 1927), p. 133.
**3** See below, p. 69.
**4** See below, pp. 52–3, 102–6.

## II The Legend

**1** Of the five printed versions three are fragmentary. None of the five provides a prime text. They naturally differ in detail one from another, but they also share a number of defects which must be derived from a common source. These include: the omission of the first line of stanza 7 and the first line of stanza 87 in all three versions which include these stanzas and the omission of the first line of stanza 98 in the two versions which include it. In all these instances one of the defective versions is a relatively late one of *c.* 1560. The defects seem to have been inherent in the known text.
**2** The main argument for an early date of *c.* 1400 is the survival in the printed text of some Middle-English forms, in particular the final *-e* and *-es* as regular inflexional word-endings (Child, iii, p. 40; Clawson, pp. 6, 128). These features appear throughout the poem. As Clawson pointed out, it is more likely that the *Gest* embodied Middle-English forms which were slowly eroded as the poem went through successive versions before it reached print, than that it was composed at a later date of component ballads all of which happened to retain *-e* and *-es* word-endings. It should be noted, however, that the question has not been re-examined in detail by linguistic scholars since Clawson wrote in 1909.
**3** The friar is named 'Tuck' in the title added by the scribe of the Percy Folio. In the ballad itself he appears simply as the 'cutted' (short-frocked) friar.

**4** See below, pp. 58–9.
**5** B Text. Passus V, lines 394–5. Ed. George Kane and E. Talbot Donaldson (London 1975), p. 331.
**6** Local guides to Alnwick (Northumberland) claim an earlier reference in a poem on the battle of Dunbar (1296) attributed to William of Coldingham, prior of Alnwick, and written *c.* 1304. This is an error apparently derived from G. Tate, *History of the Borough Castle and Barony of Alnwick* (Alnwick 1866–9) ii, pp. 12–13, where Tate mistakenly treated an analogy between William Wallace and Robin Hood drawn by Francis Peck, the eighteenth-century antiquary, in the title he gave to the poem in his collection, as part of the body of the text. This allusion, therefore, is no earlier than the eighteenth century. The poem, which Peck included with other material on the abbey of Alnwick, in his collection on Premonstratensian houses (B.L., Sloane MS 4934, fol. 103r) is edited by T. Wright (1839) pp. 160–79. On Peck's collections see H. M. Colvin, 'The Registrum Premonstratense: A Lost MS Rediscovered', *Journal of Ecclesiastical History*, viii (1957), pp. 96–7. See also below, pp. 180–1.
**7** See below, pp. 38–9.
**8** See below, p. 38.
**9** Fowler (1968), pp. 73–80.
**10** This is discussed in Chapter 5.
**11** See Clawson (1909), especially pp. 125–7. Clawson may have been a little too ready to multiply the number of separate components which must have underlain the *Gest* and to assume that those components already took the form of ballads. None the less his work remains fundamental to the study of the poem.
**12** I find the suggestion (Fowler, pp. 79–80) that *Robin Hoode his Death* was 'inspired' by the closing verses of the *Gest* unconvincing. The story in the *Gest* is restricted to five stanzas which

leave the 'false playe' of the prioress and Sir Roger of Doncaster quite un-explored. They read very much as a summary designed for listeners who would already know the tale of Robin's death in greater detail.

**13** The fragment is now preserved in the library of Trinity College, Cambridge. It is commonly argued that it is derived from the household of Sir John Paston where plays of Robin Hood were performed in 1473. This is based on the fact that in the eighteenth century the fragment was in the possession of the antiquary, Peter le Neve, who also acquired the Paston letters. However, it should be noted that le Neve collected much miscellaneous material and that the accountant in the fragment, John Sterndale, does not apparently figure in the Paston letters.

**14** The earlier version of *Robin Hoode his Death* comes from the Percy Folio; the later versions are derived from garlands. The dramatic version of *Robin Hood and the Potter* was printed in 1634, well over a century after the MS version was written. The earlier version of *Robin Hood and the Curtal Friar* comes from the Percy Folio, the later versions are from late seventeenth-century garlands and collections. There are also multiple versions of many of the later ballads, on which see below, pp. 163–74.

**15** E. J. Hobsbawm, *Primitive Rebels* (Manchester 1971), pp. 4, 13.

**16** Hilton (1958), pp. 30, 41.

**17** Wright (1839), p. 152.

*III  Who was Robin Hood?*

**1** *The Original Chronicle of Andrew de Wyntoun*, ed. F. J. Amours (Scottish Text Society 1907), v, pp. 136–7.

**2** *Johannis de Fordun Scotichronicon*, ed. T. Hearne (Oxford 1722), iii, p. 774.

**3** See below, pp. 44, 184.

**4** Gough, p. cviii. In 1715 the Yorkshire antiquary Ralph Thoresby had already commented: 'Near unto [Kirklees] the noted Robin Hood lies buried under a grave-stone that yet

remains near the park, but the Inscription scarce legible' (*Ducatus Leodensis*, p. 91).

**5** 'Apparently' because the manuscript is damaged at this point (B.L., Sloane MS 780, fols. 46–48v).

**6** Ritson, i, pp. xlvi–xlvii.

**7** Child, iii, p. 233.

**8** W. Stukeley, *Palaeographia Britannica*, part 2 (Stamford 1746), p. 115. It seems that Stukeley was primarily responsible for converting Huntington to Huntingdon. The change was probably of little significance since both spellings are recorded for the place name Huntington, although not apparently for Huntingdon itself.

**8a** Since Mr J. Lees (*The Quest for Robin Hood*, Nottingham 1987), has tried to revive Stukeley's pedigree in a revised form it may be useful to summarize a few of the salient errors. First, the critical figure for both Stukeley and Mr Lees is William 'FitzOoth', who (Stukeley) or whose heir (Lees) was transferred to the custody of Robert de Vere, earl of Oxford, in 1214. In reality the William son of Otho, whose heir or heirs were placed in the custody of Aubrey de Vere, earl of Oxford, in 1205 and transferred to Robert de Vere, earl of Oxford, in 1214, had nothing to do with the family of Kyme, or with the earls of Huntingdon, still less with Robin Hood. He is well known as an official of the Mint, holding his office in charge of the manufacture of the royal dies as a sergeanty. By 1219 he was succeeded by his son, Otho son of William, who still held office in 1242–3. It follows therefore that 'Robert fitz Ooth' is entirely fictitious; so is the alleged link between 'FitzOoth' and Kyme; and so are the grounds for seeking an original Robin Hood in the Kyme family. Secondly, there is no evidence that any Robert of Kyme mentioned by Mr Lees was outlawed. The instance on which he relies is a royal remission of wrath and indignation incurred by an appeal of rape against a Robert of Kyme at Wenlock in 1226; there is no mention of outlawry. Thirdly, Mr Lees's 'Robert of Kyme' is compounded of at least two distinct individuals, none of them an outlaw and none of them a disinherited elder son; many of the relationships he proposes within the Kyme family are quite unsupported by any contemporary evidence.

**9** Oxford, Bodleian Library, Dodsworth MS 160, fol. 64b, quoted Hunter, p. 69.

**10** Thomas Percy, *Reliques of Ancient English Poetry* (London 1765), i, p. 104.

**11** Richard Gough, *Sepulchral Monuments* (1786), p. cviii.

**12** Ritson, i, p. i.

**13** Ritson, i, pp. xlvii, xi.

**14** Hunter, p. 63.

**15** J. W. Walker, *The True History of Robin Hood* (Wakefield 1952), p. 9.

**16** When he wrote *South Yorkshire*, Joseph Hunter had access to material which included letters of Thomas of Lancaster in the papers of the Foljambe family, which cannot now be found. It may be that Walker drew on these either directly or through Hunter's transcripts. Further search in Hunter's papers in the British Library and the Jackson collection in the Sheffield City Library may reveal his source.

**17** The Latin is *Et de xxiiid, de firma v celdarum de novo edificatarum super Bichill*: 'And for 23 pence for the rent of five stalls newly built on Bitchhill'. Walker seems to have translated *firma* viz. 'farm' or 'rent' as 'farmhouse'.

**18** This roll of contrariants was printed by Thomas Taylor, *The History of Wakefield, the Rectory Manor* (Wakefield 1886), appendix, pp. lii–lxii, where it is wrongly attributed to 1342. Bitchhill appears at p. liv.

**19** J. W. Walker, 'Robin Hood Identified', *Yorkshire Archaeological Journal*, xxxvi (1944), p. 18; *The True History of Robin Hood* (Wakefield 1952), pp. 4–7.

**20** Walker, 'Robin Hood Identified', *op. cit.*, p. 40.

**21** P. Valentine Harris, *The Truth about Robin Hood* (Mansfield 1973), p. 79.

**22** Hunter, pp. 44–5.

**23** London, Public Record Office, E 101/379/6. This is a fragment of two folios of an account book of the king's chamber. The marginal entry *Gages des porteurs de la chambre* marks the relevant section of fol. 1, consisting of payments totalling £6 to thirty-four 'vadletz porteurs de la Chambres le Roi'. The recipients are the usual team, including 'Simon Hod' and 'Robyn Hod', which appears in the subsequent accounts examined by Hunter. Hunter surmised that the accounting practice of the chamber changed on 16 April 1324, the names of the porters being entered in gross up to that point and individually thereafter. This was evidently not so.

In the fragment which contains the newly discovered and critical entry on 'Robyn Hod' there is only one payment of wages to porters, clearly signalled by the marginal entry. The whole entry, which is worn and faint, has been washed with gall, the standby treatment for difficult passages before the use of ultraviolet light. Someone before the present writer used this record and appreciated the importance of the passage. But the fragment was not used by J. Conway Davies, 'The First Journal of Edward II's Chamber', *English Historical Review*, xxx (1915), pp. 662–80.

**24** Hunter, p. 46.

**25** Hunter, pp. 19–20. For the circumstances of the prelates' journey see G. W. S. Barrow, *Robert Bruce* (London 1965), pp. 215–6.

**26** Dobson and Taylor, p. 12, take a different view.

**27** The surrender of 1318 does not provide a *terminus ante quem* for the transmission of the legend from south Yorkshire to Sussex. John Warenne recovered a life-interest in Wakefield in 1326 and did not die until 1347. On the whole question of the relations between Warenne and Thomas of Lancaster see Maddicott (1970), pp.

234–7 and Hunter, *South Yorkshire*, i, p. 107 ff.

**28** Dobson and Taylor attribute Gilbert to Fletching, Sussex. This obscures the link with the honour of Leicester. Gilbert is recorded as a tenant of the Liberty of Leicester in Sussex, the court of which was based at Hungry Hatch in Fletching. See G. A. Holmes, *The Estates of the Higher Nobility in Fourteenth-Century England* (Cambridge 1957), p. 127.

**29** See Holt in Hilton (1976), p. 254.

**30** T. Wright (1846), ii, pp. 164–211, especially 208–11.

**31** *Ibid.*, i, p. ix.

**32** Hunter, pp. 7–8.

**33** Child, iii, pp. 42, 55–6.

**34** *Dictionary of National Biography*, under Hood.

**35** There are similar introductory verses to *Robin Hood and Guy of Gisborne, Robin Hood and the Potter*, and *Robin Hood and the Curtal Friar*.

**36** This tale has been ignored by most pundits on Robin Hood, perhaps because Child printed it separately from the other tales in i, pp. 109–10.

**37** Hunter, p. 69.

**38** See below, pp. 148–9.

**39** See below, pp. 149–51.

**40** E. L. G. Stones, 'The Folvilles of Ashby Folville, Leicestershire and their Associates in crime 1326–41', *Transactions of the Royal Historical Society*, 5 ser., vii (1957), pp. 134–5.

**41** See below, pp. 100–3.

**42** Maddicott (1978), p. 285.

*IV The Original Robin Hood*

**1** See below, p. 69.

**2** Public Record Office. C219/14/3, part 2, no. 101.

**3** Maddicott (1978), p. 283.

**4** Keen (1961), p. 9. Compare Holt (1961), pp. 16–17, and below, pp. 142–5.

*V The Physical Setting*

**1** At the end of fytte two, however, where the knight is stayed by the wrestling match, there is the cryptic line (135): *But as he went at a brydge ther was a wrastelyng.*

**2** This was true by the middle of the thirteenth century. At the beginning of the thirteenth century there were forests in Wharfedale and between the Ouse and Derwent in Yorkshire; Sherwood was then more extensive both to the east and north. These areas were disafforested at various dates in the first half of the thirteenth century.

**3** *The Itinerary of John Leland*, ed. L. Toulmin-Smith (London 1906–10), iv, p. 13.

**3a** The recent attempt by Mr J. Lees (*The Quest for Robin Hood*, Nottingham 1987) to alter the accepted geography of the tales by placing Barnsdale in Sherwood is quite unacceptable. It involves an elementary misreading of the *Gest*: the knight was travelling south through Barnsdale, not north, as he insists, for he was intending to voyage to the Holy Land (56, 57); it is only later, after leaving Robin in Barnsdale, that he visits St Mary's, York, in order to repay his debt (84). It is also based on a tendentious and uncritical evaluation of the place-name evidence. 'Brunnisdale' in Basford, Notts., cannot be equated with Barnsdale. 'Brunnis' is most probably 'brun', i.e. brown; 'Barn' comes from the personal name 'Beorn'. Moreover, the evidence linking Wentbridge, Sayles, Barnsdale and Watling Street is quite clear and certain. The main facts concerning the use of Watling Street as a name for the Great North Road in the Barnsdale area, which Mr Lees questions, are incontrovertibly presented in *The Place Names of the West Riding of Yorkshire*, vii, p. 145.

**4** I have found no evidence that the present main road up the Aire valley to Skipton was in use as a through route in the Middle Ages. This was only completed after the first Ordnance Survey of 1845–54. There were possible variants to the route I have described. Local antiquaries assume that the obvious route west from Pontefract was to Wakefield and thence by the Roman road to

Bradford. This ignores the administrative advantages of the route via Ferrybridge or Rothwell to Leeds, which lay entirely within the Lacy honour. The route through Wakefield would in any case have been impossible at critical times when the Warenne lords of Wakefield were political opponents of, or at odds with, the Lacys or later with Thomas of Lancaster.

5 The extent of Bradford of 1314 is printed as 'Chapter House Records', trans. J. Lister, *The Bradford Antiquary*, ii (1895), pp. 57–65.

6 The deed is entered with the date 1322 but, as Walker noted, this is plainly a slip. See *Abstracts of the Cartularies of the Priory of Monkbretton*, ed. J. W. Walker, Yorkshire Archaeological Society, Record Series, 66 (1924), pp. 105–6.

7 The ings or 'Lynges' of Skelbrooke must have run northwards down to the Skell which flows from west to east through the village. My reading of the deed is that the northern edge of the ings formed the southern, and Robin Hode's Stone the northern bounds of a half-acre plot, which cannot have been contiguous with the Great North Road since that appears as the eastern boundary to two other half-acre plots.

8 *Peniarth 53*, Prifysgol Cymru, v (Caerdydd 1927), pp. 51–2.

*VI The Audience*

1 *Polychronicon Ranulphi Higden*, ed. C. Babington (Rolls Series 1869), ii, 159–61. The first paragraph of the passage quoted is Trevisa's translation of Higden's Latin chronicle, the second is Trevisa's own comment.

2 *De Laudibus Legum Anglie*, ed. S. B. Chrimes (Cambridge 1942), p. 68.

3 *The Governance of England*, ed. Charles Plummer (Oxford 1885), p. 151.

4 Myers (1959), pp. 116–7.

5 *The Canterbury Tales*, Prologue, ll. 103–17.

6 *Gest*, 84.

7 Child, iii, p. 364.

8 See above, pp. 104–5.

9 Myers (1969), pp. 1200–1.

10 *Memorials of the Abbey of St. Mary of Fountains*, ed. J. R. Walbran, ii, part 1 (Surtees Society, lxvii, 1878), p. 90.

11 Chambers, i, p. 48.

12 Robert Laneham, *A Letter* (1575), ed. R. C. Alston (English Linguistics 1500–1800, no. 60, Menston 1968) pp. 34–6; extracts in Chambers, ii, pp. 263–6. The text is also edited with a full commentary on Cox's books and ballads in F. J. Furnivall, *Captain Cox, His Ballads and Books, or Robert Laneham's Letter* (Ballad Society publications vii, 1871). Laneham's, or more correctly, Langham's authorship of the Letter has been questioned by Brian O'Kill (*Trans. Cambridge Bibliographical Society*, vii, 1977, pp. 35–43) and David Scott (*English Literary Renaissance*, vii, 1977, pp. 297–306), both of whom attribute Langham's letter to William Patten, a view repeated in S. Halkett and J. Lang, *A Dictionary of Anonymous and Pseudonymous Publications in the English Language*, ed. J. Horden (London 1980), p. 115. This criticism has not been accepted by R. J. P. Kuin, the latest editor of the Letter, who sustains Langham's authorship. See his *Robert Langham: a Letter* (Leiden 1983), where there are considerable additions to Furnivall's comments on Captain Cox's books (pp. 131–43), and 'The Purloined *Letter*. Evidence and Probability regarding Robert Langham's Authorship', *The Library*, 6th ser. vii (1985), pp. 115–25. However this may be, 'Captain Cox of Coventry' seems altogether too alliterative to be anything but a pseudonym; he has not been traced as such in the surviving Coventry archives.

13 *Gesta Herewardi*, ed. S. H. Miller, pp. 19–20.

14 *Troilus and Criseyde*, Book II, ll. 860–1.

15 *Jack Upland, Friar Daw's Reply and Upland's Rejoinder*, ed. P. L. Heyworth (Oxford 1968), p. 80.

16 G. E. Morris, 'A Ryme of Robyn

Hode', *Modern Language Review*, xliii (1948), pp. 507–8.

**17** N. Davis (1971), no. 275.

**18** E. K. Chambers, *English Literature at the Close of the Middle Ages* (Oxford 1945), p. 131.

**19** See above, pp. 79–80.

**20** *Collections For a History of Staffordshire* (William Salt Archaeological Society, new ser., x. part I, 1907), pp. 80–1.

**21** *Rotuli Parliamentorum*, v, p. 16.

**22** Sir Ralph Winwood, *Memorials of Affairs of State* (London 1725), ii, pp. 172–3.

**23** *Wakefield Court Roll* 1329–30, Yorkshire Archaeological Society, Leeds, M D 225, m. 12d.

**24** *Wakefield Court Rolls*, iii, p. 148.

**25** 'B' text, xix, 245–7.

**26** Myers (1969), p. 1116.

**27** Piers Gaveston, Edward II's favourite.

**28** The 'West Country' is Lancashire. For an account of Sir Adam de Banastre and the disturbances in Lancashire in 1315, see *South Lancashire in the Reign of Edward II*, ed. G. H. Tupling (Chetham Society, 3rd ser., i. 1949).

**29** *The Honour and Forest of Pickering*, ed. R. B. Turton (North Riding Record Society, new ser., iii, 1896), pp. 243–4.

**30** Text B, passus v, ll. 461–76; Text C. passus, i, l. 45, passus, vii, ll. 316, 322.

**31** K. Sisam, *Fourteenth-Century Verse and Prose* (Oxford 1955), pp. 160–1.

**32** *Chronicon Henrici Knighton*, ed. J. R. Lumby (Rolls Series 1895), ii. p. 139.

**33** Ll. 72–3. Ed. W. W. Skeat (Early English Text Society 1867), p. 3.

## VII The Later Tradition

**1** See above, pp. 58–9.

**2** Hall's *Chronicle; Containing the History of England* (1809 edn), p. 582.

**3** Act I, scene I.

**4** *The Downfall of Robert Earl of Huntington*, J2, ll. 2210–15 (Malone

Society Reprints *cur*. J. C. Meagher and A. Brown 1965).

**5** See above, pp. 15–16.

**6** See below, pp. 180–1.

**7** Algernon Cecil, *Life of Robert Cecil* (London 1915), p. 379.

**8** *Calendar of Nottinghamshire Coroners' Inquests 1485–1558*, ed. R. F. Hunnisett (Thoroton Society, Record Series, xxv, 1969, no. 82.

**9** Alexander Smith, *A Complete History of the Lives and Robberies of the Most Notorious Highwaymen*, ed. A. L. Hayward (London 1926), p. 408.

**10** *The Compleat Angler* (Nelson Classics), p. 83.

**11** T. Gent, *A History of York* (York 1730), p. 234.

**12** (J. Brome), *An Historical Account of Mr Roger's Travels* (London 1694), pp. 90–1.

**13** R. Thoroton, *Antiquities of Nottinghamshire*, ed. J. Throsby (London 1797), ii, pp. 170–1.

**14** British Library, Additional MS 28638, fol. 16.

**15** A. V. Judges, *The Elizabethan Underworld* (London 1930), pp. 68–9.

**16** *Ibid*, p. 54.

**17** Smith, *op. cit.*, p. 408.

**18** See above, pp. 38–9.

**19** J. Major, *Historia Maioris Britanniae* (Edinburgh 1521), p. 55b; trans. A. Constable, *A History of Greater Britain* (Scottish Historical Society, x, 1892), pp. 156–7.

**20** J. Stow, *The Annales of England* (London 1592), p. 227.

**21** See above, pp. 44–5.

**22** Ritson, i, p. xi.

**23** *Poetical Works of John Keats*, ed. H. W. Garrod (oxford 1939), pp. 271–2.

## VIII Postscript

**1** See above, pp. 52–3.

**2** For a full discussion of Robert Hood of Wakefield see above, pp. 45–51.

**3** For more information on Robert Hod see above, pp. 53–4.

**4** These matters are further discussed above, pp. 41–2.

5   There are more details about Fulk and his legend above, pp. 63–4.

6   For more about Eustace see above, pp. 63–4.

7   The case of Roger Godberd is discussed above, pp. 97–9. For the details of the final charges against him see PRO Just 1/1222, m. 15: gaol delivery at Hereford, 16 Dec. 1275, whence Roger was sent to Newgate for trial 5 April 1276; no further record has been traced. I am grateful to Dr David Crook for bringing this to my attention.

8   It has been suggested that the carving represents the tale of Valentine and Orson, but Robin Hood and the King seem preferable. The majestic figure carries a long-bow. The archer is hooded. Orson is usually represented as a Wild Man which the archer certainly is not.

9   See above, p. 142.

10   For these instances see above pp. 69, 141–2 and also J. C. Holt and Toshiyuki Takamiya, 'A new version of a Rhyme of Robin Hood', *English Manuscript Studies*, 1989.

11   Parker and the other sources are discussed at p. 184.

12   For more details see above, pp. 159–60.

# Sources and further reading

*References cited in the Notes*

Boulton, Helen E., ed., *The Sherwood Forest Book* (Thoroton Society, Record Series, xxiii, 1965).

Chambers, E. K., *The Medieval Stage*, 2 vols (Oxford 1903).

Child, F. J., *The English and Scottish Popular Ballads*, 5 vols (Boston 1882–98; repr. New York 1962).

Clawson, W. H., *The Gest of Robin Hood* (University of Toronto 1909).

Davis, N., ed., *Paston Letters and Papers*, 2 vols (Oxford 1971, 1976).

Dobson, R. B. and Taylor, J., *Rymes of Robyn Hood* (London 1976).

Fowler, D. C., *A Literary History of the Popular Ballad* (Durham, North Carolina 1968).

Hilton, R. H., 'The Origins of Robin Hood', *Past and Present*, 14 (1958), pp. 30–44.

—, ed., *Peasants Knights and Heretics* (Cambridge 1976), which reprints the papers by Hilton above and by Holt and Keen below.

Hodgart, M. J. C., *The Ballads* (London 1950).

Holt, J. C., 'The Origins and Audience of the Ballads of Robin Hood', *Past and Present*, 18 (1960), pp. 89–110.

—, 'Robin Hood: Some Comments', *Past and Present*, 19 (1961), pp. 16–18.

Hunter, J. *The Great Hero of the Ancient English Minstrelsy of England: Robin Hood* (London 1852, Worksop 1883).

Keen, M. H., *The Outlaws of Medieval Legend* (London 1961, 1977). All references are to the second edn.

—, 'Robin Hood – Peasant or Gentleman?', *Past and Present*, 19 (1961), pp. 7–15.

Maddicott, J. R., *Thomas of Lancaster* (Oxford 1970).

—, 'The Birth and Setting of the Ballads of Robin Hood', *English Historical Review*, xciii (1978), pp. 276–99.

Myers, A. R., *The Household of Edward IV* (Manchester 1959).

—, ed., *English Historical Documents*, iv (London 1969).

Ritson, Joseph, *Robin Hood: A Collection of all the Ancient Poems, Songs and Ballads Now Extant* (London 1795, 1832, 1887). All references are to the last edn.

Wales, David, *The Early Plays of Robin Hood* (Woodbridge 1981).

Wright, T., ed., *The Political Songs of England* (Camden Society 1839).

Wright, T., *Essays on the Literature, Popular Superstitions and History of England in the Middle Ages*, 2 vols (London 1846).

*General*

The tales and ballads of Robin Hood are collected in volume 3 of F. J. Child, *The English and Scottish Popular Ballads*, 5 vols (Boston 1882–98, repr. New York 1962), from which all the passages quoted in this book are taken. His collection superseded Joseph Ritson's *Robin Hood* (London 1795), which in turn superseded Thomas Percy's *Reliques of Ancient English Poetry* (London 1765). Child's editorial notes remain invaluable, especially on the analogues to the Robin Hood stories. Ritson's introduction to his collection of ballads is also a mine of information, both sound and false.

R. B. Dobson and J. Taylor have edited a selection of the tales, including all the earliest, in *Rymes of Robyn Hood* (London 1976). Their introduction to the collection is scholarly and comprehensive, as are the appendices on ballad titles, proverbs and place names.

The best introduction to the social background to the legend is to be found in the lively account of M. H. Keen, *The Outlaws of Medieval Legend* (London 1961, 1977) which should be read in the light of the author's comments in the introduction to the second edition.

Dobson and Taylor provide a select bibliography. See also J. Harris Gable, *Bibliography of Robin Hood* (University of Nebraska, Studies in Language, Literature and Criticism, no. 17, Lincoln, Nebraska 1939).

CHAPTER ONE *Prologue*

For the discussion of the social objectives of Robin Hood see Hilton (1976) which assembles papers published in *Past and Present*, 1958–71.

*The Outlaw's Song*, or *Song of Trailbaston* of *c.* 1305 is printed with translation in Wright (1839), pp. 231–6; Isabel S. T. Aspin, ed., *Anglo-Norman Political Songs* (Anglo-Norman Text Society, xi, 1953), pp. 67–78, and Dobson and Taylor, pp. 251–4. For Robin Hood and the American outlaws, see Kent L. Steckmesser, 'Robin Hood and the American Outlaw: A Note on History and Folklore', *Journal of American Folklore*, lxxix (1966), pp. 348–55.

CHAPTER TWO *The Legend*

The dates of the original versions of the various stories are discussed by Child and more recently by Dobson and Taylor. The Percy Folio is edited by J. W. Hales and F. J. Furnivall, as *Bishop Percy's Folio Manuscript; Ballads and Romances*, 3 vols (London 1867–8). Clawson (1909) still provides the best analysis of the *Gest*. Fowler (1968) contains important sections on the 'Rymes of Robyn Hood' and the Percy Folio. For the literature which has not come down to us, see R. M. Wilson, *The Lost Literature of Medieval England* (London 1952). For the interpretation of Robin as an arche-

typal social rebel see Hilton (1978) and E. J. Hobsbawm, *Primitive Rebels* (Manchester 1959, 1971) and *Bandits* (London 1969). For the background to the *Song of the Husbandman* see J. R. Maddicott, *The English Peasantry and the Demands of the Crown* 1294–1341 (*Past and Present Supplement*, no. 1, 1975).

CHAPTER THREE *Who was Robin Hood?*

The early historical references to Robin Hood are conveniently assembled by Dobson and Taylor, pp. 1–17. They also provide an excellent critique of the Sloane MS 'life' at pp. 286–7. The best discussion of the grave is by Keen (1977), pp. 179–83. The summary account of the Hoods of Wakefield and its neighbourhood is based on the Wakefield court rolls, printed by the Yorkshire Archaeological Society and on the unprinted rolls in the Society's custody.

Attempts to identify Robin Hood and other members of his band in the Wakefield area began with Hunter (1852, 1883) and were continued by J. W. Walker, 'Robin Hood Identified', *Yorkshire Archaeological Journal*, xxxvi (1944), pp. 4–46, and *The True History of Robin Hood* (Wakefield 1952); and by P. Valentine Harris, *The Truth about Robin Hood* (p.p. and Mansfield, 1951, 1973). More recently, Professor John Bellamy (*Robin Hood: an historical enquiry*, London 1985) engaged in a complicated argument concerning Sir Richard of the Lee, suggesting that he was parson of Arksey, Yorks., but fell back on Hunter's Robert Hood of Wakefield as the original Robin. For the honour of Leicester, see Levi Fox, 'The Honor and Earldom of Leicester: Origin and Descent, 1066–1399', *English Historical Review*, liv, 1939, pp. 385–99. For Thomas of Lancaster see Maddicott (1970) and R. Somerville, *The Duchy of Lancaster*, i (London 1953). For later restatements of the argument that Robin was mere myth see Margaret Murray, *The God of the Witches* (London 1933) and Lord Raglan, *The Hero* (London 1949). For a succinct restatement of the argument against the mythological interpretation see Keen (1977), pp. 219–22, and the discussion which followed W. E. Simeone, 'The May Games and the Robin Hood Legend', *Journal of American Folklore*, lxiv, 1951, pp. 265–74 in *Journal of American Folklore*, lxv, 1952, pp. 304–5, 418–20.

On Robin of Redesdale see C. Ross, *Edward IV* (London 1974), pp. 126–7. On William Wither see Hugh Mackenzie, 'The Anti-Foreign Movement in England 1231–1232', *Anniversary Essays in Medieval History by Students of C. H. Haskins* (New York 1929), pp. 183–203. For possible sheriffs see Holt (1960) and Maddicott (1978). Mr Jeffrey Stafford's suggestion was made in letters to the author. It is advanced independently, with a full account of Eustace's career, by David Crook, 'The Sheriff of Nottingham and Robin Hood: The Genesis of the Legend?' in *Thirteenth-Century England*, ii, ed. P. R. Coss and S. D. Lloyd (Woodbridge 1989), pp. 59–68.

CHAPTER FOUR *The Original Robin Hood*

There is a succinct, level-headed account of Hereward the Wake by T. F. Tout in the *Dictionary of National Biography*. He receives fuller treatment in E. A. Freeman, *The Norman Conquest*, iv (1871), pp. 454–87, 804–12, and an excellent discussion in Keen (1977), pp. 9–38. The most accessible editions of the *De Gestis* are in Gaimar's *L'Estoire des Engles*, ed. T. D. Hardy and C. T. Martin (Rolls Series 1888) and *Fenland Notes and Queries*, iii (1897), ed. S. H. Miller and trans. W. D. Sweeting. On the career of Eustace the Monk and for a modern edition of the romance see *Le Romans de Wistasse li Moine*, ed. D. J. Conlon (University of North Carolina, Studies in Romance Languages and Literature, cxxvi, 1972). The story is summarized in Wright (1846), ii, pp. 121–46. Fulk fitz Warin is discussed in S. Painter, *The Reign of King John* (Baltimore 1952), pp. 49–52. There is

further discussion in the splendid edition of *Fouke Le Fitz Waryn*, ed. E. J. Hathaway, P. T. Ricketts, C. A. Robson and A. D. Wilshere (Anglo-Norman Text Society 1975). The earlier edition in *Chronicon Radulphi de Coggeshall*, ed. J. Stevenson (Rolls Series 1875) contains a useful translation. *Adam Bell, Johnnie Cock* and *Robyn and Gandelyn* are all printed by Child. For Alfred and the cakes see Asser, *Life of Alfred*, ed. W. H. Stevenson (Oxford 1904), pp. 41–2, 256–61. For the tale of Gamelyn see W. W. Skeat's edition of Chaucer's *Canterbury Tales* in *The Complete Works of Geoffrey Chaucer*, iv (Oxford 1894), pp. 645–67; and for a useful comment see John Bellamy, *Robin Hood: an historical enquiry* (London 1985), pp. 63–6.

Attention was first drawn to the sheriff's clerk responsible for the parliamentary returns of 1432 and 1433 by V. H. Galbraith, *An Introduction to the Study of History* (London 1964), pp. 67–8 and plate IX. The information on Sherwood is drawn from Boulton (1964) and the information on the parks of the lords of Wakefield from the Wakefield court rolls. On the history of the bow the classic work is Gad Rausing, *The Bow, Some Notes on its Origin and Development* (Acta Archaeologica Lundensia, ser. v in 8°, 6, Lund 1967). There is also a valuable and entertaining account by Robert Hardy, *Longbow, A Social and Military History* (Cambridge 1976). Another very useful survey is J. Bradbury, *The Medieval Archer* (Woodbridge 1985). On the retaining of justices see J. R. Maddicott, *Law and Lordship: Royal Justices as Retainers in Thirteenth and Fourteenth Century England* (Past and Present Supplement, no. 4, 1978).

CHAPTER FIVE *The Physical Setting*

The detail of the topography of Barnsdale is based on the 1/25,000 and 6″ Ordnance Survey maps. Further topographical information and all information on place names is drawn from the volumes issued by the English Place Name Society, especially A. H. Smith, *The Place Names of the West Riding of Yorkshire*, 8 vols (E.P.N.S. xxx–xxxvii, 1956–63). See also *West Yorkshire: An Archaeological Survey*, ed. S. A. Moorhouse and M. L. Faull (Wakefield 1981). On the Roman roads see also I. D. Margary, *Roman Roads in Britain* (London 1973).

For events in Lancashire at the time of the death of Thomas of Lancaster, see *South Lancashire in the Reign of Edward II*, ed. G. H. Tupling (Chetham Society, 3rd ser., i, 1949) and on the forest see R. Cunliffe Shaw, *The Royal Forest of Lancaster* (Preston 1956). On the Lacys and the administration of their lands see W. E. Wightman, *The Lacy Family in England and Normandy* (Oxford 1966), R. B. Smith, *Blackburnshire* (Leicester University Press 1961) and J. F. Baldwin, 'The Household Administration of Henry Lacy and Thomas of Lancaster', *English Historical Review*, xlii (1927), pp. 180–200. Relevant charters are in *Early Yorkshire Charters*, ed. W. Farrer, iii (Edinburgh 1916). Professor Bellamy has proposed an alternative for Gisburn, namely Guisborough, Yorks. (*Robin Hood: an historical enquiry*, London 1985, pp. 34–5). He is perfectly correct to say that the medieval forms of both names included common variants which were one and the same; so both places shared the form Gysburn(e). On the other hand, there is nothing else to link Guisborough, which lay in Cleveland beyond the north Yorkshire moors, with the tales. Gisburn, by contrast, fits other indications pointing to some input from the upper Ribble and Bowland areas.

Much evidence on the Robin Hood place names is conveniently summarized by Dobson and Taylor, pp. 293–311.

## CHAPTER SIX *The Audience*

For a general account of the ballads see Hodgart (1950). MacEdward Leach, *The Ballad Book* (New York 1955), is a useful collection with introduction, glossary and bibliography. Also important are Fowler (1968) and James Reed, *The Border Ballads* (London 1973). David Buchan, *The Ballad and the Folk* (London 1972), shifts some of the weight of the Scottish tradition from the borders to the north-east. For the 'popular' view of ballad origins, see F. B. Gunmere, *The Popular Ballad* (Boston 1907), supplemented by W. M. Hart, *Ballad and Epic* (Boston 1907), and criticized from the standpoint of individual authorship by Louise Pound, *Poetic Origins and the Ballad* (New York 1924). For a compromise emphasizing the folk-ballad characteristics of the component stories of the *Gest*, here stretched to 'no less than forty-three tales', see G. H. Gerould, *The Ballad of Tradition* (Oxford 1932). Lajos Vargyas, in *Researches into the Mediaeval History of Folk Ballad* (Budapest 1967), a modern Marxist interpretation, excludes the Robin Hood cycle from the genre on grounds both of style and content: 'Thus we shall leave out the Robin Hood cycle which contains only adventures often very loquaciously described.' For a general survey of continental ballads, see W. J. Entwistle, *European Balladry* (Oxford 1939).

Among the many discussions of minstrels and minstrelsy, Chambers (1903), which includes much original material, is still essential. Also important are Glynne Wickham, *Early English Stages* (London 1959), R. L. Greene's introduction to his edition of *Early English Carols* (Oxford 1977) and Constance Bullock-Davies's *Menestrellorum Multitudo* (Cardiff 1978), which takes the feast of 1306 as its starting-point. On the feudal origins of minstrel guilds in minstrel courts see the important paper of G.

R. Rastall, 'The Minstrel Court in Medieval England', *A Medieval Miscellany in honour of Professor John Le Patourel*, ed. R. L. Thomson, *Proc. Leeds Philosophical and Literary Society*, xviii (1982), pp. 96–105.

On social status and yeomen see N. Denholm-Young, *The Country Gentry in the Fourteenth Century* (Oxford 1969), F. R. H. du Boulay, 'The First English Gentlemen', *The Listener*, lx, no. 1544 (30 October 1958) and his *An Age of Ambition* (London 1970); also N. Saul, *Knights and Esquires: the Gloucestershire Gentry in the Fourteenth Century* (Oxford 1981). Mildred Campbell's *The English Yeoman* (New Haven 1942) is largely concerned with the history of the yeoman from the sixteenth century.

For discussions of courtesy see H. S. Bennett, *Chaucer and the Fifteenth Century* (Oxford 1947), pp. 156 ff; Sylvia L. Thrupp, *The Merchant Class of Medieval London* (London 1948), pp. 288–319; D. S. Brewer, 'Courtesy and the Gawain-poet', in *Patterns of Love and Courtesy*, ed. J. Lawlor (London 1966), pp. 54–85; and J. W. Nicholls, *The Matter of Courtesy* (Woodbridge 1985).

On archery, see the works listed under Chapter Four above. On fencing see Egerton Castle, *Schools and Master of Fence* (3rd edn, London 1969) and J. D. Aylward, 'The Medieval Master of Fence', *Notes and Queries*, cxcviii (1953), pp. 230–4.

On the criminal gangs of later medieval England a useful introduction is provided both by Keen (1977) and by John Bellamy, *Crime and Public Order in England in the later Middle Ages* (London 1973). See also chapter 5 of N. Saul, *Knights and Esquires*, noted above. The classic essay in this field is E. L. G. Stones, 'The Folvilles of Ashby Folville, Leicestershire, and their Associates in crime 1326–41', *Transactions of the Royal Historical Society*, 5 ser., vii (1957), pp. 117–36. See also John Bellamy, 'The Coterel Gang: An Anatomy of a Band of Fourteenth Century Criminals',

*English Historical Review*, lxxix (1964), pp. 698–717, and 'the Northern Rebellion in the Later Years of Richard II', *Bulletin of the John Rylands Library*, xlvii (1965), pp. 254–74. *Medieval Legal Records edited in memory of C. A. F. Meetings*, ed. R. F. Hunnisett, and J. B. Post (London 1978) contains essays by M. T. Clanchy on the Alston robbery of 1249, Natalie Fryde on Sir John Molyns and Alan Harding on the Trailbaston proceedings in Lincolnshire in 1305. J. B. Given, *Society and Homicide in Thirteenth Century England* (Stanford 1977) and Barbara Hanawalt, *Crime and Conflict in English Communities, 1300–1348* (Cambridge, Mass. 1979) examine crime at a lower social level. The latter is particularly useful in questioning the role of the beneficent criminal which is conventionally allotted to Robin Hood. For the continuation of characteristically medieval conditions into the sixteenth and seventeenth centuries in northern England see the study by Mervyn James, *Family Lineage and Civic Society* (Oxford 1974).

CHAPTER SEVEN   *The Later Legend*

For further general discussion of the legend since the Middle Ages see Dobson and Taylor, especially pp. 36–64, and Malcolm A. Nelson, *The Robin Hood Tradition in the English Renaissance* (Salzburg Studies in English Literature 1973). On the May Games see Chambers (1903), i, pp. 160–81, and W. E. Simeone, 'The May Games and the Robin Hood Legend', *Journal of American Folklore*, lxiv (1951), pp. 265–74. S. Anglo, *Spectacle, Pageantry and Early Tudor Policy* (Oxford 1969) provides splendid background. On Scotland see L. Spencer, 'Robin Hood in Scotland', *Chambers Journal*, ix ser., xviii (1928), pp. 94–6. For Tollet's window see Herbert Read, *English Stained Glass* (London 1926), pp. 213, 240–9.

On the widening reading public

consult R. S. Schofield, 'the Measurement of Literacy in Pre-Industrial England', in *Literacy in Traditional Societies*, ed. J. Goody (Cambridge 1968); D. Cressy, 'Levels of Illiteracy in England, 1530–1730'. *Historical Journal*, xx (1977), pp. 1–23, and his *Literacy and the Social Order* (Cambridge 1980); and Dr Margaret Spufford, *Small Books and Pleasant Histories* (London 1981).

On the development of the ballad, see Fowler (1968) and, for an interpretation which lays greater emphasis on the folk tradition, G. H. Gerould, *The Ballad of Tradition* (Oxford 1932). For the traditional tunes of the ballads, see B. H. Bronson, *The Traditional Times of the Child Ballads*, 4 vols (Princeton 1959–72), in which Robin Hood is dealt with in vol. 3. For further discussion see B. H. Bronson's collected essays *The Ballad as Song* (Berkeley 1969).

For further information on the Robin Hood place names in Nottinghamshire and Derbyshire see the volumes of the English Place Name Society and Dobson and Taylor.

A good selection of the sixteenth-century literature on crime and criminals is edited by A. V. Judges. *The Elizabethan Underworld* (London 1930, 1965) and by G. Salgado, *Cony-Catchers and Bawdy Baskets* (London 1972). There is useful comment and more general discussion in F. Aydelotte, *Elizabethan Rogues and Vagabonds* (Oxford 1913, London 1967) and in J. A. S. McPeek, *The Black Book of Knaves and Unthrift* (Storrs 1969). There is wider chronological coverage with a very useful bibliography in J. S. Cockburn, ed., *Crime in England 1550–1800* (London 1977). E. P. Thompson, *Whigs and Hunters: the Origins of the Black Act* (London 1975) continues the study of poaching and the game laws into the eighteenth century.

On almanacs see B. Capp, *English Almanacs 1500–1800* (Ithaca 1979); finally on the life of Joseph Ritson consult B. H. Bronson, *Joseph Ritson, Scholar at Arms*, 2 vols (Berkeley 1938).

CHAPTER EIGHT *Postscript*

The sources of the Robinhood surnames are all in manuscript. All the new ones are derived from the Plea Rolls. I owe them to the kindness especially of Dr Henry Summerson, who is engaged in compiling a collection of criminal nicknames, and to Dr David Crook and Professor R. C. Palmer. For the example of 1261–2 see D. Crook, 'Some further evidence concerning the dating of the origins of the legend of Robin Hood', *English Historical Review*, xcix (1984), pp. 530–4. For Robert of Wetherby and the connection with Eustace of Lowdham see David Crook, 'The Sheriff of Nottingham and Robin Hood: the Genesis of the Legend?', *Thirteenth Century England*, ii (1989), pp. 59–68. For possible literary antecedents to the *Gest* see P. R. Coss, 'Aspects of Cultural Diffusion in Medieval England: the early romances, local society and Robin Hood', *Past and Present*, no. 108 (1985), pp. 35–79.

The Beverley carvings are included in the illustrations in this volume, nos. 12, 13.

For a general account of plays at spring and other festivals see Chambers 1903. He is still one of the best authorities and perhaps the best of all on the *quête*. There is also an important modern study, David Wiles, *The Early Plays of Robin Hood* (Woodbridge 1981); the appendices include lists of the early plays and extracts of church wardens' accounts from Kingston. For the church wardens' accounts from Reading see Charles Kerry, *A History of the municipal church of St. Lawrence, Reading* (Reading 1883). There are also many extracts in J. C. Cox, *Church Wardens' Accounts* (London 1913), which still remains the classic study of the subject.

# List of illustrations

# Acknowledgments

This book is the product of intermittent work conducted over more than twenty years. During that lengthy period I have received help and information from many friends and colleagues. It would have been both cumbersome and impractical to mention each one of them at the appropriate point in the text; so I gladly record my debt to them here. I have turned to Dr D. S. Brewer for advice on Chaucer, Gower and the development of the ballad. Mr Peter Burke drew my attention to the evidence of almanacs. Dr Christine Carpenter allowed me to use material from her work on the gentry of Warwickshire in the fifteenth century. Miss Barbara Dodwell provided me with information on yeomen and the definition of yeoman status. Professor Kenneth Cameron advised me on place names and more generally on the original articles which I wrote on Robin Hood in 1960. Dr David Crook kindly checked material on Roger Godberd. Dr David Dumville supplied me with the reference to Robin Hood in Welsh. Professor G. R. Elton and Dr J. S. Morrill helped me on several points of sixteenth- and seventeenth-century history. Mr C. B. Hardman gave me information on courtesy and on books of courtesy. Dr J. R. L. Highfield supplied information on the records of Merton College, Oxford. Professor Olwen Hufton gave me bibliographical guidance on the history of crime in early modern England. Dr J. R. Maddicott helped on matters involving Thomas earl of Lancaster and the battle of Boroughbridge. Mrs Janet Martin kindly lent me her dissertation on Nathaniel Johnstone. The late Mr C. A. F. Meekings sent valuable comment on Hobbehod, *fugitivus*. Mr D. J. H. Michelmore and Mr S. A. Moorhouse helped me on the topography of Barnsdale, on roads and administrative centres in West Yorkshire and on the Hoods of Wakefield. Mr Michael Palmer provided information on the Wakefield court rolls and allowed me to use his transcript of the roll of 1311. Professor Avrom Saltman gave me valuable help on the history of Dale Abbey. Dr R. S. Schofield guided me on the problem of literacy and Dr Margaret Spufford gave me the benefit of her work on chapbooks. Mr Jeffrey Stafford made a number of suggestions about possible sheriffs of Nottingham. Professor E. L. G. Stones was most generous in sending me several references to the Folvilles and to Folville's Law. Professor R. L. Storey allowed me to see his unprinted paper on 'Gentlemen – Bureaucrats' forthcoming in *Profession, Vocation and Culture in later Medieval England*, ed. C. H. Clough, Liverpool 1981. Finally, Dr Hilary Wayment helped me in tracing Tollet's window to the Victoria and Albert Museum. To all these I am most grateful.

More generally I must thank the staff of the Public Record Office, London, of the Library of the University of Nottingham and of the Yorkshire Archaeological Society at Leeds for their assistance and courtesy. There are also some larger debts. My publishers have suffered patiently the delays which affected the composition of the book and have made some valuable suggestions on arrangement. Finally my wife, who has shared an interest which has taken us together into many excursions, both literary and topographical, helped with the proofs and the compilation of the index.

*October 1981*

# Index

*Death of Robert Earl of
Huntington, The*, Anthony
Munday 162
Deepdale (Derbs.) 180, 181
*De Gestis Herewardi Saxonis*
63, 73, 74, 113
*Dives and Pauper* 142
Dobson, R. B. and Taylor, J.
101, 123
Dodsworth, Roger 44, 176
Dogs and hounds 71; *14, 24*
Doncaster (Yorks.) 83, 85;
entertainers from 138;
Roger of 48; *see also* Roger
of Doncaster
*Downfall of Robert Earl of
Huntington, The*, Anthony
Munday 162
Drabyl, Thomas, and his gang
153
Duels and personal combats;
with staff 167–71; with
sword 146, 171; with sword
against staff 33, 171
Duffield Frith (Derbys.) 97
Dugdale, William 42
Dunbar, William 100
*Durham Field* 57

Eden, river (Cumb.) 61
Edward I, King 12, 52, 77, 78,
111, 115
Edward II, King 45, 46, 47,
49, 52, 61, 101, 102, 103,
105, 111, 112, 122, 139, 143,
155, 197; Isabella, wife of 78
Edward III, King 144
Edward IV, King 128, 145
Edward, Black Prince 158
Edward, 'our comely king'
37, 38, 45, 56, 77, 100, 101,
103, 104, 105, 174, 192, 197
Edwinstowe (Notts.) 179; *10,
11*
Egan, Pierce 185
English *see* Anglo-Saxons;
Language
Erlinton 57
Essex 187
Eustace the Monk 55, 62, 63,
64, 80, 189, 191
Evesham (Worcs.), battle of
40
Ewyas, Walter of 98

Falstaff, Sir John 154, 158
Fareham (Hants.) 188
Feast of Fools 159
Fencing, art of 145–6
Fenwick (Yorks.), castle of
98, 99

Ferrers, Robert de, earl of
Derby 97
Ferrybridge (Yorks.) 54, 83,
84
Ferry Fryston (Yorks.) 84
Fevere, Fevre, William son of
Robert le (William
Robehod) 188–91
Field of the Cloth of Gold 145
Finchampstead (Berks.) 195
fitz Gilbert, Richard, of Clare
42, 43; Rohaise, daughter of
42; Richard (Strongbow),
earl of Pembroke 143
fitz Ooth, fictitious family 43,
201
fitz Otuel, fitz Othuer,
William 43
fitz Stephen, Ralph 97
fitz Walter, Lord 154; Robert
162; Matilda, daughter of
162
fitz Warin, Fulk 55, 57, 62, 63,
64, 65, 189, 191
Fletching (Sussex) 59, 187,
188; Hungry Hatch in 52
Flodden 127
Flodden, battle of 143
Foliot, Sir Richard 98, 99
Folville, family 152, 154, 155;
Eustace de 154
Folville's Law 155, 157
Fordun, John 40
Forests and chases 85–6, 97;
contraction of royal forest
in later Middle Ages 77–8;
depredation of 78–9, 101–2;
poaching in 78, 97, 99, 102;
*see also* parks
Foresters 99, as yeomen 121–
2; attacks on 58–9, 99, 153;
hostility to among local
community 78, 155–6
*Foresters, The*, Tennyson 186
Fortescue, Sir John 119, 120
*Fouke le Fitz Waryn* 63, 65, 71,
73, 74, 113, 114
Fountain Dale (Notts.) 179
Fountains abbey (Yorks.) 137,
138, 179
Framlingham (Suffolk), castle
of 116
France, King John of 158
Franklin *see* Social ranks
Fraser, Simon 112, 114
*Fraternity of Vagabonds*, John
Awdeley 181
French *see* Language
Friar Tuck 16, 33, 58, 59, 73,
160, 162, 167, 179, 182, 192,
197, 200; *29*

Gadshill (Kent) 158

Gale, Thomas 41, 42, 189
*Gamelyn, The Tale of* 70–4, 77,
164
Gamwell 164–7
Gangs, recruitment to 172
Gant, Gilbert de 42
Garendon (Leics.), abbey of
97
Garlands 162–3
'Gathering' 149; *see also Quête*
*Gawain and the Green Knight*
125, 140
Gentlemen *see* Social ranks
George a'Green, *see* Robin
Hood, tales of; *The Jolly
Pinder of Wakefield*
Gerald of Wales 79, 143
Gilbert of the White Hand 48
Gloucester, Richard duke of,
players of 137
Godberd, Roger 97, 98, 99,
191, 196
Goldburgh, William 41, 43
Gough, Richard 41, 44
*Governour, The*, Sir Thomas
Elyot 143
Gower, John 147, 160, 192; *5*
Grafton, Richard 41, 162
Great North Road 11, 53, 71,
83, 84, 85, 107, 176, 203; *2*
Greenwood, as a literary
convention 34, 56, 161
Grey, Reginald de, of Codnor
97, 98
Grimston (Notts.) 98, 99
Grosseteste, Robert, bishop of
Lincoln 159
Gunpowder plotters 170
Guy of Gisborne, 11, 16, 30–
33, 61, 116, 144, 164, 180,
191; *see also* Robin Hood,
Tales
Guy of Warwick 70, 165
Gwent, archers of 143

Hales, Sir Robert, Treasurer
157
Halle, Adam de la 160
Hampshire 187
Harman, Thomas 181, 182
Harrington, Sir James, players
of 138
Harris, P. Valentine 48, 49
Hathersage, Hathershead
(Derbs.) 44, 58, 176; *31*
Haworth (Yorks.) 104, 106,
128
Hearne, Thomas 43
Henley (Oxon.) 195
Henry II, King 45, 181, 183
Henry III, King 45, 77, 98, 189
Henry VIII, King 41, 119,
143, 145, 161, 183